MznLnx

Missing Links Exam Preps

Exam Prep for

Fundamentals of Corporate Finance Alternate Edition

Ross, Westerfield, & Jordan, 8th Edition

The MznLnx Exam Prep is your link from the texbook and lecture to your exams.

The MznLnx Exam Preps are unauthorized and comprehensive reviews of your textbooks.

All material provided by MznLnx and Rico Publications (c) 2010

Textbook publishers and textbook authors do not particpate in or contribute to these reviews.

MznLnx

Rico
Publications

Exam Prep for Fundamentals of Corporate Finance Alternate Edition
8th Edition
Ross, Westerfield, & Jordan

Publisher: Raymond Houge

Assistant Editor: Michael Rouger

Text and Cover Designer: Lisa Buckner

Marketing Manager: Sara Swagger

Project Manager, Editorial Production: Jerry Emerson

Art Director: Vernon Lowerui

Product Manager: Dave Mason

Editorial Assitant: Rachel Guzmanji

Pedagogy: Debra Long

Cover Image: Jim Reed/Getty Images

Text and Cover Printer: City Printing, Inc.

Compositor: Media Mix, Inc.

For more information about our products, contact us at:

Dave.Mason@RicoPublications.com

For permission to use material from this text or

product, submit a request online to:

Dave.Mason@RicoPublications.com

Printed in the United States
ISBN:

Contents

Contents (Cont.)

TO THE STUDENT

COMPREHENSIVE

The *MznLnx* Exam Prep series is designed to help you pass your exams. Editors at MznLnx review your textbooks and then prepare these practice exams to help you master the textbook material. Unlike study guides, workbooks, and practice tests provided by the texbook publisher and textbook authors, *MznLnx* gives you **all** of the material in each chapter in exam form, not just samples, so you can be sure to nail your exam.

MECHANICAL

The MznLnx Exam Prep series creates exams that will help you learn the subject matter as well as test you on your understanding. Each question is designed to help you master the concept. Just working through the exams, you gain an understanding of the subject--its a simple mechanical process that produces success.

INTEGRATED STUDY GUIDE AND REVIEW

MznLnx is not just a set of exams designed to test you, its also a comprehensive review of the subject content. Each exam question is also a review of the concept, making sure that you will get the answer correct without having to go to other sources of material. You learn as you go! Its the easiest way to pass an exam.

HUMOR

Studying can be tedious and dry. MznLnx's instructional design includes moderate humor within the exam questions on occassion, to break the tedium and revitalize the brain

1. _____ is an area of finance dealing with the financial decisions corporations make and the tools and analysis used to make these decisions. The primary goal of _____ is to maximize corporate value while managing the firm's financial risks. Although it is in principle different from managerial finance which studies the financial decisions of all firms, rather than corporations alone, the main concepts in the study of _____ are applicable to the financial problems of all kinds of firms.

   a. Cash flow
   b. Corporate finance
   c. Special purpose entity
   d. Gross profit

2. In finance, _____ (or gearing) is borrowing money to supplement existing funds for investment in such a way that the potential positive or negative outcome is magnified and/or enhanced. It generally refers to using borrowed funds, or debt, so as to attempt to increase the returns to equity. Deleveraging is the action of reducing borrowings.

   a. Pension fund
   b. Limited partnership
   c. Financial endowment
   d. Leverage

3. A _____ is a financial contract between two parties, the buyer and the seller of this type of option. Often it is simply labeled a 'call'. The buyer of the option has the right, but not the obligation to buy an agreed quantity of a particular commodity or financial instrument (the underlying instrument) from the seller of the option at a certain time (the expiration date) for a certain price (the strike price.)

   a. Bear spread
   b. Bull spread
   c. Bear call spread
   d. Call option

4. _____ is the planning process used to determine whether a firm's long term investments such as new machinery, replacement machinery, new plants, new products, and research development projects are worth pursuing. It is budget for major capital, or investment, expenditures.

Many formal methods are used in _____, including the techniques such as

- Net present value
- Profitability index
- Internal rate of return
- Modified Internal Rate of Return
- Equivalent annuity

These methods use the incremental cash flows from each potential investment, or project. Techniques based on accounting earnings and accounting rules are sometimes used - though economists consider this to be improper - such as the accounting rate of return, and 'return on investment.' Simplified and hybrid methods are used as well, such as payback period and discounted payback period.

   a. Preferred stock
   b. Financial distress
   c. Capital budgeting
   d. Shareholder value

5. An _____ is a contract written by a seller that conveys to the buyer the right -- but not the obligation -- to buy (in the case of a call _____) or to sell (in the case of a put _____) a particular asset, such as a piece of property such as, among others, a futures contract. In return for granting the _____, the seller collects a payment (the premium) from the buyer.

For example, buying a call _____ provides the right to buy a specified quantity of a security at a set strike price at some time on or before expiration, while buying a put _____ provides the right to sell.

   a. Amortization

   c. Annuity

   b. AT'T Mobility LLC

   d. Option

6.   In finance, _____ is the process of estimating the potential market value of a financial asset or liability. they can be done on assets (for example, investments in marketable securities such as stocks, options, business enterprises, or intangible assets such as patents and trademarks) or on liabilities (e.g., Bonds issued by a company.) _____s are required in many contexts including investment analysis, capital budgeting, merger and acquisition transactions, financial reporting, taxable events to determine the proper tax liability, and in litigation.

   a. Share

   c. Margin

   b. Procter ' Gamble

   d. Valuation

7.   In finance, _____ refers to the way a corporation finances its assets through some combination of equity, debt, or hybrid securities. A firm's _____ is then the composition or 'structure' of its liabilities. For example, a firm that sells $20 billion in equity and $80 billion in debt is said to be 20% equity-financed and 80% debt-financed.

   a. Capital structure

   c. Book building

   b. Rights issue

   d. Market for corporate control

8.   _____ is a financial metric which represents operating liquidity available to a business. Along with fixed assets such as plant and equipment, _____ is considered a part of operating capital. It is calculated as current assets minus current liabilities.

   a. 529 plan

   c. Working capital

   b. 4-4-5 Calendar

   d. Working capital management

9.   Decisions relating to working capital and short term financing are referred to as _____. These involve managing the relationship between a firm's short-term assets and its short-term liabilities. The goal of _____ is to ensure that the firm is able to continue its operations and that it has sufficient cash flow to satisfy both maturing short-term debt and upcoming operational expenses.

   a. Working capital

   c. 529 plan

   b. Working capital management

   d. 4-4-5 Calendar

10.   In the commercial and legal parlance of most countries, a _____ or simply a partnership, refers to an association of persons or an unincorporated company with the following major features:

- Created by agreement, proof of existence and estoppel.
- Formed by two or more persons
- The owners are all personally liable for any legal actions and debts the company may face

It is a partnership in which partners share equally in both responsibility and liability.

Partnerships have certain default characteristics relating to both the relationship between the individual partners and (b) the relationship between the partnership and the outside world. The former can generally be overridden by agreement between the partners, whereas the latter generally cannot be.

The assets of the business are owned on behalf of the other partners, and they are each personally liable, jointly and severally, for business debts, taxes or tortious liability.

a. The Depository Trust ' Clearing Corporation

c. First Prudential Markets

b. Federal Home Loan Mortgage Corporation

d. General partnership

11. In the most general sense, a _____ is anything that is a hindrance, or puts individuals at a disadvantage.

Before we discuss the financial terms, we should note that a _____ can also have a much more important slang meaning.

This is best described in an example.

a. McFadden Act

c. Limited liability

b. Covenant

d. Liability

12. A _____ is a form of partnership similar to a general partnership, except that in addition to one or more general partners (GPs), there are one or more limited partners (_____s). It is a partnership in which only one partner is required to be a general partner.

The GPs are, in all major respects, in the same legal position as partners in a conventional firm, i.e. they have management control, share the right to use partnership property, share the profits of the firm in predefined proportions, and have joint and several liability for the debts of the partnership.

a. Limited partnership

c. Leverage

b. Fund of funds

d. Limited liability company

13. A _____ is a type of business entity in which partners (owners) share with each other the profits or losses of the business undertaking in which all have invested. _____s are often favored over corporations for taxation purposes, as the _____ structure does not generally incur a tax on profits before it is distributed to the partners (i.e. there is no dividend tax levied.) However, depending on the _____ structure and the jurisdiction in which it operates, owners of a _____ may be exposed to greater personal liability than they would as shareholders of a corporation.

a. National Securities Markets Improvement Act of 1996

c. Fiduciary

b. Clayton Antitrust Act

d. Partnership

14. _____ is a voluntary contract between two or among more than two persons to place their capital, labor, and skills, and corporation in business with the understanding that there will be a sharing of the profits and losses between/among partners. Outside of North America, it is normally referred to simply as a partnership agreement.

a. Economic depreciation

c. Economies of scale

b. Express warranty

d. Articles of Partnership

15. A sole _____, or simply _____ is a type of business entity which legally has no separate existence from its owner. Hence, the limitations of liability enjoyed by a corporation and limited liability partnerships do not apply to sole proprietors. All debts of the business are debts of the owner.

a. Product life cycle

b. Proprietorship

c. Free cash flow

d. Just-in-time

16.   The _____ are the primary rules governing the management of a corporation in the United States and Canada, and are filed with a state or other regulatory agency. The equivalent in the United Kingdom and various other countries is Articles of Association.

A corporation's _____ generally provide information such as:

- The corporation's name, which has to be unique from any other corporation in that jurisdiction. As part of the corporation's name, certain words such as 'incorporated', 'limited', 'corporation', (or their abbreviations) or some equivalent term in countries whose language is not English, are usually required as part of the name as a 'flag' to indicate to persons doing business with the organization that it is a corporation as opposed to an individual or partnership (with unlimited liability.) In some cases, certain types of names are prohibited except by special permission, such as words implying the corporation is a government agency or has powers to act in ways it is not otherwise allowed.
- The name of the person(s) organizing the corporation (usually members of the board of directors.)
- Whether the corporation is a stock corporation or a non-stock corporation.
- Whether the corporation's existence is permanent or limited for a specific period of time. Generally the rule is that a corporation existence is forever, or until (1) it stops paying the yearly corporate renewal fees or otherwise fails to do something required to continue its existence such as file certain paperwork each year; or (2) it files a request to 'wind up and dissolve.'
- In some cases, a corporation must state the purposes for which it is formed. Some jurisdictions permit a general statement such as 'any lawful purpose' but some require explicit specifications.
- If a non-stock corporation, whether it is for profit or non-profit. However, some jurisdictions differentiate by 'for profit' or 'non profit' and some by 'stock or non-stock'.
- In the United States, if a corporation is to be organized as a non-profit, to be recognized as such by the Internal Revenue Service, such as for eligibility for tax exemption, certain specific wording must be included stating no part of the assets of the corporation are to benefit the members.
- If a stock corporation, the number of shares the corporation is authorized to issue, or the maximum amount in a specific currency of stock that may be issued, e.g. a maximum of $25,000.
- The number and names of the corporation's initial Board of Directors (though this is optional in most cases.)
- The initial director(s) of the corporation (in some cases the incorporator or the registered agent must be a director, if not an attorney or another corporation.)
- The location of the corporation's 'registered office' - the location at which legal papers can be served to the corporation if necessary. Some states further require the designation of a Registered Agent: a person to whom such papers could be delivered.

Most states permit a corporation to be formed by one person; in some cases (such as non-profit corporations) it may require three or five or more. This change has come about as a result of Delaware liberalizing its corporation rules to allow corporations to be formed by one person, and states not wanting to lose corporate charters to Delaware had to revise their rules as a result.

a. Expedited Funds Availability Act

b. Articles of Partnership

c. External risks

d. Articles of incorporation

17. The institution most often referenced by the word '_____' is a public or publicly traded _____, the shares of which are traded on a public stock exchange (e.g., the New York Stock Exchange or Nasdaq in the United States) where shares of stock of _____s are bought and sold by and to the general public. Most of the largest businesses in the world are publicly traded _____s. However, the majority of _____s are said to be closely held, privately held or close _____s, meaning that no ready market exists for the trading of shares.

a. Federal Home Loan Mortgage Corporation

b. Protect

c. Depository Trust Company

d. Corporation

18. _____ is the imposition of two or more taxes on the same income (in the case of income taxes), asset (in the case of capital taxes), or financial transaction (in the case of sales taxes.) It refers to two distinct situations:

- taxation of dividend income without relief or credit for taxes paid by the company paying the dividend on the income from which the dividend is paid. This arises in the so-called 'classical' system of corporate taxation, used in the United States.
- taxation by two or more countries of the same income, asset or transaction, for example income paid by an entity of one country to a resident of a different country. The double liability is often mitigated by tax treaties between countries.

It is not unusual for a business or individual who is resident in one country to make a taxable gain (earnings, profits) in another. This person may find that he is obliged by domestic laws to pay tax on that gain locally and pay again in the country in which the gain was made. Since this is inequitable, many nations make bilateral _____ agreements with each other.

a. 4-4-5 Calendar

b. 529 plan

c. 7-Eleven

d. Double taxation

19. _____ is a concept whereby a person's financial liability is limited to a fixed sum, most commonly the value of a person's investment in a company or partnership with _____. A shareholder in a limited company is not personally liable for any of the debts of the company, other than for the value of his investment in that company. The same is true for the members of a _____ partnership and the limited partners in a limited partnership.

a. Beneficial owner

b. Sarbanes-Oxley Act

c. Personal property

d. Limited liability

20. A _____ in the law of the vast majority of United States jurisdictions is a legal form of business company that provides limited liability to its owners. It is a hybrid business entity having certain characteristics of both a corporation and a partnership or sole proprietorship (depending on how many owners there are.) The primary characteristic an _____ shares with a corporation is limited liability, and the primary characteristic it shares with a partnership is the availability of pass-through income taxation.

a. Limited liability company

b. Financial endowment

c. Pension fund

d. Fund of funds

21. A _____ is a type of business entity: it is a type of corporation or partnership between two companies. Certificates of ownership (or stocks) are issued by the company in return for each contribution, and the shareholders are free to transfer their ownership interest at any time by selling their stockholding to others.

There are two kinds of _____. The private company kind and the open market. The shares are usually only held by the directors and Company Secretary. Debt for which they agree to be liable.

a. Subsidiary   b. 529 plan
c. Joint stock company   d. 4-4-5 Calendar

22.   A _____ is a type of limited company in the United Kingdom and the Republic of Ireland which is permitted to offer its shares to the public.
a. 4-4-5 Calendar   b. 529 plan
c. 7-Eleven   d. Public limited company

23.   In business, _____ is income that a company receives from its normal business activities, usually from the sale of goods and services to customers. Some companies also receive _____ from interest, dividends or royalties paid to them by other companies. _____ may refer to business income in general, or it may refer to the amount, in a monetary unit, received during a period of time, as in 'Last year, Company X had _____ of $32 million.'

In many countries, including the UK, _____ is referred to as turnover.

a. Furniture, Fixtures and Equipment   b. Bottom line
c. Matching principle   d. Revenue

24.   _____ is the difference between price and the costs of bringing to market whatever it is that is accounted as an enterprise (whether by harvest, extraction, manufacture, or purchase) in terms of the component costs of delivered goods and/or services and any operating or other expenses.

A key difficulty in measuring profit is in defining costs. Pure economic monetary profits can be zero or negative even in competitive equilibrium when accounted monetized costs exceed monetized price.

a. Economic profit   b. A Random Walk Down Wall Street
c. AAB   d. Accounting profit

25.   In economics, _____ is the process by which a firm determines the price and output level that returns the greatest profit. There are several approaches to this problem. The total revenue--total cost method relies on the fact that profit equals revenue minus cost, and the marginal revenue--marginal cost method is based on the fact that total profit in a perfectly competitive market reaches its maximum point where marginal revenue equals marginal cost.
a. Profit maximization   b. Profit margin
c. Net profit margin   d. 4-4-5 Calendar

26.   In financial accounting, a _____ or statement of financial position is a summary of a person's or organization's balances. Assets, liabilities and ownership equity are listed as of a specific date, such as the end of its financial year. A _____ is often described as a snapshot of a company's financial condition.

a. Financial statements   b. Statement on Auditing Standards No. 70: Service Organizations
c. Balance sheet   d. Statement of retained earnings

27. The _____ of 2002 (Pub.L. 107-204, 116 Stat. 745, enacted July 30, 2002), also known as the Public Company Accounting Reform and Investor Protection Act of 2002 and commonly called Sarbanes-Oxley, Sarbox or SOX, is a United States federal law enacted on July 30, 2002 in response to a number of major corporate and accounting scandals including those affecting Enron, Tyco International, Adelphia, Peregrine Systems and WorldCom.

a. Blue sky law
b. Foreign Corrupt Practices Act
c. Sarbanes-Oxley Act
d. Duty of loyalty

28. A _____ is a fungible, negotiable instrument representing financial value. They are broadly categorized into debt securities (such as banknotes, bonds and debentures), and equity securities; e.g., common stocks. The company or other entity issuing the _____ is called the issuer.

a. Securities lending
b. Book entry
c. Tracking stock
d. Security

29. The U.S. _____ is an independent agency of the United States government which holds primary responsibility for enforcing the federal securities laws and regulating the securities industry, the nation's stock and options exchanges, and other electronic securities markets. The SEC was created by section 4 of the SEC of 1934 (now codified as 15 U.S.C. § 78d and commonly referred to as the 1934 Act.)

a. 529 plan
b. Securities and Exchange Commission
c. 7-Eleven
d. 4-4-5 Calendar

30. An _____ is an economic concept that relates to the cost incurred by an entity (such as organizations) associated with problems such as divergent management-shareholder objectives and information asymmetry. The costs consist of two main sources:

1. The costs inherently associated with using an agent (e.g., the risk that agents will use organizational resource for their own benefit) and
2. The costs of techniques used to mitigate the problems associated with using an agent (e.g., the costs of producing financial statements or the use of stock options to align executive interests to shareholder interests.)

Though effects of _____ are present in any agency relationship, the term is most used in business contexts.

The information asymmetry that exists between shareholders and the Chief Executive Officer is generally considered to be a classic example of a principal-agent problem. The agent (the manager) is working on behalf of the principal (the shareholders), who does not observe the actions of the agent.

a. AAB
b. ABN Amro
c. A Random Walk Down Wall Street
d. Agency cost

31. In political science and economics, the _____ or agency dilemma treats the difficulties that arise under conditions of incomplete and asymmetric information when a principal hires an agent. Various mechanisms may be used to try to align the interests of the agent with those of the principal, such as piece rates/commissions, profit sharing, efficiency wages, performance measurement (including financial statements), the agent posting a bond, or fear of firing. The _____ is found in most employer/employee relationships, for example, when stockholders hire top executives of corporations.

a. 4-4-5 Calendar

b. Principal-agent problem

c. 7-Eleven

d. 529 plan

32.   In economics, business, and accounting, a _____ is the value of money that has been used up to produce something, and hence is not available for use anymore. In business, the _____ may be one of acquisition, in which case the amount of money expended to acquire it is counted as _____. In this case, money is the input that is gone in order to acquire the thing.

a. Sliding scale fees

b. Fixed costs

c. Cost

d. Marginal cost

33.   A _____ or secondary offering is an issuance of stock subsequent to the company's initial public offering. A _____ can be either of two types (or a mixture of both): dilutive and non-dilutive. A secondary offering is an offering of securities by a shareholder of the company (as opposed to the company itself, which is a primary offering).

a. Capital structure

b. Follow-on offering

c. Shareholder value

d. Second lien loan

34.   A _____ is an event that may occur when a corporation's stockholders develop opposition to some aspect of the corporate governance, often focusing on directorial and management positions. Corporate activists may attempt to persuade shareholders to use their proxy votes (i.e. votes by one individual or institution as the authorized representative of another) to install new management for any of a variety of reasons.

In a _____, incumbent directors and management have the odds stacked in their favor over those trying to force the corporate change.

a. Procurement

b. Proxy fight

c. Trade finance

d. Forfaiting

35.   _____ is a fee paid on borrowed assets. It is the price paid for the use of borrowed money , or, money earned by deposited funds . Assets that are sometimes lent with _____ include money, shares, consumer goods through hire purchase, major assets such as aircraft, and even entire factories in finance lease arrangements.

a. A Random Walk Down Wall Street

b. Insolvency

c. AAB

d. Interest

36.   In economics, the concept of the _____ refers to the decision-making time frame of a firm in which at least one factor of production is fixed. Costs which are fixed in the _____ have no impact on a firms decisions. For example a firm can raise output by increasing the amount of labour through overtime.

a. 529 plan

b. 4-4-5 Calendar

c. Long-run

d. Short-run

37.   In business, a _____ is the purchase of one company (the target) by another (the acquirer or bidder). In the UK the term refers to the acquisition of a public company whose shares are listed on a stock exchange, in contrast to the acquisition of a private company.

Before a bidder makes an offer for another company, it usually first informs that company's board of directors.

a. 529 plan

b. Stock swap

c. 4-4-5 Calendar

d. Takeover

38. _____ is the balance of the amounts of cash being received and paid by a business during a defined period of time, sometimes tied to a specific project. Measurement of _____ can be used

- to evaluate the state or performance of a business or project.
- to determine problems with liquidity. Being profitable does not necessarily mean being liquid. A company can fail because of a shortage of cash, even while profitable.
- to generate project rate of returns. The time of _____s into and out of projects are used as inputs to financial models such as internal rate of return, and net present value.
- to examine income or growth of a business when it is believed that accrual accounting concepts do not represent economic realities. Alternately, _____ can be used to 'validate' the net income generated by accrual accounting.

_____ as a generic term may be used differently depending on context, and certain _____ definitions may be adapted by analysts and users for their own uses. Common terms include operating _____ and free _____.

_____s can be classified into:

1. Operational _____s: Cash received or expended as a result of the company's core business activities.
2. Investment _____s: Cash received or expended through capital expenditure, investments or acquisitions.
3. Financing _____s: Cash received or expended as a result of financial activities, such as interests and dividends.

All three together - the net _____ - are necessary to reconcile the beginning cash balance to the ending cash balance. Loan draw downs or equity injections, that is just shifting of capital but no expenditure as such, are not considered in the net _____.

a. Real option

b. Shareholder value

c. Corporate finance

d. Cash flow

39. In economics, a _____ is a mechanism that allows people to easily buy and sell (trade) financial securities (such as stocks and bonds), commodities (such as precious metals or agricultural goods), and other fungible items of value at low transaction costs and at prices that reflect the efficient-market hypothesis.

_____s have evolved significantly over several hundred years and are undergoing constant innovation to improve liquidity.

Both general markets (where many commodities are traded) and specialized markets (where only one commodity is traded) exist.

a. Financial market

b. Cost of carry

c. Delta hedging

d. Secondary market

40.   The _____ is an American stock exchange. It is the largest electronic screen-based equity securities trading market in the United States. With approximately 3,200 companies, it has more trading volume per day than any other stock exchange in the world.

a. 4-4-5 Calendar

b. 529 plan

c. 7-Eleven

d. NASDAQ

41.   In the United States, the Financial Industry Regulatory Authority (FINRA) is a self-regulatory organization (SRO) under the Securities Exchange Act of 1934, successor to the _____, Inc.

FINRA is responsible for regulatory oversight of all securities firms that do business with the public; professional training, testing and licensing of registered persons; arbitration and mediation; market regulation by contract for The NASDAQ Stock Market, Inc., the American Stock Exchange LLC, and the International Securities Exchange, LLC; and industry utilities, such as Trade Reporting Facilities and other over-the-counter operations.

a. 4-4-5 Calendar

b. 529 plan

c. National Association of Securities Dealers

d. 7-Eleven

42.   The _____ is that part of the capital markets that deals with the issuance of new securities. Companies, governments or public sector institutions can obtain funding through the sale of a new stock or bond issue. This is typically done through a syndicate of securities dealers.

a. Peer group analysis

b. Volatility clustering

c. Primary market

d. Sector rotation

43.   The _____ is the financial market where previously issued securities and financial instruments such as stock, bonds, options, and futures are bought and sold. The term '_____' is also used refer to the market for any used goods or assets, or an alternative use for an existing product or asset where the customer base is the second market

With primary issuances of securities or financial instruments, or the primary market, investors purchase these securities directly from issuers such as corporations issuing shares in an IPO or private placement, or directly from the federal government in the case of treasuries.

a. Delta neutral

b. Financial market

c. Performance attribution

d. Secondary market

44.   The _____ is the market for securities, where companies and governments can raise longterm funds. The _____ includes the stock market and the bond market. Financial regulators, such as the U.S. Securities and Exchange Commission, oversee the _____s in their designated countries to ensure that investors are protected against fraud.

a. Spot rate

b. Forward market

c. Delta neutral

d. Capital Market

45.   The _____ is a stock exchange based in New York City, New York. It is the largest stock exchange in the world by dollar value of its listed companies securities. As of October 2008, the combined capitalization of all domestic _____ listed companies was $10.1 trillion.

a. 4-4-5 Calendar

b. 529 plan

c. 7-Eleven

d. New York Stock Exchange

46.   A _____, securities exchange or (in Europe) bourse is a corporation or mutual organization which provides 'trading' facilities for stock brokers and traders, to trade stocks and other securities. _____s also provide facilities for the issue and redemption of securities as well as other financial instruments and capital events including the payment of income and dividends. The securities traded on a _____ include: shares issued by companies, unit trusts and other pooled investment products and bonds.

a. 7-Eleven

b. 529 plan

c. 4-4-5 Calendar

d. Stock Exchange

47.   In finance, a _____ is a debt security, in which the authorized issuer owes the holders a debt and, depending on the terms of the _____, is obliged to pay interest (the coupon) and/or to repay the principal at a later date, termed maturity.

Thus a _____ is a loan: the issuer is the borrower, the _____ holder is the lender, and the coupon is the interest. _____s provide the borrower with external funds to finance long-term investments, or, in the case of government _____s, to finance current expenditure.

a. Puttable bond

b. Bond

c. Catastrophe bonds

d. Convertible bond

48.   _____ is typically a higher ranking stock than voting shares, and its terms are negotiated between the corporation and the investor.

_____ usually carry no voting rights, but may carry superior priority over common stock in the payment of dividends and upon liquidation. _____ may carry a dividend that is paid out prior to any dividends to common stock holders.

a. Preferred Stock

b. Follow-on offering

c. Second lien loan

d. Trade-off theory

49.   In financial accounting, _____s are precautions for which the amount or probability of occurrence are not known. Typical examples are _____s for warranty costs and _____ for taxes the term reserve is used instead of term _____; such a use, however, is inconsistent with the terminology suggested by International Accounting Standards Board.

a. Petty cash

b. Provision

c. Money measurement concept

d. Momentum Accounting and Triple-Entry Bookkeeping

1. In finance, a _____ is a debt security, in which the authorized issuer owes the holders a debt and, depending on the terms of the _____, is obliged to pay interest (the coupon) and/or to repay the principal at a later date, termed maturity.

Thus a _____ is a loan: the issuer is the borrower, the _____ holder is the lender, and the coupon is the interest. _____s provide the borrower with external funds to finance long-term investments, or, in the case of government _____s, to finance current expenditure.

a. Puttable bond

b. Bond

c. Catastrophe bonds

d. Convertible bond

2. In banking and finance, _____ denotes all activities from the time a commitment is made for a transaction until it is settled. _____ is necessary because the speed of trades is much faster than the cycle time for completing the underlying transaction.

In its widest sense _____ involves the management of post-trading, pre-settlement credit exposures, to ensure that trades are settled in accordance with market rules, even if a buyer or seller should become insolvent prior to settlement.

a. Procter ' Gamble

b. Clearing

c. Share

d. Clearing house

3. In business and accounting, _____s are everything of value that is owned by a person or company. The balance sheet of a firm records the monetary value of the _____s owned by the firm. The two major _____ classes are tangible _____s and intangible _____s.

a. EBITDA

b. Asset

c. Accounts payable

d. Income

4. In financial accounting, a _____ or statement of financial position is a summary of a person's or organization's balances. Assets, liabilities and ownership equity are listed as of a specific date, such as the end of its financial year. A _____ is often described as a snapshot of a company's financial condition.

a. Statement of retained earnings

b. Financial statements

c. Statement on Auditing Standards No. 70: Service Organizations

d. Balance sheet

5. A _____ is a party (e.g. person, organization, company, or government) that has a claim to the services of a second party. The first party, in general, has provided some property or service to the second party under the assumption (usually enforced by contract) that the second party will return an equivalent property or service. The second party is frequently called a debtor or borrower.

a. Creditor

b. False billing

c. NOPLAT

d. Redemption value

6. In accounting, a _____ is an asset on the balance sheet which is expected to be sold or otherwise used up in the near future, usually within one year, or one business cycle - whichever is longer. Typical _____s include cash, cash equivalents, accounts receivable, inventory, the portion of prepaid accounts which will be used within a year, and short-term investments.

On the balance sheet, assets will typically be classified into _____s and long-term assets.

a. Write-off
c. Historical cost

b. Long-term liabilities
d. Current asset

7.   In accounting, _____ are considered liabilities of the business that are to be settled in cash within the fiscal year or the operating cycle, whichever period is longer.

For example accounts payable for goods, services or supplies that were purchased for use in the operation of the business and payable within a normal period of time would be _____.

Bonds, mortgages and loans that are payable over a term exceeding one year would be fixed liabilities.

a. Gross sales
c. Net income

b. Closing entries
d. Current liabilities

8.   _____ plant, and equipment, is a term used in accountancy for assets and property which cannot easily be converted into cash. This can be compared with current assets such as cash or bank accounts, which are described as liquid assets. In most cases, only tangible assets are referred to as fixed.

a. Fixed asset
c. Petty cash

b. Percentage of Completion
d. Remittance advice

9.   In economic models, the _____ time frame assumes no fixed factors of production. Firms can enter or leave the marketplace, and the cost (and availability) of land, labor, raw materials, and capital goods can be assumed to vary. In contrast, in the short-run time frame, certain factors are assumed to be fixed, because there is not sufficient time for them to change.

a. Short-run
c. 529 plan

b. Long-run
d. 4-4-5 Calendar

10.   _____ is the task of determining how a business will afford to achieve its strategic goals and objectives. Usually, a company creates a Financial Plan immediately after the vision and objectives have been set. The Financial Plan describes each of the activities, resources, equipment and materials that are needed to achieve these objectives, as well as the timeframes involved.

a. Management by exception
c. Corporate Transparency

b. Financial planning
d. Performance measurement

11.   _____ is a financial metric which represents operating liquidity available to a business. Along with fixed assets such as plant and equipment, _____ is considered a part of operating capital. It is calculated as current assets minus current liabilities.

a. Working capital management
c. 529 plan

b. Working capital
d. 4-4-5 Calendar

12.   _____ is a measure of the ability of a debtor to pay their debts as and when they fall due. It is usually expressed as a ratio or a percentage of current liabilities.

For a corporation with a published balance sheet there are various ratios used to calculate a measure of liquidity.

a. Operating profit margin
c. Invested capital

b. Operating leverage
d. Accounting liquidity

13.   In accounting, _____ or *Carrying value* is the value of an asset according to its balance sheet account balance. For assets, the value is based on the original cost of the asset less any depreciation, amortization or impairment costs made against the asset. A company's _____ is its total assets minus intangible assets and liabilities.

a. Pro forma
c. Retained earnings

b. Current liabilities
d. Book value

14.   In economics, business, and accounting, a _____ is the value of money that has been used up to produce something, and hence is not available for use anymore. In business, the _____ may be one of acquisition, in which case the amount of money expended to acquire it is counted as _____. In this case, money is the input that is gone in order to acquire the thing.

a. Marginal cost
c. Fixed costs

b. Sliding scale fees
d. Cost

15.   _____ is that which is owed; usually referencing assets owed, but the term can cover other obligations. In the case of assets, _____ is a means of using future purchasing power in the present before a summation has been earned. Some companies and corporations use _____ as a part of their overall corporate finance strategy.

a. Cross-collateralization
c. Debt

b. Credit cycle
d. Partial Payment

16.   _____ is the standard framework of guidelines for financial accounting used in the United States of America. It includes the standards, conventions, and rules accountants follow in recording and summarizing transactions, and in the preparation of financial statements. _____ are now issued by the Financial Accounting Standards Board (FASB).

a. Revenue
c. Generally Accepted Accounting Principles

b. Net income
d. Depreciation

17.   In accounting, _____ is the original monetary value of an economic item. In some circumstances, assets and liabilities may be shown at their _____, as if there had been no change in value since the date of acquisition. The balance sheet value of the item may therefore differ from the 'true' value.

a. Deferred income
c. Treasury stock

b. Pro forma
d. Historical cost

18.   _____ is the price at which an asset would trade in a competitive Walrasian auction setting. _____ is often used interchangeably with open _____, fair value or fair _____, although these terms have distinct definitions in different standards, and may differ in some circumstances.

International Valuation Standards defines _____ as 'the estimated amount for which a property should exchange on the date of valuation between a willing buyer and a willing seller in an arm'e;s-length transaction after proper marketing wherein the parties had each acted knowledgeably, prudently, and without compulsion.'

_____ is a concept distinct from market price, which is 'e;the price at which one can transact'e;, while _____ is 'e;the true underlying value'e; according to theoretical standards.

a. Wrap account

c. Debt restructuring

b. T-Model

d. Market value

19.   A _____ is a financial contract between two parties, the buyer and the seller of this type of option. Often it is simply labeled a 'call'. The buyer of the option has the right, but not the obligation to buy an agreed quantity of a particular commodity or financial instrument (the underlying instrument) from the seller of the option at a certain time (the expiration date) for a certain price (the strike price.)

a. Call option

c. Bear spread

b. Bear call spread

d. Bull spread

20.   In finance, the _____ is the minimum rate of return a firm must offer shareholders to compensate for waiting for their returns, and for bearing some risk.

The _____ capital for a particular company is the rate of return on investment that is required by the company's ordinary shareholders. The return consists both of dividend and capital gains, e.g. increases in the share price.

a. Round-tripping

c. Net pay

b. Cost of Equity

d. Residual value

21.   In finance, _____ (or gearing) is borrowing money to supplement existing funds for investment in such a way that the potential positive or negative outcome is magnified and/or enhanced. It generally refers to using borrowed funds, or debt, so as to attempt to increase the returns to equity. Deleveraging is the action of reducing borrowings.

a. Limited partnership

c. Financial endowment

b. Pension fund

d. Leverage

22.   An _____ is a contract written by a seller that conveys to the buyer the right -- but not the obligation -- to buy (in the case of a call _____) or to sell (in the case of a put _____) a particular asset, such as a piece of property such as, among others, a futures contract. In return for granting the _____, the seller collects a payment (the premium) from the buyer.

For example, buying a call _____ provides the right to buy a specified quantity of a security at a set strike price at some time on or before expiration, while buying a put _____ provides the right to sell.

a. Annuity

c. AT'T Mobility LLC

b. Amortization

d. Option

23.   _____, refers to consumption opportunity gained by an entity within a specified time frame, which is generally expressed in monetary terms. However, for households and individuals, '_____ is the sum of all the wages, salaries, profits, interests payments, rents and other forms of earnings received... in a given period of time.' For firms, _____ generally refers to net-profit: what remains of revenue after expenses have been subtracted.

a. OIBDA

b. Annual report

c. Accrual

d. Income

24. An _____ is a financial statement for companies that indicates how Revenue is transformed into net income The purpose of the _____ is to show managers and investors whether the company made or lost money during the period being reported.

The important thing to remember about an _____ is that it represents a period of time.

a. Income statement

b. A Random Walk Down Wall Street

c. AAB

d. ABN Amro

25. _____ are the earnings returned on the initial investment amount.

In the US, the Financial Accounting Standards Board (FASB) requires companies' income statements to report _____ for each of the major categories of the income statement: continuing operations, discontinued operations, extraordinary items, and net income.

The _____ formula does not include preferred dividends for categories outside of continued operations and net income.

a. Earnings per share

b. Average accounting return

c. Assets turnover

d. Inventory turnover

26. _____ is equal to the income that a firm has after subtracting costs and expenses from the total revenue. _____ can be distributed among holders of common stock as a dividend or held by the firm as retained earnings. _____ is an accounting term; in some countries (such as the UK) profit is the usual term.

a. Net income

b. Historical cost

c. Furniture, Fixtures and Equipment

d. Write-off

27. The _____ principle is a cornerstone of accrual accounting together with matching principle. They both determine the accounting period, in which revenues and expenses are recognized. According to the principle, revenues are recognized when they are (1) realized or realizable, and are (2) earned (usually when goods are transferred or services rendered), no matter when cash is received.

a. Commodity Pool Operator

b. Regulation FD

c. Tail risk

d. Revenue recognition

28. In business and finance, a _____ (also referred to as equity _____) of stock means a _____ of ownership in a corporation (company.) In the plural, stocks is often used as a synonym for _____s especially in the United States, but it is less commonly used that way outside of North America.

In the United Kingdom, South Africa, and Australia, stock can also refer to completely different financial instruments such as government bonds or, less commonly, to all kinds of marketable securities.

a. Margin   b. Bucket shop

c. Share   d. Procter ' Gamble

29. _____ is a term used in accounting, economics and finance to spread the cost of an asset over the span of several years.

In simple words we can say that _____ is the reduction in the value of an asset due to usage, passage of time, wear and tear, technological outdating or obsolescence, depletion or other such factors.

In accounting, _____ is a term used to describe any method of attributing the historical or purchase cost of an asset across its useful life, roughly corresponding to normal wear and tear.

a. Matching principle   b. Bottom line

c. Deferred financing costs   d. Depreciation

30. _____ is a cornerstone of accrual accounting together with revenue recognition. They both determine the point, at which expenses and revenues are recognized. According to the principle, expenses are recognized when they are (1) incurred and (2) offset against recognized revenues, which were generated from those expenses (related on the cause-and-effect basis), no matter when cash is paid out.

a. Retained earnings   b. Pro forma

c. Gross sales   d. Matching principle

31. _____ is the balance of the amounts of cash being received and paid by a business during a defined period of time, sometimes tied to a specific project. Measurement of _____ can be used

- to evaluate the state or performance of a business or project.
- to determine problems with liquidity. Being profitable does not necessarily mean being liquid. A company can fail because of a shortage of cash, even while profitable.
- to generate project rate of returns. The time of _____s into and out of projects are used as inputs to financial models such as internal rate of return, and net present value.
- to examine income or growth of a business when it is believed that accrual accounting concepts do not represent economic realities. Alternately, _____ can be used to 'validate' the net income generated by accrual accounting.

_____ as a generic term may be used differently depending on context, and certain _____ definitions may be adapted by analysts and users for their own uses. Common terms include operating _____ and free _____.

_____s can be classified into:

1. Operational _____s: Cash received or expended as a result of the company's core business activities.
2. Investment _____s: Cash received or expended through capital expenditure, investments or acquisitions.
3. Financing _____s: Cash received or expended as a result of financial activities, such as interests and dividends.

All three together - the net _____ - are necessary to reconcile the beginning cash balance to the ending cash balance. Loan draw downs or equity injections, that is just shifting of capital but no expenditure as such, are not considered in the net _____.

a. Real option   b. Shareholder value
c. Corporate finance   d. Cash flow

32.   In financial accounting, a _____ or statement of cash flows is a financial statement that shows a company's flow of cash. The money coming into the business is called cash inflow, and money going out from the business is called cash outflow. The statement shows how changes in balance sheet and income accounts affect cash and cash equivalents, and breaks the analysis down to operating, investing, and financing activities.

a. 529 plan   b. 4-4-5 Calendar
c. 7-Eleven   d. Cash flow statement

33.   In financial accounting, _____ , cash flow provided by operations or cash flow from operating activities, refers to the amount of cash a company generates from the revenues it brings in, excluding costs associated with long-term investment on capital items or investment in securities.

_____ = Cash generated from operations less taxation and interest paid, investment income received and less dividends paid gives rise to _____s per International Financial Reporting Standards.

To calculate cash generated from operations, one must calculate cash generated from customers and cash paid to suppliers.

a. Other Comprehensive Basis of Accounting   b. A Random Walk Down Wall Street
c. Appreciation   d. Operating cash flow

34.   In economics, the concept of the _____ refers to the decision-making time frame of a firm in which at least one factor of production is fixed. Costs which are fixed in the _____ have no impact on a firms decisions. For example a firm can raise output by increasing the amount of labour through overtime.

a. Short-run   b. 529 plan
c. Long-run   d. 4-4-5 Calendar

35.   In economics and business, specifically cost accounting, the _____ is the point at which cost or expenses and revenue are equal: there is no net loss or gain, and one has 'broken even'. A profit or a loss has not been made, although opportunity costs have been paid, and capital has received the risk-adjusted, expected return.

For example, if the business sells less than 200 tables each month, it will make a loss, if it sells more, it will be a profit.

a. Market microstructure   b. Fixed asset turnover
c. Break-even point   d. Defined contribution plan

36.   In corporate finance, _____ is a cash flow available for distribution among all the security holders of a company. They include equity holders, debt holders, preferred stock holders, convertible security holders, and so on.

Note that the first three lines above are calculated for you on the standard Statement of Cash Flows.

a. Funding

b. Safety stock

c. Forfaiting

d. Free cash flow

37. A mutual shareholder or _____ is an individual or company (including a corporation) that legally owns one or more shares of stock in a joint stock company. A company's shareholders collectively own that company. Thus, the typical goal of such companies is to enhance shareholder value.

a. Trading curb

b. Stock market bubble

c. Limit order

d. Stockholder

38. In political science and economics, the _____ or agency dilemma treats the difficulties that arise under conditions of incomplete and asymmetric information when a principal hires an agent. Various mechanisms may be used to try to align the interests of the agent with those of the principal, such as piece rates/commissions, profit sharing, efficiency wages, performance measurement (including financial statements), the agent posting a bond, or fear of firing. The _____ is found in most employer/employee relationships, for example, when stockholders hire top executives of corporations.

a. 4-4-5 Calendar

b. Principal-agent problem

c. 529 plan

d. 7-Eleven

39. _____ are formal records of a business' financial activities.

_____ provide an overview of a business' financial condition in both short and long term. There are four basic _____:

1. **Balance sheet**: also referred to as statement of financial position or condition, reports on a company's assets, liabilities, and net equity as of a given point in time.
2. **Income statement**: also referred to as Profit and Loss statement (or a 'P'L'), reports on a company's income, expenses, and profits over a period of time.
3. **Statement of retained earnings**: explains the changes in a company's retained earnings over the reporting period.
4. **Statement of cash flows**: reports on a company's cash flow activities, particularly its operating, investing and financing activities.

a. Statement of retained earnings

b. Notes to the Financial Statements

c. Financial statements

d. Statement on Auditing Standards No. 70: Service Organizations

1. _____ are formal records of a business' financial activities.

_____ provide an overview of a business' financial condition in both short and long term. There are four basic _____:

1. **Balance sheet**: also referred to as statement of financial position or condition, reports on a company's assets, liabilities, and net equity as of a given point in time.
2. **Income statement**: also referred to as Profit and Loss statement (or a 'P'L'), reports on a company's income, expenses, and profits over a period of time.
3. **Statement of retained earnings**: explains the changes in a company's retained earnings over the reporting period.
4. **Statement of cash flows**: reports on a company's cash flow activities, particularly its operating, investing and financing activities.

a. Statement of retained earnings

b. Financial statements

c. Notes to the Financial Statements

d. Statement on Auditing Standards No. 70: Service Organizations

2. In finance, a _____ is a debt security, in which the authorized issuer owes the holders a debt and, depending on the terms of the _____, is obliged to pay interest (the coupon) and/or to repay the principal at a later date, termed maturity.

Thus a _____ is a loan: the issuer is the borrower, the _____ holder is the lender, and the coupon is the interest. _____s provide the borrower with external funds to finance long-term investments, or, in the case of government _____s, to finance current expenditure.

a. Catastrophe bonds

b. Convertible bond

c. Bond

d. Puttable bond

3. A _____ is the price of a single share of a no. of saleable stocks of the company. Once the stock is purchased, the owner becomes a shareholder of the company that issued the share.

a. Stock split

b. Trading curb

c. Share price

d. Whisper numbers

4. In financial accounting, a _____ or statement of financial position is a summary of a person's or organization's balances. Assets, liabilities and ownership equity are listed as of a specific date, such as the end of its financial year. A _____ is often described as a snapshot of a company's financial condition.

a. Statement on Auditing Standards No. 70: Service Organizations

b. Balance sheet

c. Financial statements

d. Statement of retained earnings

5. In financial accounting, a _____ or statement of cash flows is a financial statement that shows a company's flow of cash. The money coming into the business is called cash inflow, and money going out from the business is called cash outflow. The statement shows how changes in balance sheet and income accounts affect cash and cash equivalents, and breaks the analysis down to operating, investing, and financing activities.

a. 7-Eleven

b. 4-4-5 Calendar

c. Cash flow statement

d. 529 plan

6. _____ is the balance of the amounts of cash being received and paid by a business during a defined period of time, sometimes tied to a specific project. Measurement of _____ can be used

- to evaluate the state or performance of a business or project.
- to determine problems with liquidity. Being profitable does not necessarily mean being liquid. A company can fail because of a shortage of cash, even while profitable.
- to generate project rate of returns. The time of _____s into and out of projects are used as inputs to financial models such as internal rate of return, and net present value.
- to examine income or growth of a business when it is believed that accrual accounting concepts do not represent economic realities. Alternately, _____ can be used to 'validate' the net income generated by accrual accounting.

_____ as a generic term may be used differently depending on context, and certain _____ definitions may be adapted by analysts and users for their own uses. Common terms include operating _____ and free _____.

_____s can be classified into:

1. Operational _____s: Cash received or expended as a result of the company's core business activities.
2. Investment _____s: Cash received or expended through capital expenditure, investments or acquisitions.
3. Financing _____s: Cash received or expended as a result of financial activities, such as interests and dividends.

All three together - the net _____ - are necessary to reconcile the beginning cash balance to the ending cash balance. Loan draw downs or equity injections, that is just shifting of capital but no expenditure as such, are not considered in the net _____.

a. Corporate finance

b. Cash flow

c. Shareholder value

d. Real option

7. _____, refers to consumption opportunity gained by an entity within a specified time frame, which is generally expressed in monetary terms. However, for households and individuals, '_____ is the sum of all the wages, salaries, profits, interests payments, rents and other forms of earnings received... in a given period of time.' For firms, _____ generally refers to net-profit: what remains of revenue after expenses have been subtracted.

a. Annual report

b. Accrual

c. OIBDA

d. Income

8. An _____ is a financial statement for companies that indicates how Revenue is transformed into net income The purpose of the _____ is to show managers and investors whether the company made or lost money during the period being reported.

The important thing to remember about an _____ is that it represents a period of time.

a. ABN Amro   b. Income statement

c. A Random Walk Down Wall Street   d. AAB

9.   In finance, a _____ or accounting ratio is a ratio of two selected numerical values taken from an enterprise's financial statements. There are many standard ratios used to try to evaluate the overall financial condition of a corporation or other organization. They may be used by managers within a firm, by current and potential shareholders (owners) of a firm, and by a firm's creditors. Security analysts use these to compare the strengths and weaknesses in various companies.

a. Financial ratio   b. Return on capital employed

c. Sustainable growth rate   d. Price/cash flow ratio

10.   The _____ is a financial ratio that measures whether or not a firm has enough resources to pay its debts over the next 12 months. It compares a firm's current assets to its current liabilities. It is expressed as follows:

$$\text{Current ratio} = \frac{\text{Current Assets}}{\text{Current Liabilities}}$$

For example, if WXY Company's current assets are $50,000,000 and its current liabilities are $40,000,000, then its _____ would be $50,000,000 divided by $40,000,000, which equals 1.25.

a. Sustainable growth rate   b. Debt service coverage ratio

c. PEG ratio   d. Current ratio

11.   _____ is a measure of the ability of a debtor to pay their debts as and when they fall due. It is usually expressed as a ratio or a percentage of current liabilities.

For a corporation with a published balance sheet there are various ratios used to calculate a measure of liquidity.

a. Invested capital   b. Operating leverage

c. Operating profit margin   d. Accounting liquidity

12.   The _____ is used by business and government to classify and measure economic activity in Canada, Mexico and the United States. It has largely replaced the older Standard Industrial Classification (SIC) system; however, certain government departments and agencies, such as the U.S. Securities and Exchange Commission (SEC), still use the SIC codes.

The _____ numbering system is a six-digit code.

a. 529 plan   b. 7-Eleven

c. 4-4-5 Calendar   d. NAICS

13.   In economics, the concept of the _____ refers to the decision-making time frame of a firm in which at least one factor of production is fixed. Costs which are fixed in the _____ have no impact on a firms decisions. For example a firm can raise output by increasing the amount of labour through overtime.

a. Long-run

b. 4-4-5 Calendar

c. 529 plan

d. Short-run

14.   In finance, _____ is the ability of an entity to pay its debts with available cash. _____ can also be described as the ability of a corporation to meet its long-term fixed expenses and to accomplish long-term expansion and growth. The better a company's _____, the better it is financially.

a. Solvency

b. Political risk

c. Mid price

d. Capital asset

15.   In finance, the Acid-test or _____ or liquid ratio measures the ability of a company to use its near cash or quick assets to immediately extinguish or retire its current liabilities. Quick assets include those current assets that presumably can be quickly converted to cash at close to their book values.

Generally, the acid test ratio should be 1:1 or better, however this varies widely by industry.

a. Quick ratio

b. Net assets

c. P/E ratio

d. Financial ratio

16.   The _____ is a bank regulation that sets the minimum reserves each bank must hold to customer deposits and notes. These reserves are designed to satisfy withdrawal demands, and would normally be in the form of fiat currency stored in a bank vault (vault cash), or with a central bank.

The reserve ratio is sometimes used as a tool in the monetary policy, influencing the country's economy, borrowing, and interest rates.

a. Wall Street Journal prime rate

b. Prime rate

c. Reserve requirement

d. Variable rate mortgage

17.   _____ is a fee paid on borrowed assets. It is the price paid for the use of borrowed money , or, money earned by deposited funds . Assets that are sometimes lent with _____ include money, shares, consumer goods through hire purchase, major assets such as aircraft, and even entire factories in finance lease arrangements.

a. A Random Walk Down Wall Street

b. Insolvency

c. AAB

d. Interest

18.   In finance, _____ (or gearing) is borrowing money to supplement existing funds for investment in such a way that the potential positive or negative outcome is magnified and/or enhanced. It generally refers to using borrowed funds, or debt, so as to attempt to increase the returns to equity. Deleveraging is the action of reducing borrowings.

a. Leverage

b. Pension fund

c. Financial endowment

d. Limited partnership

19.   In economic models, the _____ time frame assumes no fixed factors of production. Firms can enter or leave the marketplace, and the cost (and availability) of land, labor, raw materials, and capital goods can be assumed to vary. In contrast, in the short-run time frame, certain factors are assumed to be fixed, because there is not sufficient time for them to change.

   a. 4-4-5 Calendar   b. Short-run

   c. 529 plan   d. Long-run

20.   _____ is a financial metric which represents operating liquidity available to a business. Along with fixed assets such as plant and equipment, _____ is considered a part of operating capital. It is calculated as current assets minus current liabilities.

   a. Working capital   b. Working capital management

   c. 529 plan   d. 4-4-5 Calendar

21.   In business and accounting, _____s are everything of value that is owned by a person or company. The balance sheet of a firm records the monetary value of the _____s owned by the firm. The two major _____ classes are tangible _____s and intangible _____s.

   a. Asset   b. EBITDA

   c. Income   d. Accounts payable

22.   _____ is that which is owed; usually referencing assets owed, but the term can cover other obligations. In the case of assets, _____ is a means of using future purchasing power in the present before a summation has been earned. Some companies and corporations use _____ as a part of their overall corporate finance strategy.

   a. Cross-collateralization   b. Debt

   c. Partial Payment   d. Credit cycle

23.   _____ is a financial ratio that indicates the percentage of a company's assets are provided via debt. It is the ratio of total debt (the sum of current liabilities and long-term liabilities) and total assets (the sum of current assets, fixed assets, and other assets such as 'goodwill'.)

or alternatively:

For example, a company with $2 million in total assets and $500,000 in total liabilities would have a _____ of 25%

Like all financial ratios, a company's _____ should be compared with their industry average or other competing firms.

   a. Cash concentration   b. Debt ratio

   c. Capitalization rate   d. Cash management

24.   Times interest earned (TIE) or _____ is a measure of a company's ability to honor its debt payments. It may be calculated as either EBIT or EBITDA divided by the total interest payable.

$$\text{Times-Interest-Earned} = \frac{\text{EBIT or EBITDA}}{\text{Interest Charges}}$$

- Financial ratio
- Financial leverage
- EBIT
- EBITDA
- Debt service coverage ratio

Interest Charges = Traditionally 'charges' refers to interest expense found on the income statement.

Times Interest Earned or Interest Coverage is a great tool when measuring a company's ability to meet its debt obligations.

a. Earnings per share

c. Assets turnover

b. Information ratio

d. Interest coverage ratio

25.   _____ or interest coverage ratio is a measure of a company's ability to honor its debt payments. It may be calculated as either EBIT or EBITDA divided by the total interest payable.

$$\text{Times-Interest-Earned} = \frac{\text{EBIT or EBITDA}}{\text{Interest Charges}}$$

- Financial ratio
- Financial leverage
- EBIT
- EBITDA
- Debt service coverage ratio

Interest Charges = Traditionally 'charges' refers to interest expense found on the income statement.

_____ or Interest Coverage is a great tool when measuring a company's ability to meet its debt obligations.

a. Net assets

c. Return of capital

b. Cash conversion cycle

d. Times interest earned

26. _____ is the process of decreasing an amount over a period of time. The word comes from Middle English amortisen to kill, alienate in mortmain, from Anglo-French amorteser, alteration of amortir, from Vulgar Latin admortire to kill, from Latin ad- + mort-, mors death. Particular instances of the term include:

- _____ (business), the allocation of a lump sum amount to different time periods, particularly for loans and other forms of finance, including related interest or other finance charges.
    ○ _____ schedule, a table detailing each periodic payment on a loan (typically a mortgage), as generated by an _____ calculator.
    ○ Negative _____, an _____ schedule where the loan amount actually increases through not paying the full interest
- Amortized analysis, analyzing the execution cost of algorithms over a sequence of operations.
- _____ of capital expenditures of certain assets under accounting rules, particularly intangible assets, in a manner analogous to depreciation.
- _____ (tax law)

_____ is also used in the context of zoning regulations and describes the time in which a property owner has to relocate when the property's use constitutes a preexisting nonconforming use under zoning regulations.

- Depreciation

a. Intrinsic value   b. Amortization
c. AT'T Inc.   d. Option

27.   The term _____ is often used to refer to the investment management of collective investments, (not necessarily) whilst the more generic fund management may refer to all forms of institutional investment as well as investment management for private investors. Investment managers who specialize in advisory or discretionary management on behalf of (normally wealthy) private investors may often refer to their services as wealth management or portfolio management often within the context of so-called 'private banking'.

The provision of 'investment management services' includes elements of financial analysis, asset selection, stock selection, plan implementation and ongoing monitoring of investments.

a. AAB   b. ABN Amro
c. A Random Walk Down Wall Street   d. Asset management

28.   _____ is a term used in accounting, economics and finance to spread the cost of an asset over the span of several years.

In simple words we can say that _____ is the reduction in the value of an asset due to usage, passage of time, wear and tear, technological outdating or obsolescence, depletion or other such factors.

In accounting, _____ is a term used to describe any method of attributing the historical or purchase cost of an asset across its useful life, roughly corresponding to normal wear and tear.

a. Bottom line

b. Depreciation

c. Deferred financing costs

d. Matching principle

29.   In financial and business accounting, _____ is a measure of a firm's profitability that excludes interest and income tax expenses.

EBIT = Operating Revenue - Operating Expenses (OPEX) + Non-operating Income

Operating Income = Operating Revenue - Operating Expenses

Operating income is the difference between operating revenues and operating expenses, but it is also sometimes used as a synonym for EBIT and operating profit. This is true if the firm has no non-operating income.

a. Earnings before interest and taxes

b. AAB

c. A Random Walk Down Wall Street

d. ABN Amro

30.   Earnings before interest, taxes, depreciation and amortization (_____) is a non-GAAP metric that can be used to evaluate a company's profitability.

_____ = Operating Revenue - Operating Expenses + Other Revenue

Its name comes from the fact that Operating Expenses do not include interest, taxes, or amortization. _____ is not a defined measure according to Generally Accepted Accounting Principles (GAAP), and thus can be calculated however a company wishes.

a. Invoice processing

b. Accounts payable

c. Accrual

d. EBITDA

31.   _____ is a list for goods and materials held available in stock by a business. It is also used for a list of the contents of a household and for a list for testamentary purposes of the possessions of someone who has died. In accounting _____ is considered an asset.

a. ABN Amro

b. AAB

c. A Random Walk Down Wall Street

d. Inventory

32.   The _____ is an equation that equals the cost of goods sold divided by the average inventory. Average inventory equals beginning inventory plus ending inventory divided by 2.

The formula for _____:

$$\text{Inventory Turnover} = \frac{\text{Cost of Goods Sold}}{\text{Average Inventory}}$$

The formula for average inventory:

$$\text{Average Inventory} = \frac{\text{Beginning inventory} + \text{Ending inventory}}{2}$$

A low turnover rate may point to overstocking, obsolescence, or deficiencies in the product line or marketing effort.

a. Information ratio

b. Operating leverage

c. Earnings yield

d. Inventory turnover

33. _____ is one of the Accounting Liquidity ratios, a financial ratio. This ratio measures the number of times, on average, the inventory is sold during the period. Its purpose is to measure the liquidity of the inventory.

a. A Random Walk Down Wall Street

b. AAB

c. ABN Amro

d. Inventory turnover ratio

34. _____ (EBITDA) is a non-GAAP metric that can be used to evaluate a company's profitability.

EBITDA = Operating Revenue - Operating Expenses + Other Revenue

Its name comes from the fact that Operating Expenses do not include interest, taxes, or amortization. EBITDA is not a defined measure according to Generally Accepted Accounting Principles (GAAP), and thus can be calculated however a company wishes.

a. Earnings before interest, taxes, depreciation and amortization

b. Accrued liabilities

c. Annual report

d. Accounting methods

35. _____ is one of the accounting liquidity ratios, a financial ratio. This ratio measures the number of times, on average, receivables (e.g. Accounts Receivable) are collected during the period. A popular variant of the _____ is to convert it into an Average Collection Period in terms of days.

a. Return on equity

b. Receivables turnover ratio

c. PEG ratio

d. Sharpe ratio

36. _____ is a financial ratio that measures the efficiency of a company's use of its assets in generating sales revenue or sales income to the company.

$$Asset\ Turnover = \frac{Sales}{Average\,Total\,Assets}$$

- 'Sales' is the value of 'Net Sales' or 'Sales' from the company's income statement
- 'Average Total Assets' is the value of 'Total assets' from the company's balance sheet in the beginning and the end of the fiscal period divided by 2.

- Assets turnover

a. Average accounting return	b. Earnings yield
c. Inventory turnover	d. Asset turnover

37. _____ plant, and equipment, is a term used in accountancy for assets and property which cannot easily be converted into cash. This can be compared with current assets such as cash or bank accounts, which are described as liquid assets. In most cases, only tangible assets are referred to as fixed.

a. Percentage of Completion	b. Petty cash
c. Fixed asset	d. Remittance advice

38. _____ is the ratio of sales (on the Profit and loss account) to the value of fixed assets (on the balance sheet.) It indicates how well the business is using its fixed assets to generate sales.

Generally speaking, the higher the ratio, the better, because a high ratio indicates the business has less money tied up in fixed assets for each dollar of sales revenue.

a. Defined contribution plan	b. Total revenue
c. Market microstructure	d. Fixed asset turnover

39. _____ is the difference between price and the costs of bringing to market whatever it is that is accounted as an enterprise (whether by harvest, extraction, manufacture, or purchase) in terms of the component costs of delivered goods and/or services and any operating or other expenses.

A key difficulty in measuring profit is in defining costs. Pure economic monetary profits can be zero or negative even in competitive equilibrium when accounted monetized costs exceed monetized price.

a. AAB	b. A Random Walk Down Wall Street
c. Accounting profit	d. Economic profit

40. _____, Net Margin, Net _____ or Net Profit Ratio all refer to a measure of profitability. It is calculated using a formula and written as a percentage or a number.

$$\text{Net profit margin} = \frac{\text{Net profit after taxes}}{\text{Net Sales}}$$

The _____ is mostly used for internal comparison.

a. Profit maximization
c. Net profit margin

b. 4-4-5 Calendar
d. Profit margin

41. The _____ percentage shows how profitable a company's assets are in generating revenue.

_____ can be computed as:

$$\text{ROA} = \frac{\text{Net Income}}{\text{Total Assets}}$$

This number tells you 'what the company can do with what it's got', i.e. how many dollars of earnings they derive from each dollar of assets they control. It's a useful number for comparing competing companies in the same industry.

a. P/E ratio
c. Receivables turnover ratio

b. Return on sales
d. Return on assets

42. _____ measures the rate of return on the ownership interest (shareholders' equity) of the common stock owners. _____ is viewed as one of the most important financial ratios. It measures a firm's efficiency at generating profits from every dollar of shareholders' equity (also known as net assets or assets minus liabilities.)

a. Return of capital
c. Diluted Earnings Per Share

b. Return on sales
d. Return on equity

43. The _____ is the average project earnings after taxes and depreciation, divided by the average book value of the investment during its life.

There are three steps to calculating the _____.

First, determine the average net income of each year of the project's life. Second, determine the average investment, taking depreciation into account. Third, determine the _____ by dividing the average net income by the average investment.

a. Assets turnover
c. Information ratio

b. Operating leverage
d. Average accounting return

44. A _____ is a financial contract between two parties, the buyer and the seller of this type of option. Often it is simply labeled a 'call'. The buyer of the option has the right, but not the obligation to buy an agreed quantity of a particular commodity or financial instrument (the underlying instrument) from the seller of the option at a certain time (the expiration date) for a certain price (the strike price.)

a. Bear call spread

b. Call option

c. Bull spread

d. Bear spread

45. In finance, a _____ is collateral that the holder of a position in securities, options, or futures contracts has to deposit to cover the credit risk of his counterparty (most often his broker.) This risk can arise if the holder has done any of the following:

- borrowed cash from the counterparty to buy securities or options,
- sold securities or options short, or
- entered into a futures contract.

The collateral can be in the form of cash or securities, and it is deposited in a _____ account. On U.S. futures exchanges, '_____' was formally called performance bond.

_____ buying is buying securities with cash borrowed from a broker, using other securities as collateral.

a. Credit

b. Procter ' Gamble

c. Margin

d. Share

46. In business, _____ is the total assets minus total outside liabilities of an individual or a company. For a company, this is called shareholders' equity and may be referred to as book value. _____ is stated as at a particular point in time.

a. Net worth

b. Restructuring

c. Certified International Investment Analyst

d. Moneylender

47. An _____ is a contract written by a seller that conveys to the buyer the right -- but not the obligation -- to buy (in the case of a call _____) or to sell (in the case of a put _____) a particular asset, such as a piece of property such as, among others, a futures contract. In return for granting the _____, the seller collects a payment (the premium) from the buyer.

For example, buying a call _____ provides the right to buy a specified quantity of a security at a set strike price at some time on or before expiration, while buying a put _____ provides the right to sell.

a. AT'T Mobility LLC

b. Annuity

c. Amortization

d. Option

48. _____ is the price at which an asset would trade in a competitive Walrasian auction setting. _____ is often used interchangeably with open _____, fair value or fair _____, although these terms have distinct definitions in different standards, and may differ in some circumstances.

International Valuation Standards defines _____ as 'the estimated amount for which a property should exchange on the date of valuation between a willing buyer and a willing seller in an arm'e;s-length transaction after proper marketing wherein the parties had each acted knowledgeably, prudently, and without compulsion.'

_____ is a concept distinct from market price, which is 'e;the price at which one can transact'e;, while _____ is 'e;the true underlying value'e; according to theoretical standards.

a. T-Model

c. Wrap account

b. Debt restructuring

d. Market value

49.   The _____ is a financial ratio used to compare a company's book value to its current market price. Book value is an accounting term denoting the portion of the company held by the shareholders; in other words, the company's total tangible assets less its total liabilities. The calculation can be performed in two ways, but the result should be the same each way. In the first way, the company's market capitalization can be divided by the company's total book value from its balance sheet. The second way, using per-share values, is to divide the company's current share price by the book value per share (i.e. its book value divided by the number of outstanding shares).

a. Stop order

c. Whisper numbers

b. Stock repurchase

d. Price-to-book ratio

50.   _____ is the process of comparing the cost, time or quality of what one organization does against what another organization does. The result is often a business case for making changes in order to make improvements.

Also referred to as 'best practice _____' or 'process _____', it is a process used in management and particularly strategic management, in which organizations evaluate various aspects of their processes in relation to best practice, usually within their own sector.

a. 7-Eleven

c. 529 plan

b. 4-4-5 Calendar

d. Benchmarking

51.   The _____ is a United States government system for classifying industries by a four-digit code. Established in 1937, it is being supplanted by the six-digit North American Industry Classification System, which was released in 1997; however certain government departments and agencies, such as the U.S. Securities and Exchange Commission (SEC), still use the _____ codes.

The following table is from the SEC's site, which allows searching for companies by _____ code in its database of filings.

a. 529 plan

c. 4-4-5 Calendar

b. Standard Industrial Classification

d. 7-Eleven

52.   _____ is the practice of comparing a firm's results to those of similar companies or competitors.

a. Trade date

c. False billing

b. Capital guarantee

d. Peer group analysis

53.   _____ is the value on a given date of a future payment or series of future payments, discounted to reflect the time value of money and other factors such as investment risk. _____ calculations are widely used in business and economics to provide a means to compare cash flows at different times on a meaningful 'like to like' basis.

The most commonly applied model of the time value of money is compound interest.

a. Present value	b. Present value of benefits
c. Negative gearing	d. Net present value

54.   The _____ or _____ is used by business and government to classify and measure economic activity in Canada, Mexico and the United States. It has largely replaced the older Standard Industrial Classification (SIC) system; however, certain government departments and agencies, such as the U.S. Securities and Exchange Commission (SEC), still use the SIC codes.

The _____ numbering system is a six-digit code.

a. 7-Eleven	b. North American Industry Classification System
c. 529 plan	d. 4-4-5 Calendar

55.   _____ is the discipline of identifying, monitoring and limiting risks. In some cases the acceptable risk may be near zero. Risks can come from accidents, natural causes and disasters as well as deliberate attacks from an adversary.

a. Penny stock	b. FIFO
c. 4-4-5 Calendar	d. Risk Management

56.   _____ is the standard framework of guidelines for financial accounting used in the United States of America. It includes the standards, conventions, and rules accountants follow in recording and summarizing transactions, and in the preparation of financial statements. _____ are now issued by the Financial Accounting Standards Board (FASB).

a. Net income	b. Generally Accepted Accounting Principles
c. Revenue	d. Depreciation

57.   In finance, a _____ is a type of bond that can be converted into shares of stock in the issuing company, usually at some pre-announced ratio. It is a hybrid security with debt- and equity-like features. Although it typically has a low coupon rate, the holder is compensated with the ability to convert the bond to common stock, usually at a substantial discount to the stock's market value.

a. Bond fund	b. Gilts
c. Corporate bond	d. Convertible bond

1. _____ is the task of determining how a business will afford to achieve its strategic goals and objectives. Usually, a company creates a Financial Plan immediately after the vision and objectives have been set. The Financial Plan describes each of the activities, resources, equipment and materials that are needed to achieve these objectives, as well as the timeframes involved.

   a. Corporate Transparency   b. Management by exception

   c. Performance measurement   d. Financial planning

2. The _____ is the amount of time an organization will look into the future when preparing a strategic plan. Many commercial companies use a five-year _____, but other organizations such as the Forestry Commission in the UK have to use a much longer _____ to form effective plans.

   a. First-mover advantage   b. Trade finance

   c. Debtor-in-possession financing   d. Planning horizon

3. An _____ is a contract written by a seller that conveys to the buyer the right -- but not the obligation -- to buy (in the case of a call _____) or to sell (in the case of a put _____) a particular asset, such as a piece of property such as, among others, a futures contract. In return for granting the _____, the seller collects a payment (the premium) from the buyer.

For example, buying a call _____ provides the right to buy a specified quantity of a security at a set strike price at some time on or before expiration, while buying a put _____ provides the right to sell.

   a. Option   b. AT'T Mobility LLC

   c. Amortization   d. Annuity

4. The term _____ is a term applied to practices that are perfunctory, or seek to satisfy the minimum requirements or to conform to a convention or doctrine. It has different meanings in different fields.

In accounting, _____ earnings are those earnings of companies in addition to actual earnings calculated under the Generally Accepted Accounting Principles (GAAP) in their quarterly and yearly financial reports.

   a. Deferred income   b. Pro forma

   c. Deferred financing costs   d. Long-term liabilities

5. _____ are formal records of a business' financial activities.

_____ provide an overview of a business' financial condition in both short and long term. There are four basic _____:

1. **Balance sheet**: also referred to as statement of financial position or condition, reports on a company's assets, liabilities, and net equity as of a given point in time.
2. **Income statement**: also referred to as Profit and Loss statement (or a 'P'L'), reports on a company's income, expenses, and profits over a period of time.
3. **Statement of retained earnings**: explains the changes in a company's retained earnings over the reporting period.
4. **Statement of cash flows**: reports on a company's cash flow activities, particularly its operating, investing and financing activities.

a. Statement of retained earnings

b. Statement on Auditing Standards No. 70: Service Organizations

c. Notes to the Financial Statements

d. Financial statements

6.   In business and accounting, _____s are everything of value that is owned by a person or company. The balance sheet of a firm records the monetary value of the _____s owned by the firm. The two major _____ classes are tangible _____s and intangible _____s.

a. EBITDA

b. Income

c. Accounts payable

d. Asset

7.   In economics, the concept of the _____ refers to the decision-making time frame of a firm in which at least one factor of production is fixed. Costs which are fixed in the _____ have no impact on a firms decisions. For example a firm can raise output by increasing the amount of labour through overtime.

a. 4-4-5 Calendar

b. Long-run

c. 529 plan

d. Short-run

8.   A _____ is a payment made by a corporation to its shareholder members. When a corporation earns a profit or surplus, that money can be put to two uses: it can either be re-invested in the business (called retained earnings), or it can be paid to the shareholders as a _____. Many corporations retain a portion of their earnings and pay the remainder as a _____.

a. Dividend

b. Dividend yield

c. Dividend puzzle

d. Special dividend

9.   In finance, a _____ or accounting ratio is a ratio of two selected numerical values taken from an enterprise's financial statements. There are many standard ratios used to try to evaluate the overall financial condition of a corporation or other organization. They may be used by managers within a firm, by current and potential shareholders (owners) of a firm, and by a firm's creditors. Security analysts use these to compare the strengths and weaknesses in various companies.

a. Financial ratio

b. Price/cash flow ratio

c. Return on capital employed

d. Sustainable growth rate

10.   _____ is the standard framework of guidelines for financial accounting used in the United States of America. It includes the standards, conventions, and rules accountants follow in recording and summarizing transactions, and in the preparation of financial statements. _____ are now issued by the Financial Accounting Standards Board (FASB).

a. Net income

b. Revenue

c. Depreciation

d. Generally Accepted Accounting Principles

11. _____ is the fraction of net income a firm pays to its stockholders in dividends:

The part of the earnings not paid to investors is left for investment to provide for future earnings growth. Investors seeking high current income and limited capital growth prefer companies with high _____. However investors seeking capital growth may prefer lower payout ratio because capital gains are taxed at a lower rate.

a. Dividend yield

b. Dividend puzzle

c. Dividend imputation

d. Dividend payout ratio

12. _____, refers to consumption opportunity gained by an entity within a specified time frame, which is generally expressed in monetary terms. However, for households and individuals, '_____ is the sum of all the wages, salaries, profits, interests payments, rents and other forms of earnings received... in a given period of time.' For firms, _____ generally refers to net-profit: what remains of revenue after expenses have been subtracted.

a. Income

b. Annual report

c. OIBDA

d. Accrual

13. An _____ is a financial statement for companies that indicates how Revenue is transformed into net income The purpose of the _____ is to show managers and investors whether the company made or lost money during the period being reported.

The important thing to remember about an _____ is that it represents a period of time.

a. AAB

b. Income statement

c. A Random Walk Down Wall Street

d. ABN Amro

14. In financial accounting, a _____ or statement of financial position is a summary of a person's or organization's balances. Assets, liabilities and ownership equity are listed as of a specific date, such as the end of its financial year. A _____ is often described as a snapshot of a company's financial condition.

a. Statement of retained earnings

b. Financial statements

c. Statement on Auditing Standards No. 70: Service Organizations

d. Balance sheet

15. _____ is the term in economics for the amount of fixed or real capital present in relation to other factors of production, especially labor. At the level of either a production process or the aggregate economy, it may be estimated by the capital/labor ratio, such as from the points along a capital/labor isoquant.

Since the use of tools and machinery makes labor more effective, rising _____ pushes up the productivity of labor, so a society that is more capital intensive tends to have a higher standard of living over the long run than one with low _____.

a. Weighted average cost of capital   b. Capital intensity

c. Cost of capital   d. 4-4-5 Calendar

16.   The _____ is used by business and government to classify and measure economic activity in Canada, Mexico and the United States. It has largely replaced the older Standard Industrial Classification (SIC) system; however, certain government departments and agencies, such as the U.S. Securities and Exchange Commission (SEC), still use the SIC codes.

The _____ numbering system is a six-digit code.

    a. 7-Eleven   b. 529 plan

    c. 4-4-5 Calendar   d. NAICS

17.   _____ indicates the percentage of a company's earnings that are not paid out in dividends but credited to retained earnings. It is the opposite of the dividend payout ratio, so that also called the retention rate.

_____ = 1 - Dividend Payout Ratio

    a. Dow Jones Indexes   b. Retention ratio

    c. Bankassurer   d. Fair market value

18.   In the theory of capital structure, _____ is the phrase used to describe funds that firms obtain from outside of the firm. It is contrasted to internal financing which consists mainly of profits retained by the firm for investment. There are many kinds of _____.

    a. Adjustment   b. Asset-backed commercial paper

    c. Ownership equity   d. External financing

19.   _____ or financing is to provide capital (funds), which means money for a project, a person, a business or any other private or public institutions.

Those funds can be allocated for either short term or long term purposes. The health fund is a new way of _____ private healthcare centers.

    a. Proxy fight   b. Synthetic CDO

    c. Product life cycle   d. Funding

20.   A _____ is an international bond that is denominated in a currency not native to the country where it is issued. It can be categorised according to the currency in which it is issued. London is one of the centers of the _____ market, but _____s may be traded throughout the world - for example in Singapore or Tokyo.

    a. Economic entity   b. Education production function

    c. Interest rate option   d. Eurobond

21.   _____ is the maximum rate at which a company can grow revenue without having to invest new equity capital. If a company earns a 15% return on equity (ROE), it can grow 15% simply by reinvesting all the earnings in new opportunities and maintaining a stable debt to equity ratio. In order to grow faster, the company would have to invest more equity capital or increase its financial leverage.

a. Price/cash flow ratio   b. Current ratio
c. Sustainable growth rate   d. Return on capital employed

22.   In finance, _____ is that risk which is common to an entire market and not to any individual entity or component thereof. It should be distinguished from systemic risk which is the risk that the entire financial system will collapse as a result of some catastrophic event.

Risks can be reduced in four main ways: Avoidance, Reduction, Retention and Transfer.

a. Conglomerate merger   b. Systematic risk
c. Capital surplus   d. Primary market

23.   _____ is the difference between price and the costs of bringing to market whatever it is that is accounted as an enterprise (whether by harvest, extraction, manufacture, or purchase) in terms of the component costs of delivered goods and/or services and any operating or other expenses.

A key difficulty in measuring profit is in defining costs. Pure economic monetary profits can be zero or negative even in competitive equilibrium when accounted monetized costs exceed monetized price.

a. Accounting profit   b. AAB
c. Economic profit   d. A Random Walk Down Wall Street

24.   _____, Net Margin, Net _____ or Net Profit Ratio all refer to a measure of profitability. It is calculated using a formula and written as a percentage or a number.

$$\text{Net profit margin} = \frac{\text{Net profit after taxes}}{\text{Net Sales}}$$

The _____ is mostly used for internal comparison.

a. 4-4-5 Calendar   b. Profit maximization
c. Net profit margin   d. Profit margin

25.   In finance, a _____ is collateral that the holder of a position in securities, options, or futures contracts has to deposit to cover the credit risk of his counterparty (most often his broker.) This risk can arise if the holder has done any of the following:

• borrowed cash from the counterparty to buy securities or options,
• sold securities or options short, or
• entered into a futures contract.

The collateral can be in the form of cash or securities, and it is deposited in a _____ account. On U.S. futures exchanges, '_____' was formally called performance bond.

_____ buying is buying securities with cash borrowed from a broker, using other securities as collateral.

a. Credit

c. Procter ' Gamble

b. Share

d. Margin

26.   In finance, a _____ is a debt security, in which the authorized issuer owes the holders a debt and, depending on the terms of the _____, is obliged to pay interest (the coupon) and/or to repay the principal at a later date, termed maturity.

Thus a _____ is a loan: the issuer is the borrower, the _____ holder is the lender, and the coupon is the interest. _____s provide the borrower with external funds to finance long-term investments, or, in the case of government _____s, to finance current expenditure.

a. Convertible bond

c. Catastrophe bonds

b. Puttable bond

d. Bond

27.   In finance, a _____ is a type of bond that can be converted into shares of stock in the issuing company, usually at some pre-announced ratio. It is a hybrid security with debt- and equity-like features. Although it typically has a low coupon rate, the holder is compensated with the ability to convert the bond to common stock, usually at a substantial discount to the stock's market value.

a. Bond fund

c. Corporate bond

b. Gilts

d. Convertible bond

1.   In finance, the value of an option consists of two components, its intrinsic value and its _____. Time value is simply the difference between option value and intrinsic value. _____ is also known as theta, extrinsic value, or instrumental value.
   - a. Conservatism
   - b. Time value
   - c. Global Squeeze
   - d. Debt buyer

2.   Simply put, _____ is the value of money figuring in a given amount of interest for a given amount of time. For example 100 dollars of todays money held for a year at 5 percent interest is worth 105 dollars, therefore 100 dollars paid now or 105 dollars paid exactly one year from now is the same amount of payment of money with that given intersest at that given amount of time. This notion dates at least to Martín de Azpilcueta of the School of Salamanca.

All of the standard calculations for _____ derive from the most basic algebraic expression for the present value of a future sum, 'discounted' to the present by an amount equal to the _____. For example, a sum of FV to be received in one year is discounted (at the rate of interest r) to give a sum of PV at present: $PV = FV -- r·PV = FV/(1+r)$.

   - a. Coefficient of variation
   - b. Time value of money
   - c. Zero-coupon bond
   - d. Current account

3.   _____ is the concept of adding accumulated interest back to the principal, so that interest is earned on interest from that moment on. The act of declaring interest to be principal is called compounding (i.e., interest is compounded.) A loan, for example, may have its interest compounded every month: in this case, a loan with $100 principal and 1% interest per month would have a balance of $101 at the end of the first month.
   - a. Penny stock
   - b. 4-4-5 Calendar
   - c. Risk management
   - d. Compound interest

4.   _____ or financing is to provide capital (funds), which means money for a project, a person, a business or any other private or public institutions.

Those funds can be allocated for either short term or long term purposes. The health fund is a new way of _____ private healthcare centers.

   - a. Product life cycle
   - b. Proxy fight
   - c. Synthetic CDO
   - d. Funding

5.   _____ measures the nominal future sum of money that a given sum of money is 'worth' at a specified time in the future assuming a certain interest rate rate of return; it is the present value multiplied by the accumulation function.

The value does not include corrections for inflation or other factors that affect the true value of money in the future. This is used in time value of money calculations.

   - a. Present value of costs
   - b. Discounted cash flow
   - c. Future-oriented
   - d. Future value

6.   _____ is a fee paid on borrowed assets. It is the price paid for the use of borrowed money , or, money earned by deposited funds . Assets that are sometimes lent with _____ include money, shares, consumer goods through hire purchase, major assets such as aircraft, and even entire factories in finance lease arrangements.

a. A Random Walk Down Wall Street

b. Insolvency

c. AAB

d. Interest

7.   A '_____' is a 'Charge' that is paid to obtain the right to delay a payment. Essentially, the payer purchases the right to make a given payment in the future instead of in the Present. The '_____', or 'Charge' that must be paid to delay the payment, is simply the difference between what the payment amount would be if it were paid in the present and what the payment amount would be paid if it were paid in the future.

a. Risk aversion

b. Risk modeling

c. Discount

d. Value at risk

8.   _____ is the value on a given date of a future payment or series of future payments, discounted to reflect the time value of money and other factors such as investment risk. _____ calculations are widely used in business and economics to provide a means to compare cash flows at different times on a meaningful 'like to like' basis.

The most commonly applied model of the time value of money is compound interest.

a. Present value of benefits

b. Negative gearing

c. Net present value

d. Present value

9.   A _____ is a payment made by a corporation to its shareholder members. When a corporation earns a profit or surplus, that money can be put to two uses: it can either be re-invested in the business (called retained earnings), or it can be paid to the shareholders as a _____. Many corporations retain a portion of their earnings and pay the remainder as a

_____.

a. Special dividend

b. Dividend puzzle

c. Dividend

d. Dividend yield

10.   The _____ is an interest rate a central bank charges depository institutions that borrow reserves from it.

The term _____ has two meanings:

- the same as interest rate; the term 'discount' does not refer to the meaning of the word, but to the purpose of using the quantity, such as computations of present value, e.g. net present value / discounted cash flow

- the annual effective _____, which is the annual interest divided by the capital including that interest; this rate is lower than the interest rate; it corresponds to using the value after a year as the nominal value, and seeing the initial value as the nominal value minus a discount; it is used for Treasury Bills and similar financial instruments

The annual effective _____ is the annual interest divided by the capital including that interest, which is the interest rate divided by 100% plus the interest rate. It is the annual discount factor to be applied to the future cash flow, to find the discount, subtracted from a future value to find the value one year earlier.

For example, suppose there is a government bond that sells for $95 and pays $100 in a year's time.

a. Fisher equation
c. Black-Scholes

b. Discount rate
d. Stochastic volatility

11.   In finance, the _____ approach describes a method of valuing a project, company, or asset using the concepts of the time value of money. All future cash flows are estimated and discounted to give their present values. The discount rate used is generally the appropriate cost of capital and may incorporate judgments of the uncertainty (riskiness) of the future cash flows.

a. Future-oriented
c. Present value of benefits

b. Discounted cash flow
d. Net present value

12.   _____ is the balance of the amounts of cash being received and paid by a business during a defined period of time, sometimes tied to a specific project. Measurement of _____ can be used

- to evaluate the state or performance of a business or project.
- to determine problems with liquidity. Being profitable does not necessarily mean being liquid. A company can fail because of a shortage of cash, even while profitable.
- to generate project rate of returns. The time of _____s into and out of projects are used as inputs to financial models such as internal rate of return, and net present value.
- to examine income or growth of a business when it is believed that accrual accounting concepts do not represent economic realities. Alternately, _____ can be used to 'validate' the net income generated by accrual accounting.

_____ as a generic term may be used differently depending on context, and certain _____ definitions may be adapted by analysts and users for their own uses. Common terms include operating _____ and free _____.

_____s can be classified into:

1.   Operational _____s: Cash received or expended as a result of the company's core business activities.
2.   Investment _____s: Cash received or expended through capital expenditure, investments or acquisitions.
3.   Financing _____s: Cash received or expended as a result of financial activities, such as interests and dividends.

All three together - the net _____ - are necessary to reconcile the beginning cash balance to the ending cash balance. Loan draw downs or equity injections, that is just shifting of capital but no expenditure as such, are not considered in the net _____.

a. Real option
c. Corporate finance

b. Shareholder value
d. Cash flow

13.   In finance, _____ is the process of estimating the potential market value of a financial asset or liability. they can be done on assets (for example, investments in marketable securities such as stocks, options, business enterprises, or intangible assets such as patents and trademarks) or on liabilities (e.g., Bonds issued by a company.) _____s are required in many contexts including investment analysis, capital budgeting, merger and acquisition transactions, financial reporting, taxable events to determine the proper tax liability, and in litigation.

a. Margin

c. Share

b. Valuation

d. Procter ' Gamble

14.   An _____ can be defined as a contract which provides an income stream in return for an initial payment.

An immediate _____ is an _____ for which the time between the contract date and the date of the first payment is not longer than the time interval between payments. A common use for an immediate _____ is to provide a pension to a retired person or persons.

a. Intrinsic value

c. AT'T Inc.

b. Amortization

d. Annuity

15.   _____ or net present worth (NPW) is defined as the total present value (PV) of a time series of cash flows. It is a standard method for using the time value of money to appraise long-term projects. Used for capital budgeting, and widely throughout economics, it measures the excess or shortfall of cash flows, in present value terms, once financing charges are met.

a. Present value of costs

c. Net Present value

b. Negative gearing

d. Tax shield

16.   _____ is a type of private equity capital typically provided to early-stage, high-potential, growth companies in the interest of generating a return through an eventual realization event such as an IPO or trade sale of the company. _____ investments are generally made as cash in exchange for shares in the invested company. It is typical for _____ investors to identify and back companies in high technology industries such as biotechnology and ICT.

a. Probability distribution

c. Tail risk

b. Venture capital

d. Treasury Inflation-Protected Securities

17.   In finance, a _____ is a debt security, in which the authorized issuer owes the holders a debt and, depending on the terms of the _____, is obliged to pay interest (the coupon) and/or to repay the principal at a later date, termed maturity.

Thus a _____ is a loan: the issuer is the borrower, the _____ holder is the lender, and the coupon is the interest. _____s provide the borrower with external funds to finance long-term investments, or, in the case of government _____s, to finance current expenditure.

a. Bond

c. Puttable bond

b. Catastrophe bonds

d. Convertible bond

18.   In finance, the term _____ describes the amount in cash that returns to the owners of a security. Normally it does not include the price variations, at the difference of the total return. _____ applies to various stated rates of return on stocks (common and preferred, and convertible), fixed income instruments (bonds, notes, bills, strips, zero coupon), and some other investment type insurance products (e.g. annuities.)

a. Yield

c. Macaulay duration

b. Yield to maturity

d. 4-4-5 Calendar

1. In finance, the _____ approach describes a method of valuing a project, company, or asset using the concepts of the time value of money. All future cash flows are estimated and discounted to give their present values. The discount rate used is generally the appropriate cost of capital and may incorporate judgments of the uncertainty (riskiness) of the future cash flows.
    a. Future-oriented
    c. Net present value
    b. Present value of benefits
    d. Discounted cash flow

2. _____ or financing is to provide capital (funds), which means money for a project, a person, a business or any other private or public institutions.

    Those funds can be allocated for either short term or long term purposes. The health fund is a new way of _____ private healthcare centers.

    a. Proxy fight
    c. Product life cycle
    b. Synthetic CDO
    d. Funding

3. _____ measures the nominal future sum of money that a given sum of money is 'worth' at a specified time in the future assuming a certain interest rate rate of return; it is the present value multiplied by the accumulation function.

    The value does not include corrections for inflation or other factors that affect the true value of money in the future. This is used in time value of money calculations.

    a. Present value of costs
    c. Future value
    b. Future-oriented
    d. Discounted cash flow

4. _____ is the balance of the amounts of cash being received and paid by a business during a defined period of time, sometimes tied to a specific project. Measurement of _____ can be used

    - to evaluate the state or performance of a business or project.
    - to determine problems with liquidity. Being profitable does not necessarily mean being liquid. A company can fail because of a shortage of cash, even while profitable.
    - to generate project rate of returns. The time of _____s into and out of projects are used as inputs to financial models such as internal rate of return, and net present value.
    - to examine income or growth of a business when it is believed that accrual accounting concepts do not represent economic realities. Alternately, _____ can be used to 'validate' the net income generated by accrual accounting.

    _____ as a generic term may be used differently depending on context, and certain _____ definitions may be adapted by analysts and users for their own uses. Common terms include operating _____ and free _____.

_____s can be classified into:

1. Operational _____s: Cash received or expended as a result of the company's core business activities.
2. Investment _____s: Cash received or expended through capital expenditure, investments or acquisitions.
3. Financing _____s: Cash received or expended as a result of financial activities, such as interests and dividends.

All three together - the net _____ - are necessary to reconcile the beginning cash balance to the ending cash balance. Loan draw downs or equity injections, that is just shifting of capital but no expenditure as such, are not considered in the net _____.

a. Corporate finance
c. Shareholder value

b. Cash flow
d. Real option

5. In finance, _____ is the process of estimating the potential market value of a financial asset or liability. they can be done on assets (for example, investments in marketable securities such as stocks, options, business enterprises, or intangible assets such as patents and trademarks) or on liabilities (e.g., Bonds issued by a company.) _____s are required in many contexts including investment analysis, capital budgeting, merger and acquisition transactions, financial reporting, taxable events to determine the proper tax liability, and in litigation.

a. Share
c. Margin

b. Procter ' Gamble
d. Valuation

6. _____ is the value on a given date of a future payment or series of future payments, discounted to reflect the time value of money and other factors such as investment risk. _____ calculations are widely used in business and economics to provide a means to compare cash flows at different times on a meaningful 'like to like' basis.

The most commonly applied model of the time value of money is compound interest.

a. Negative gearing
c. Present value of benefits

b. Net present value
d. Present value

7. In finance, a _____ is a debt security, in which the authorized issuer owes the holders a debt and, depending on the terms of the _____, is obliged to pay interest (the coupon) and/or to repay the principal at a later date, termed maturity.

Thus a _____ is a loan: the issuer is the borrower, the _____ holder is the lender, and the coupon is the interest. _____s provide the borrower with external funds to finance long-term investments, or, in the case of government _____s, to finance current expenditure.

a. Convertible bond
c. Puttable bond

b. Catastrophe bonds
d. Bond

8. In finance, the term _____ describes the amount in cash that returns to the owners of a security. Normally it does not include the price variations, at the difference of the total return. _____ applies to various stated rates of return on stocks (common and preferred, and convertible), fixed income instruments (bonds, notes, bills, strips, zero coupon), and some other investment type insurance products (e.g. annuities.)

  a. 4-4-5 Calendar   b. Macaulay duration

  c. Yield to maturity   d. Yield

9. An _____ can be defined as a contract which provides an income stream in return for an initial payment.

An immediate _____ is an _____ for which the time between the contract date and the date of the first payment is not longer than the time interval between payments. A common use for an immediate _____ is to provide a pension to a retired person or persons.

  a. AT'T Inc.   b. Amortization

  c. Annuity   d. Intrinsic value

10. _____ are formal records of a business' financial activities.

_____ provide an overview of a business' financial condition in both short and long term. There are four basic _____:

1. **Balance sheet**: also referred to as statement of financial position or condition, reports on a company's assets, liabilities, and net equity as of a given point in time.
2. **Income statement**: also referred to as Profit and Loss statement (or a 'P'L'), reports on a company's income, expenses, and profits over a period of time.
3. **Statement of retained earnings**: explains the changes in a company's retained earnings over the reporting period.
4. **Statement of cash flows**: reports on a company's cash flow activities, particularly its operating, investing and financing activities.

  a. Notes to the Financial Statements   b. Statement on Auditing Standards No. 70: Service Organizations

  c. Statement of retained earnings   d. Financial statements

11. _____ is a fee paid on borrowed assets. It is the price paid for the use of borrowed money , or, money earned by deposited funds . Assets that are sometimes lent with _____ include money, shares, consumer goods through hire purchase, major assets such as aircraft, and even entire factories in finance lease arrangements.

  a. Interest   b. A Random Walk Down Wall Street

  c. AAB   d. Insolvency

12. A _____ is an annuity in which the periodic payments begin on a fixed date and continue indefinitely. It is sometimes referred to as a perpetual annuity. Fixed coupon payments on permanently invested (irredeemable) sums of money are prime examples of these. Scholarships paid perpetually from an endowment fit the definition of _____.

  a. Stochastic volatility   b. LIBOR market model

  c. Current yield   d. Perpetuity

13. _____ is typically a higher ranking stock than voting shares, and its terms are negotiated between the corporation and the investor.

_____ usually carry no voting rights, but may carry superior priority over common stock in the payment of dividends and upon liquidation. _____ may carry a dividend that is paid out prior to any dividends to common stock holders.

a. Preferred stock

b. Trade-off theory

c. Second lien loan

d. Follow-on offering

14. _____ is the concept of adding accumulated interest back to the principal, so that interest is earned on interest from that moment on. The act of declaring interest to be principal is called compounding (i.e., interest is compounded.) A loan, for example, may have its interest compounded every month: in this case, a loan with $100 principal and 1% interest per month would have a balance of $101 at the end of the first month.

a. Penny stock

b. Compound interest

c. Risk management

d. 4-4-5 Calendar

15. The _____, effective annual interest rate, Annual Equivalent Rate (AER) or simply effective rate is the interest rate on a loan or financial product restated from the nominal interest rate as an interest rate with annual compound interest. It is used to compare the annual interest between loans with different compounding terms (daily, monthly, annually, or other.)

The _____ differs in two important respects from the annual percentage rate (APR):

1. the _____ generally does not incorporate one-time charges such as front-end fees;
2. the _____ is (generally) not defined by legal or regulatory authorities (as APR is in many jurisdictions.)

By contrast, the 'effective APR' is used as a legal term, where front-fees and other costs can be included, as defined by local law.

Annual Percentage Yield or effective annual yield is the analogous concept used for savings or investment products, such as a certificate of deposit.

a. AAB

b. ABN Amro

c. A Random Walk Down Wall Street

d. Effective interest rate

16. An _____ is the price a borrower pays for the use of money they do not own, and the return a lender receives for deferring the use of funds, by lending it to the borrower. _____s are normally expressed as a percentage rate over the period of one year.

_____s targets are also a vital tool of monetary policy and are used to control variables like investment, inflation, and unemployment.

a. AAB   b. A Random Walk Down Wall Street
c. ABN Amro   d. Interest rate

17.   The terms _____ , nominal _____, and effective _____ describe the interest rate for a whole year (annualized), rather than just a monthly fee/rate, as applied on a loan, mortgage, credit card, etc. Those terms have formal, legal definitions in some countries or legal jurisdictions, but in general:

- The nominal _____ is the simple-interest rate (for a year.)
- The effective _____ is the fee+compound interest rate (calculated across a year.)

The nominal _____ is calculated as: the rate, for a payment period, multiplied by the number of payment periods in a year. However, the exact legal definition of 'effective _____' can vary greatly in each jurisdiction, depending on the type of fees included, such as participation fees, loan origination fees, monthly service charges, or late fees. The effective _____ has been called the 'mathematically-true' interest rate for each year. The computation for the effective _____, as the fee+compound interest rate, can also vary depending on whether the up-front fees, such as origination or participation fees, are added to the entire amount, or treated as a short-term loan due in the first payment.

a. AAB   b. A Random Walk Down Wall Street
c. ABN Amro   d. Annual percentage rate

18.   _____ expresses an annual rate of interest taking into account the effect of compounding, usually for deposit or investment products (such as a certificate of deposit.) It is analogous to the Annual percentage rate (APR), which is used for loans. In some jurisdictions, the use and definition of _____ may be regulated by a government agency, in which case it would generally be capitalized.
a. A Random Walk Down Wall Street   b. ABN Amro
c. AAB   d. Annual percentage yield

19.   An _____ is a loan in which for a set term the borrower pays only the interest on the principal balance, with the principal balance unchanged. At the end of the interest-only term the borrower may enter an interest-only mortgage, pay the principal, or (with some lenders) convert the loan to a principal and interest payment (or amortized) loan at his/her option.

In the United States, a five- or ten-year interest-only period is typical.

a. AAB   b. Interest-only loan
c. A Random Walk Down Wall Street   d. ABN Amro

20.   _____ mature in one year or less. Like zero-coupon bonds, they do not pay interest prior to maturity; instead they are sold at a discount of the par value to create a positive yield to maturity. Many regard _____ as the least risky investment available to U.S. investors.
a. Treasury securities   b. Treasury Inflation Protected Securities
c. 4-4-5 Calendar   d. Treasury bills

21. _____ is the process of decreasing an amount over a period of time. The word comes from Middle English amortisen to kill, alienate in mortmain, from Anglo-French amorteser, alteration of amortir, from Vulgar Latin admortire to kill, from Latin ad- + mort-, mors death. Particular instances of the term include:

- _____ (business), the allocation of a lump sum amount to different time periods, particularly for loans and other forms of finance, including related interest or other finance charges.
  - _____ schedule, a table detailing each periodic payment on a loan (typically a mortgage), as generated by an _____ calculator.
  - Negative _____, an _____ schedule where the loan amount actually increases through not paying the full interest
- Amortized analysis, analyzing the execution cost of algorithms over a sequence of operations.
- _____ of capital expenditures of certain assets under accounting rules, particularly intangible assets, in a manner analogous to depreciation.
- _____ (tax law)

_____ is also used in the context of zoning regulations and describes the time in which a property owner has to relocate when the property's use constitutes a preexisting nonconforming use under zoning regulations.

- Depreciation

a. Option	b. Intrinsic value
c. AT'T Inc.	d. Amortization

22. A '_____' is a 'Charge' that is paid to obtain the right to delay a payment. Essentially, the payer purchases the right to make a given payment in the future instead of in the Present. The '_____', or 'Charge' that must be paid to delay the payment, is simply the difference between what the payment amount would be if it were paid in the present and what the payment amount would be paid if it were paid in the future.

a. Risk aversion	b. Value at risk
c. Risk modeling	d. Discount

23. The phrase _____ or bullet payment refers to one of two ways for repaying a loan; the other type is called amortizing payment or Amortization (business).

With a balloon loan, a _____ is paid back when the loan comes to its contractual maturity, e.g. reaches the deadline set to repayment at the time the loan was granted, representing the full loan amount (also called principal.) Periodic interest payments are generally made throughout the life of the loan.

a. Present value of costs	b. Refinancing risk
c. Future-oriented	d. Balloon payment

24. An _____ is a table detailing each periodic payment on a amortizing loan (typically a mortgage), as generated by an amortization calculator.

While a portion of every payment is applied towards both the interest and the principal balance of the loan, the exact amount applied to principal each time varies (with the remainder going to interest.) An _____ reveals the specific monetary amount put towards interest, as well as the specific put towards the Principal balance, with each payment.

a. Amortization schedule   b. Annual report

c. Adjusted basis   d. Adjusting entries

1.   In finance, a _____ is a debt security, in which the authorized issuer owes the holders a debt and, depending on the terms of the _____, is obliged to pay interest (the coupon) and/or to repay the principal at a later date, termed maturity.

Thus a _____ is a loan: the issuer is the borrower, the _____ holder is the lender, and the coupon is the interest. _____s provide the borrower with external funds to finance long-term investments, or, in the case of government _____s, to finance current expenditure.

a. Bond	b. Convertible bond
c. Puttable bond	d. Catastrophe bonds

2.   The coupon or _____ of a bond is the amount of interest paid per year expressed as a percentage of the face value of the bond.

For example if you hold $10,000 nominal of a bond described as a 4.5% loan stock, you will receive $450 in interest each year (probably in two installments of $225 each.)

Not all bonds have coupons.

a. Zero-coupon bond	b. Revenue bonds
c. Puttable bond	d. Coupon rate

3.   A _____ is an international bond that is denominated in a currency not native to the country where it is issued. It can be categorised according to the currency in which it is issued. London is one of the centers of the _____ market, but _____s may be traded throughout the world - for example in Singapore or Tokyo.

a. Education production function	b. Interest rate option
c. Eurobond	d. Economic entity

4.   In economics, the _____ is the proposition by Irving Fisher that the real interest rate is independent of monetary measures, especially the nominal interest rate. The Fisher equation is

$$r_r = r_n >- >\pi^e.$$

This means, the real interest rate (r_r) equals the nominal interest rate (r_n) minus expected rate of inflation ($>\pi^e$.) Here all the rates are continuously compounded.

a. Fisher hypothesis	b. 529 plan
c. 7-Eleven	d. 4-4-5 Calendar

5.   _____ is a life of security. It may also refer to the final payment date of a loan or other financial instrument, at which point all remaining interest and principal is due to be paid.

1, 3, 6 months _____ band can be calculated by using 30-day per month periods.

a. Primary market

b. False billing

c. Replacement cost

d. Maturity

6. _____, in finance and accounting, means stated value or face value. From this comes the expressions at par (at the _____), over par (over _____) and under par (under _____.)

The term '_____' has several meanings depending on context and geography.

a. FIDC

b. Par value

c. Sinking fund

d. Global Squeeze

7. In finance, the term _____ describes the amount in cash that returns to the owners of a security. Normally it does not include the price variations, at the difference of the total return. _____ applies to various stated rates of return on stocks (common and preferred, and convertible), fixed income instruments (bonds, notes, bills, strips, zero coupon), and some other investment type insurance products (e.g. annuities.)

a. Yield

b. Macaulay duration

c. 4-4-5 Calendar

d. Yield to maturity

8. The _____ or redemption yield is the yield promised to the bondholder on the assumption that the bond or other fixed-interest security such as gilts will be held to maturity, that all coupon and principal payments will be made and coupon payments are reinvested at the bond's promised yield at the same rate as invested. It is a measure of the return of the bond. This technique in theory allows investors to calculate the fair value of different financial instruments.

a. Yield to maturity

b. Yield

c. 4-4-5 Calendar

d. Macaulay duration

9. In finance, a _____ is a type of bond that can be converted into shares of stock in the issuing company, usually at some pre-announced ratio. It is a hybrid security with debt- and equity-like features. Although it typically has a low coupon rate, the holder is compensated with the ability to convert the bond to common stock, usually at a substantial discount to the stock's market value.

a. Gilts

b. Bond fund

c. Convertible bond

d. Corporate bond

10. A '_____' is a 'Charge' that is paid to obtain the right to delay a payment. Essentially, the payer purchases the right to make a given payment in the future instead of in the Present. The '_____', or 'Charge' that must be paid to delay the payment, is simply the difference between what the payment amount would be if it were paid in the present and what the payment amount would be paid if it were paid in the future.

a. Value at risk

b. Discount

c. Risk modeling

d. Risk aversion

11. A _____ is a bond bought at a price lower than its face value, with the face value repaid at the time of maturity. It does not make periodic interest payments, or so-called 'coupons,' hence the term zero-coupon bond. Investors earn return from the compounded interest all paid at maturity plus the difference between the discounted price of the bond and its par value.

a. Callable bond

b. Bowie bonds

c. Municipal bond

d. Zero coupon bond

12. A _____ is a generic term for any bond selling for more than 100% of par value, i.e., at a price greater than 100.00, which typically occurs for high coupon bonds in a falling interest rate climate.
   a. Revenue bonds
   b. Premium bond
   c. Municipal bond
   d. Nominal yield

13. _____ is a fee paid on borrowed assets. It is the price paid for the use of borrowed money , or, money earned by deposited funds . Assets that are sometimes lent with _____ include money, shares, consumer goods through hire purchase, major assets such as aircraft, and even entire factories in finance lease arrangements.
   a. A Random Walk Down Wall Street
   b. Interest
   c. Insolvency
   d. AAB

14. An _____ is the price a borrower pays for the use of money they do not own, and the return a lender receives for deferring the use of funds, by lending it to the borrower. _____s are normally expressed as a percentage rate over the period of one year.

_____s targets are also a vital tool of monetary policy and are used to control variables like investment, inflation, and unemployment.

   a. A Random Walk Down Wall Street
   b. ABN Amro
   c. Interest rate
   d. AAB

15. _____ is the risk (variability in value) borne by an interest-bearing asset, such as a loan or a bond, due to variability of interest rates. In general, as rates rise, the price of a fixed rate bond will fall, and vice versa. _____ is commonly measured by the bond's duration.
   a. Interest rate risk
   b. A Random Walk Down Wall Street
   c. Official bank rate
   d. International Fisher effect

16. In business, _____ is income that a company receives from its normal business activities, usually from the sale of goods and services to customers. Some companies also receive _____ from interest, dividends or royalties paid to them by other companies. _____ may refer to business income in general, or it may refer to the amount, in a monetary unit, received during a period of time, as in 'Last year, Company X had _____ of $32 million.'

In many countries, including the UK, _____ is referred to as turnover.

   a. Revenue
   b. Bottom line
   c. Matching principle
   d. Furniture, Fixtures and Equipment

17. The _____, interest yield, income yield, flat yield or running yield is a financial term used in reference to bonds and other fixed-interest securities such as gilts. It is the ratio of the annual interest payment and the bond's current price.

The _____ only therefore refers to the yield of the bond at the current moment. It does not reflect the total return over the life of the bond. In particular, it takes no account of reinvestment risk (the uncertainty about the rate at which future cashflows can be reinvested) or the fact that bonds usually mature at par value, which can be an important component of a bond's return.

a. Current yield

b. Perpetuity

c. Stochastic volatility

d. Modified Internal Rate of Return

18. In accounting, _____ or *Carrying value* is the value of an asset according to its balance sheet account balance. For assets, the value is based on the original cost of the asset less any depreciation, amortization or impairment costs made against the asset. A company's _____ is its total assets minus intangible assets and liabilities.

a. Current liabilities

b. Retained earnings

c. Pro forma

d. Book value

19. A _____ is a party (e.g. person, organization, company, or government) that has a claim to the services of a second party. The first party, in general, has provided some property or service to the second party under the assumption (usually enforced by contract) that the second party will return an equivalent property or service. The second party is frequently called a debtor or borrower.

a. NOPLAT

b. Creditor

c. Redemption value

d. False billing

20. _____ is that which is owed; usually referencing assets owed, but the term can cover other obligations. In the case of assets, _____ is a means of using future purchasing power in the present before a summation has been earned. Some companies and corporations use _____ as a part of their overall corporate finance strategy.

a. Partial Payment

b. Cross-collateralization

c. Credit cycle

d. Debt

21. In economics a _____ is simply an entity that owes a debt to someone else, the entity could be an individual, a firm, a government, or an organization. The counterparty of this arrangement is called a creditor. When the counterparty of this debt arrangement is a bank, the _____ is more often referred to as a borrower.

a. Biweekly Mortgage

b. Tick size

c. Financial rand

d. Debtor

22. In economic models, the _____ time frame assumes no fixed factors of production. Firms can enter or leave the marketplace, and the cost (and availability) of land, labor, raw materials, and capital goods can be assumed to vary. In contrast, in the short-run time frame, certain factors are assumed to be fixed, because there is not sufficient time for them to change.

a. Short-run

b. 529 plan

c. Long-run

d. 4-4-5 Calendar

23. In business and accounting, _____s are everything of value that is owned by a person or company. The balance sheet of a firm records the monetary value of the _____s owned by the firm. The two major _____ classes are tangible _____s and intangible _____s.

a. Accounts payable

b. Income

c. EBITDA

d. Asset

24. A _____ is a financial contract between two parties, the buyer and the seller of this type of option. Often it is simply labeled a 'call'. The buyer of the option has the right, but not the obligation to buy an agreed quantity of a particular commodity or financial instrument (the underlying instrument) from the seller of the option at a certain time (the expiration date) for a certain price (the strike price.)

a. Call option

b. Bear call spread

c. Bull spread

d. Bear spread

25.   In economics, business, and accounting, a _____ is the value of money that has been used up to produce something, and hence is not available for use anymore. In business, the _____ may be one of acquisition, in which case the amount of money expended to acquire it is counted as _____. In this case, money is the input that is gone in order to acquire the thing.

a. Fixed costs

b. Sliding scale fees

c. Marginal cost

d. Cost

26.   In finance, the _____ is the minimum rate of return a firm must offer shareholders to compensate for waiting for their returns, and for bearing some risk.

The _____ capital for a particular company is the rate of return on investment that is required by the company's ordinary shareholders. The return consists both of dividend and capital gains, e.g. increases in the share price.

a. Cost of Equity

b. Net pay

c. Round-tripping

d. Residual value

27.   _____ is the price at which an asset would trade in a competitive Walrasian auction setting. _____ is often used interchangeably with open _____, fair value or fair _____, although these terms have distinct definitions in different standards, and may differ in some circumstances.

International Valuation Standards defines _____ as 'the estimated amount for which a property should exchange on the date of valuation between a willing buyer and a willing seller in an arm'e;s-length transaction after proper marketing wherein the parties had each acted knowledgeably, prudently, and without compulsion.'

_____ is a concept distinct from market price, which is 'e;the price at which one can transact'e;, while _____ is 'e;the true underlying value'e; according to theoretical standards.

a. Debt restructuring

b. Market value

c. T-Model

d. Wrap account

28.   An _____ is a contract written by a seller that conveys to the buyer the right -- but not the obligation -- to buy (in the case of a call _____) or to sell (in the case of a put _____) a particular asset, such as a piece of property such as, among others, a futures contract. In return for granting the _____, the seller collects a payment (the premium) from the buyer.

For example, buying a call _____ provides the right to buy a specified quantity of a security at a set strike price at some time on or before expiration, while buying a put _____ provides the right to sell.

a. AT'T Mobility LLC

b. Amortization

c. Option

d. Annuity

29. A _____ is a fungible, negotiable instrument representing financial value. They are broadly categorized into debt securities (such as banknotes, bonds and debentures), and equity securities; e.g., common stocks. The company or other entity issuing the _____ is called the issuer.

    a. Book entry   b. Securities lending

    c. Tracking stock   d. Security

30. A _____ is defined as a certificate of agreement of loans which is given under the company's stamp and carries an undertaking that the _____ holder will get a fixed return (fixed on the basis of interest rates) and the principal amount whenever the _____ matures.

In finance, a _____ is a long-term debt instrument used by governments and large companies to obtain funds. It is defined as 'a debt secured only by the debtor's earning power, not by a lien on any specific asset.' It is similar to a bond except the securitization conditions are different.

    a. Collateral Management   b. Partial Payment

    c. Debenture   d. Collection agency

31. In economics, the concept of the _____ refers to the decision-making time frame of a firm in which at least one factor of production is fixed. Costs which are fixed in the _____ have no impact on a firms decisions. For example a firm can raise output by increasing the amount of labour through overtime.

    a. Short-run   b. Long-run

    c. 529 plan   d. 4-4-5 Calendar

32. A _____ is a document that indicates that the bearer of the document has title to property, such as shares or bonds. They differ from normal registered instruments, in that no records are kept of who owns the underlying property, or of the transactions involving transfer of ownership. Whoever physically holds the bearer bond papers owns the property.

    a. Marketable   b. Bearer instrument

    c. Securities lending   d. Book entry

33. In financial accounting, _____s are precautions for which the amount or probability of occurrence are not known. Typical examples are _____s for warranty costs and _____ for taxes the term reserve is used instead of term _____; such a use, however, is inconsistent with the terminology suggested by International Accounting Standards Board.

    a. Money measurement concept   b. Momentum Accounting and Triple-Entry Bookkeeping

    c. Provision   d. Petty cash

34. A _____ is a single mortgage that covers more than one parcel of real estate.

    a. Commercial mortgage   b. Construction loan

    c. Blanket mortgage   d. Reverse mortgage

35. In lending agreements, _____ is a borrower's pledge of specific property to a lender, to secure repayment of a loan. The _____ serves as protection for a lender against a borrower's risk of default - that is, a borrower failing to pay the principal and interest under the terms of a loan obligation. If a borrower does default on a loan (due to insolvency or other event), that borrower forfeits (gives up) the property pledged as _____ *ollateral -* and the lender then becomes the owner of the _____.

a. Future-oriented

c. Collateral

b. Refinancing risk

d. Nominal value

36. A _____ is a fund established by a government agency or business for the purpose of reducing debt.

The _____ was first used in Great Britain in the 18th century to reduce national debt. While used by Robert Walpole in 1716 and effectively in the 1720s and early 1730s, it originated in the commercial tax syndicates of the Italian peninsula of the 14th century to retire redeemable public debt of those cities.

a. Sinking fund

c. Debtor

b. Modern portfolio theory

d. Security interest

37. In finance, _____ is debt which ranks after other debts should a company fall into receivership or be closed.

Such debt is referred to as subordinate, because the debt providers have subordinate status in relationship to the normal debt. A typical example for this would be when a promoter of a company invests money in the form of debt, rather than in the form of stock.

a. Subordinated debt

c. Cross-collateralization

b. Credit rating

d. Participation loan

38. _____ (also trust indenture or deed of trust) is a legal document issued to lenders and describes key terms such as the interest rate, maturity date, convertibility, pledge, promises, representations, covenants, and other terms of the bond offering. When the Offering Memorandum is prepared in advance of marketing a Bond, the indenture will typically be summarised in the 'Description of Notes' section.

a. Bond indenture

c. Fair Labor Standards Act

b. Court of Audit of Belgium

d. McFadden Act

39. _____, in accrual accounting, is any account where the asset or liability is not realized until a future date, e.g. annuities, charges, taxes, income, etc. The _____ item may be carried, dependent on type of deferral, as either an asset or liability.See also: accrual

_____ is also used in the university admissions process. It is the action by which a school rejects a student for early admission but still opts to review that student in the general admissions pool.

a. Deferred

c. Revenue

b. Net profit

d. Current asset

40. _____ mature in one year or less. Like zero-coupon bonds, they do not pay interest prior to maturity; instead they are sold at a discount of the par value to create a positive yield to maturity. Many regard _____ as the least risky investment available to U.S. investors.

a. Treasury securities

c. Treasury Inflation Protected Securities

b. Treasury bills

d. 4-4-5 Calendar

41. A _____, in its most general sense, is a solemn promise to engage in or refrain from a specified action.

More specifically, a _____, in contrast to a contract, is a one-way agreement whereby the _____er is the only party bound by the promise. A _____ may have conditions and prerequisites that qualify the undertaking, including the actions of second or third parties, but there is no inherent agreement by such other parties to fulfill those requirements.

a. Partnership

b. Clayton Antitrust Act

c. Federal Trade Commission Act

d. Covenant

42.   A _____ is a bond issued by a national government denominated in the country's own currency. Bonds issued by national governments in foreign currencies are normally referred to as sovereign bonds. The first ever _____ was issued by the British government in 1693 to raise money to fund a war against France.

a. Municipal bond

b. Zero-coupon bond

c. Government bond

d. Collateralized debt obligations

43.   In finance, a _____ (non-investment grade bond, speculative grade bond or junk bond) is a bond that is rated below investment grade at the time of purchase. These bonds have a higher risk of default or other adverse credit events, but typically pay higher yields than better quality bonds in order to make them attractive to investors.

a. Sharpe ratio

b. Private equity

c. Volatility

d. High yield bond

44.   In the United States, a _____ is a bond issued by a city or other local government, or their agencies. Potential issuers of these bonds include cities, counties, redevelopment agencies, school districts, publicly owned airports and seaports, and any other governmental entity (or group of governments) below the state level. They may be general obligations of the issuer or secured by specified revenues.

a. Puttable bond

b. Senior debt

c. Municipal bond

d. Premium bond

45.   _____ are risk-linked securities that transfer a specified set of risks from a sponsor to investors. They are often structured as floating rate corporate bonds whose principal is forgiven if specified trigger conditions are met. They are typically used by insurers as an alternative to traditional catastrophe reinsurance.

a. Brady bonds

b. Catastrophe bonds

c. Clean price

d. Callable bond

46.   _____, refers to consumption opportunity gained by an entity within a specified time frame, which is generally expressed in monetary terms. However, for households and individuals, '_____ is the sum of all the wages, salaries, profits, interests payments, rents and other forms of earnings received... in a given period of time.' For firms, _____ generally refers to net-profit: what remains of revenue after expenses have been subtracted.

a. OIBDA

b. Income

c. Accrual

d. Annual report

47.   _____ are bonds where the principal is indexed to inflation. They are thus designed to cut out the inflation risk of an investment. _____ pay a periodic coupon that is equal to the product of the inflation index and the nominal coupon rate. The relationship between coupon payments, breakeven inflation and real interest rates is given by the Fisher equation.

a. Inflation-indexed bonds

b. ABN Amro

c. A Random Walk Down Wall Street

d. AAB

48. _____ are the inflation-indexed bonds issued by the U.S. Treasury. The principal is adjusted to the Consumer Price Index, the commonly used measure of inflation. The coupon rate is constant, but generates a different amount of interest when multiplied by the inflation-adjusted principal, thus protecting the holder against inflation. _____ are currently offered in 5-year, 10-year and 20-year maturities.

a. Treasury securities

b. Treasury Inflation-Protected Securities

c. 4-4-5 Calendar

d. Treasury Inflation Protected Securities

49. In finance, a _____ is a security that entitles the holder to buy stock of the company that issued it at a specified price, which is usually higher than the stock price at time of issue.

_____s are frequently attached to bonds or preferred stock as a sweetener, allowing the issuer to pay lower interest rates or dividends. They can be used to enhance the yield of the bond, and make them more attractive to potential buyers.

a. Credit

b. Clearing house

c. Clearing

d. Warrant

50. A _____ occurs when a financial sponsor acquires a controlling interest in a company's equity and where a significant percentage of the purchase price is financed through leverage (borrowing.) The assets of the acquired company are used as collateral for the borrowed capital, sometimes with assets of the acquiring company. The bonds or other paper issued for _____s are commonly considered not to be investment grade because of the significant risks involved.

a. Leverage

b. Pension fund

c. Limited partnership

d. Leveraged buyout

51. The _____ is a financial market where participants buy and sell debt securities, usually in the form of bonds. As of 2006, the size of the international _____ is an estimated $45 trillion, of which the size of the outstanding U.S. _____ debt was $25.2 trillion.

Nearly all of the $923 billion average daily trading volume in the U.S. _____ takes place between broker-dealers and large institutions in a decentralized, over-the-counter market.

a. Bond market

b. Fixed income

c. 529 plan

d. 4-4-5 Calendar

52. _____ is a combination of straight bond and embedded put option. The holder of the _____ has the right, but not the obligation, to demand early repayment of the principal. The put option is usually exercisable on specified dates.

a. Brady bonds

b. Puttable bond

c. Callable bond

d. Convertible bond

53. A _____ is the highest price that a buyer (i.e., bidder) is willing to pay for a good. It is usually referred to simply as the 'bid.'

In bid and ask, the _____ stands in contrast to the ask price or 'offer', and the difference between the two is called the bid/ask spread.

An unsolicited bid or offer is when a person or company receives a bid even though they are not looking to sell.

a. Political risk   b. Mid price
c. Bid price   d. Settlement date

54.   A _____ or market-based mechanism is any of a wide variety of ways to match up buyers and sellers.

An example of a _____ uses announced bid and ask prices. Generally speaking, when two parties wish to engage in a trade, the purchaser will announce a price he is willing to pay (the bid price) and seller will announce a price he is willing to accept (the ask price).

a. 4-4-5 Calendar   b. 529 plan
c. Price mechanism   d. 7-Eleven

55.   The _____ for securities is the difference between the price quoted by a market maker for an immediate sale and an immediate purchase The size of the bid-offer spread in a given commodity is a measure of the liquidity of the market.

The trader initiating the transaction is said to demand liquidity, and the other party to the transaction supplies liquidity.

a. Trade-off   b. Capital outflow
c. Defined contribution plan   d. Bid/offer spread

56.   The _____ is a stock exchange based in New York City, New York. It is the largest stock exchange in the world by dollar value of its listed companies securities. As of October 2008, the combined capitalization of all domestic _____ listed companies was $10.1 trillion.
a. 529 plan   b. 4-4-5 Calendar
c. 7-Eleven   d. New York Stock Exchange

57.   A _____, securities exchange or (in Europe) bourse is a corporation or mutual organization which provides 'trading' facilities for stock brokers and traders, to trade stocks and other securities. _____s also provide facilities for the issue and redemption of securities as well as other financial instruments and capital events including the payment of income and dividends. The securities traded on a _____ include: shares issued by companies, unit trusts and other pooled investment products and bonds.
a. 4-4-5 Calendar   b. 7-Eleven
c. Stock Exchange   d. 529 plan

58.   In finance, the _____ is the price of a bond excluding any interest that has accrued since issue or the most recent coupon payment. This is to be compared with the dirty price, which is the price of a bond including the accrued interest.

When bond prices are quoted on a Bloomberg Terminal or Reuters they are quoted using the _____.

a. Gilts

c. Bowie bonds

b. Bond valuation

d. Clean price

59.   The _____ of a bond represents the value of a bond, exclusive of any commissions or fees. The _____ is also called the 'full price.'

Bonds, as well as a variety of other fixed income securities, provide for coupon payments to be made to bond holders on a fixed schedule. The _____ of a bond will decrease on the days coupons are paid, resulting in a saw-tooth pattern for the bond value.

a. Premium bond

c. Serial bond

b. Dirty price

d. Collateralized debt obligations

60.   In economics, _____ is a rise in the general level of prices of goods and services in an economy over a period of time. The term '_____' once referred to increases in the money supply (monetary _____); however, economic debates about the relationship between money supply and price levels have led to its primary use today in describing price _____. _____ can also be described as a decline in the real value of money--a loss of purchasing power in the medium of exchange which is also the monetary unit of account.

a. A Random Walk Down Wall Street

c. ABN Amro

b. AAB

d. Inflation

61.   _____ is the value on a given date of a future payment or series of future payments, discounted to reflect the time value of money and other factors such as investment risk. _____ calculations are widely used in business and economics to provide a means to compare cash flows at different times on a meaningful 'like to like' basis.

The most commonly applied model of the time value of money is compound interest.

a. Net present value

c. Present value of benefits

b. Negative gearing

d. Present value

62.   In finance, the yield curve is the relation between the interest rate (or cost of borrowing) and the time to maturity of the debt for a given borrower in a given currency. For example, the current U.S. dollar interest rates paid on U.S. Treasury securities for various maturities are closely watched by many traders, and are commonly plotted on a graph such as the one on the right which is informally called 'the yield curve.' More formal mathematical descriptions of this relation are often called the _____.

The yield of a debt instrument is the annualized percentage increase in the value of the investment.

a. 7-Eleven

c. 529 plan

b. 4-4-5 Calendar

d. Term structure of interest rates

63.

In finance, the _____ can be the expected rate of return above the risk-free interest rate. When measuring risk, a common sense approach is to compare the risk-free return on T-bills and the very risky return on other investments. The difference between these two returns can be interpreted as a measure of the excess return on the average risky asset. This excess return is known as the _____.

a. Risk adjusted return on capital

b. Risk premium

c. Risk aversion

d. Risk modeling

64.   In finance, the _____ is the relation between the interest rate (or cost of borrowing) and the time to maturity of the debt for a given borrower in a given currency. For example, the current U.S. dollar interest rates paid on U.S. Treasury securities for various maturities are closely watched by many traders, and are commonly plotted on a graph such as the one on the right which is informally called 'the _____.' More formal mathematical descriptions of this relation are often called the term structure of interest rates.

The yield of a debt instrument is the annualized percentage increase in the value of the investment.

a. 529 plan

b. 7-Eleven

c. 4-4-5 Calendar

d. Yield curve

65.   In finance, _____ occurs when a debtor has not met its legal obligations according to the debt contract, e.g. it has not made a scheduled payment, or has violated a loan covenant (condition) of the debt contract. _____ may occur if the debtor is either unwilling or unable to pay their debt. This can occur with all debt obligations including bonds, mortgages, loans, and promissory notes.

a. Debt validation

b. Vendor finance

c. Default

d. Credit crunch

66.   _____ is the risk of loss due to a debtor's non-payment of a loan or other line of credit (either the principal or interest (coupon) or both)

Most lenders employ their own models (credit scorecards) to rank potential and existing customers according to risk, and then apply appropriate strategies. With products such as unsecured personal loans or mortgages, lenders charge a higher price for higher risk customers and vice versa. With revolving products such as credit cards and overdrafts, risk is controlled through careful setting of credit limits.

a. Credit risk

b. Market risk

c. Transaction risk

d. Liquidity risk

67.   _____ is a measure of the ability of a debtor to pay their debts as and when they fall due. It is usually expressed as a ratio or a percentage of current liabilities.

For a corporation with a published balance sheet there are various ratios used to calculate a measure of liquidity.

a. Operating leverage

b. Invested capital

c. Operating profit margin

d. Accounting liquidity

68. _____ is a term used to explain a difference between two types of financial securities (e.g. stocks), that have all the same qualities except liquidity. For example:

_____ is a segment of a three-part theory that works to explain the behavior of yield curves for interest rates. The upwards-curving component of the interest yield can be explained by the _____.

a. 529 plan

b. 4-4-5 Calendar

c. 7-Eleven

d. Liquidity premium

69. _____ or financing is to provide capital (funds), which means money for a project, a person, a business or any other private or public institutions.

Those funds can be allocated for either short term or long term purposes. The health fund is a new way of _____ private healthcare centers.

a. Synthetic CDO

b. Product life cycle

c. Funding

d. Proxy fight

1. _____ is the balance of the amounts of cash being received and paid by a business during a defined period of time, sometimes tied to a specific project. Measurement of _____ can be used

- to evaluate the state or performance of a business or project.
- to determine problems with liquidity. Being profitable does not necessarily mean being liquid. A company can fail because of a shortage of cash, even while profitable.
- to generate project rate of returns. The time of _____s into and out of projects are used as inputs to financial models such as internal rate of return, and net present value.
- to examine income or growth of a business when it is believed that accrual accounting concepts do not represent economic realities. Alternately, _____ can be used to 'validate' the net income generated by accrual accounting.

_____ as a generic term may be used differently depending on context, and certain _____ definitions may be adapted by analysts and users for their own uses. Common terms include operating _____ and free _____.

_____s can be classified into:

1. Operational _____s: Cash received or expended as a result of the company's core business activities.
2. Investment _____s: Cash received or expended through capital expenditure, investments or acquisitions.
3. Financing _____s: Cash received or expended as a result of financial activities, such as interests and dividends.

All three together - the net _____ - are necessary to reconcile the beginning cash balance to the ending cash balance. Loan draw downs or equity injections, that is just shifting of capital but no expenditure as such, are not considered in the net _____.

a. Cash flow
c. Corporate finance

b. Shareholder value
d. Real option

2. _____ is a form of corporation equity ownership represented in the securities. It is dangerous in comparison to preferred shares and some other investment options, in that in the event of bankruptcy, _____ investors receive their funds after preferred stockholders, bondholders, creditors, etc. On the other hand, common shares on average perform better than preferred shares or bonds over time.

a. Stock split
c. Stop-limit order

b. Stock market bubble
d. Common stock

3. _____ is an estimate of the fair value of corporations and their stocks, by using fundamental economic criteria. This theoretical valuation has to be perfected with market criteria, as the final purpose is to determine potential market prices.

a. 4-4-5 Calendar
c. Security Analysis

b. Stock valuation
d. Growth stocks

4. In finance, _____ is the process of estimating the potential market value of a financial asset or liability. they can be done on assets (for example, investments in marketable securities such as stocks, options, business enterprises, or intangible assets such as patents and trademarks) or on liabilities (e.g., Bonds issued by a company.) _____s are required in many contexts including investment analysis, capital budgeting, merger and acquisition transactions, financial reporting, taxable events to determine the proper tax liability, and in litigation.

a. Margin

b. Valuation

c. Share

d. Procter ' Gamble

5. In finance, _____ are stocks that appreciate in value and yield a high return on equity (ROE.) Analysts compute ROE by taking the company's net income and dividing it by the company's equity. To be classified as a growth stock, analysts expect to see at least 15 percent return on equity.

a. Stock valuation

b. Security Analysis

c. Growth stocks

d. 4-4-5 Calendar

6. A _____ is a payment made by a corporation to its shareholder members. When a corporation earns a profit or surplus, that money can be put to two uses: it can either be re-invested in the business (called retained earnings), or it can be paid to the shareholders as a _____. Many corporations retain a portion of their earnings and pay the remainder as a

_____.

a. Dividend

b. Dividend yield

c. Dividend puzzle

d. Special dividend

7. _____ are those dividends paid out in form of additional stock shares of the issuing corporation or other corporation They are usually issued in proportion to shares owned (for example for every 100 shares of stock owned, 5% stock dividend will yield 5 extra shares). If this payment involves the issue of new shares, this is very similar to a stock split in that it increases the total number of shares while lowering the price of each share and does not change the market capitalization or the total value of the shares held

a. Time-based currency

b. Database auditing

c. The Hong Kong Securities Institute

d. Stock or scrip dividends

8. In business and finance, a _____ (also referred to as equity _____) of stock means a _____ of ownership in a corporation (company.) In the plural, stocks is often used as a synonym for _____s especially in the United States, but it is less commonly used that way outside of North America.

In the United Kingdom, South Africa, and Australia, stock can also refer to completely different financial instruments such as government bonds or, less commonly, to all kinds of marketable securities.

a. Bucket shop

b. Procter ' Gamble

c. Share

d. Margin

9. A _____ is an annuity in which the periodic payments begin on a fixed date and continue indefinitely. It is sometimes referred to as a perpetual annuity. Fixed coupon payments on permanently invested (irredeemable) sums of money are prime examples of these. Scholarships paid perpetually from an endowment fit the definition of _____.

a. Stochastic volatility

b. Current yield

c. LIBOR market model

d. Perpetuity

10.　Procter is a surname, and may also refer to:

- Bryan Waller Procter (pseud. Barry Cornwall), English poet
- Goodwin Procter, American law firm
- _____, consumer products multinational

a. Procter ' Gamble

b. Valuation

c. Clearing house

d. Bucket shop

11.　_____ is a theory that all economic activities and policies should be oriented towards achieving a state of equilibrium, a steady state.

The theory asserts that the continuous growth model is inherently unstable resulting in a 'boom/bust' cycle, and that continuous growth in the context of finite resources is unlikely to support current levels of prosperity indefinitely.

Proponents of this theory also explicitly challenge the popular equation of economic growth with progress - an equation they have labelled Growth Fetish - and posit that sustainability has inherent value.

a. 4-4-5 Calendar

b. 529 plan

c. 7-Eleven

d. Zero growth

12.　A _____ rocket is a rocket that uses two or more stages, each of which contains its own engines and propellant. A tandem or serial stage is mounted on top of another stage; a parallel stage is attached alongside another stage. The result is effectively two or more rockets stacked on top of or attached next to each other.

a. 7-Eleven

b. 4-4-5 Calendar

c. Multistage

d. 529 plan

13.　A _____ is a profit that results from investments into a capital asset, such as stocks, bonds or real estate, which exceeds the purchase price. It is the difference between a higher selling price and a lower purchase price, resulting in a financial gain for the seller. Conversely, a capital loss arises if the proceeds from the sale of a capital asset are less than the purchase price.

a. Capital gains tax

b. Tax brackets

c. Payroll tax

d. Capital gain

14.　The _____ on a company stock is the company's annual dividend payments divided by its market cap, or the dividend per share divided by the price per share. It is often expressed as a percentage.

Dividend payments on preferred shares are stipulated by the prospectus.

a. Special dividend

b. Dividend reinvestment plan

c. Dividend imputation

d. Dividend yield

15.   In finance, the term _____ describes the amount in cash that returns to the owners of a security. Normally it does not include the price variations, at the difference of the total return. _____ applies to various stated rates of return on stocks (common and preferred, and convertible), fixed income instruments (bonds, notes, bills, strips, zero coupon), and some other investment type insurance products (e.g. annuities.)

    a. Yield to maturity   b. 4-4-5 Calendar

    c. Macaulay duration   d. Yield

16.   The institution most often referenced by the word '_____' is a public or publicly traded _____, the shares of which are traded on a public stock exchange (e.g., the New York Stock Exchange or Nasdaq in the United States) where shares of stock of _____s are bought and sold by and to the general public. Most of the largest businesses in the world are publicly traded _____s. However, the majority of _____s are said to be closely held, privately held or close _____s, meaning that no ready market exists for the trading of shares.

    a. Corporation   b. Federal Home Loan Mortgage Corporation

    c. Depository Trust Company   d. Protect

17.   _____ is a multiple-winner voting system intended to promote proportional representation while also being simple to understand.

_____ is used frequently in corporate governance, where it is mandated by many U.S. states, and it was used to elect the Illinois House of Representatives from 1870 until its repeal in 1980. It was used in England in the late 19th century to elect school boards.

    a. 4-4-5 Calendar   b. 529 plan

    c. 7-Eleven   d. Cumulative voting

18.   _____ is commonly used in corporations for voting by members or shareholders, because it allows members who have confidence in the judgment of other members to vote for them and allows the assembly to have a quorum of votes when it is difficult for all members to attend, or there are too many members for all of them to conveniently meet and deliberate.

    a. 7-Eleven   b. Proxy voting

    c. 4-4-5 Calendar   d. 529 plan

19.   A mutual shareholder or _____ is an individual or company (including a corporation) that legally owns one or more shares of stock in a joint stock company. A company's shareholders collectively own that company. Thus, the typical goal of such companies is to enhance shareholder value.

    a. Stock market bubble   b. Trading curb

    c. Limit order   d. Stockholder

20.   The _____ is a stock exchange based in New York City, New York. It is the largest stock exchange in the world by dollar value of its listed companies securities. As of October 2008, the combined capitalization of all domestic _____ listed companies was $10.1 trillion.

    a. New York Stock Exchange   b. 7-Eleven

    c. 4-4-5 Calendar   d. 529 plan

21.   A _____ is a right to acquire certain property in preference to any other person. It usually refers to property newly coming into existence. A right to acquire existing property in preference to any other person is usually referred to as a right of first refusal.

In practice, the most common form of _____ is the right of existing shareholders to acquire newly issued shares issued by a company in a rights issue, a usually but not always public offering.

a. Down payment   b. Court of Audit of Belgium
c. Fraud deterrence   d. Pre-emption right

22.   A _____ is an event that may occur when a corporation's stockholders develop opposition to some aspect of the corporate governance, often focusing on directorial and management positions. Corporate activists may attempt to persuade shareholders to use their proxy votes (i.e. votes by one individual or institution as the authorized representative of another) to install new management for any of a variety of reasons.

In a _____, incumbent directors and management have the odds stacked in their favor over those trying to force the corporate change.

a. Procurement   b. Forfaiting
c. Trade finance   d. Proxy fight

23.   A _____, securities exchange or (in Europe) bourse is a corporation or mutual organization which provides 'trading' facilities for stock brokers and traders, to trade stocks and other securities. _____s also provide facilities for the issue and redemption of securities as well as other financial instruments and capital events including the payment of income and dividends. The securities traded on a _____ include: shares issued by companies, unit trusts and other pooled investment products and bonds.

a. 529 plan   b. 4-4-5 Calendar
c. 7-Eleven   d. Stock Exchange

24.   _____ is typically a higher ranking stock than voting shares, and its terms are negotiated between the corporation and the investor.

_____ usually carry no voting rights, but may carry superior priority over common stock in the payment of dividends and upon liquidation. _____ may carry a dividend that is paid out prior to any dividends to common stock holders.

a. Trade-off theory   b. Follow-on offering
c. Preferred stock   d. Second lien loan

25.   In business, _____ is income that a company receives from its normal business activities, usually from the sale of goods and services to customers. Some companies also receive _____ from interest, dividends or royalties paid to them by other companies. _____ may refer to business income in general, or it may refer to the amount, in a monetary unit, received during a period of time, as in 'Last year, Company X had _____ of $32 million.'

In many countries, including the UK, _____ is referred to as turnover.

a. Bottom line

b. Furniture, Fixtures and Equipment

c. Matching principle

d. Revenue

26. In finance, a _____ is a debt security, in which the authorized issuer owes the holders a debt and, depending on the terms of the _____, is obliged to pay interest (the coupon) and/or to repay the principal at a later date, termed maturity.

Thus a _____ is a loan: the issuer is the borrower, the _____ holder is the lender, and the coupon is the interest. _____s provide the borrower with external funds to finance long-term investments, or, in the case of government _____s, to finance current expenditure.

a. Catastrophe bonds

b. Convertible bond

c. Puttable bond

d. Bond

27. _____ is that which is owed; usually referencing assets owed, but the term can cover other obligations. In the case of assets, _____ is a means of using future purchasing power in the present before a summation has been earned. Some companies and corporations use _____ as a part of their overall corporate finance strategy.

a. Partial Payment

b. Cross-collateralization

c. Credit cycle

d. Debt

28. The _____ is an American stock exchange. It is the largest electronic screen-based equity securities trading market in the United States. With approximately 3,200 companies, it has more trading volume per day than any other stock exchange in the world.

a. 4-4-5 Calendar

b. NASDAQ

c. 7-Eleven

d. 529 plan

29. In the United States, the Financial Industry Regulatory Authority (FINRA) is a self-regulatory organization (SRO) under the Securities Exchange Act of 1934, successor to the _____, Inc.

FINRA is responsible for regulatory oversight of all securities firms that do business with the public; professional training, testing and licensing of registered persons; arbitration and mediation; market regulation by contract for The NASDAQ Stock Market, Inc., the American Stock Exchange LLC, and the International Securities Exchange, LLC; and industry utilities, such as Trade Reporting Facilities and other over-the-counter operations.

a. 529 plan

b. 4-4-5 Calendar

c. 7-Eleven

d. National Association of Securities Dealers

30. The _____ is that part of the capital markets that deals with the issuance of new securities. Companies, governments or public sector institutions can obtain funding through the sale of a new stock or bond issue. This is typically done through a syndicate of securities dealers.

a. Sector rotation

b. Volatility clustering

c. Peer group analysis

d. Primary market

31. The _____ is the financial market where previously issued securities and financial instruments such as stock, bonds, options, and futures are bought and sold. The term '_____' is also used refer to the market for any used goods or assets, or an alternative use for an existing product or asset where the customer base is the second market

With primary issuances of securities or financial instruments, or the primary market, investors purchase these securities directly from issuers such as corporations issuing shares in an IPO or private placement, or directly from the federal government in the case of treasuries.

a. Secondary market

b. Financial market

c. Performance attribution

d. Delta neutral

32. A _____ is a fungible, negotiable instrument representing financial value. They are broadly categorized into debt securities (such as banknotes, bonds and debentures), and equity securities; e.g., common stocks. The company or other entity issuing the _____ is called the issuer.

a. Book entry

b. Security

c. Securities lending

d. Tracking stock

33. A _____ is a fund established by a government agency or business for the purpose of reducing debt.

The _____ was first used in Great Britain in the 18th century to reduce national debt. While used by Robert Walpole in 1716 and effectively in the 1720s and early 1730s, it originated in the commercial tax syndicates of the Italian peninsula of the 14th century to retire redeemable public debt of those cities.

a. Security interest

b. Debtor

c. Modern portfolio theory

d. Sinking fund

34. A _____ is a private or public market for the trading of company stock and derivatives of company stock at an agreed price; these are securities listed on a stock exchange as well as those only traded privately.

The size of the world _____ is estimated at about $36.6 trillion US at the beginning of October 2008 . The world derivatives market has been estimated at about $480 trillion face or nominal value, 12 times the size of the entire world economy.

a. Adolph Coors

b. Anton Gelonkin

c. Andrew Tobias

d. Stock market

35. In business and accounting, _____s are everything of value that is owned by a person or company. The balance sheet of a firm records the monetary value of the _____s owned by the firm. The two major _____ classes are tangible _____s and intangible _____s.

a. Income

b. Accounts payable

c. Asset

d. EBITDA

36. A _____ is a financial contract between two parties, the buyer and the seller of this type of option. Often it is simply labeled a 'call'. The buyer of the option has the right, but not the obligation to buy an agreed quantity of a particular commodity or financial instrument (the underlying instrument) from the seller of the option at a certain time (the expiration date) for a certain price (the strike price.)

a. Call option

b. Bull spread

c. Bear spread

d. Bear call spread

37.   In economics, business, and accounting, a _____ is the value of money that has been used up to produce something, and hence is not available for use anymore. In business, the _____ may be one of acquisition, in which case the amount of money expended to acquire it is counted as _____. In this case, money is the input that is gone in order to acquire the thing.

a. Fixed costs   b. Cost

c. Sliding scale fees   d. Marginal cost

38.   In finance, the _____ is the minimum rate of return a firm must offer shareholders to compensate for waiting for their returns, and for bearing some risk.

The _____ capital for a particular company is the rate of return on investment that is required by the company's ordinary shareholders. The return consists both of dividend and capital gains, e.g. increases in the share price.

a. Round-tripping   b. Net pay

c. Residual value   d. Cost of Equity

39.   _____, refers to consumption opportunity gained by an entity within a specified time frame, which is generally expressed in monetary terms. However, for households and individuals, '_____ is the sum of all the wages, salaries, profits, interests payments, rents and other forms of earnings received... in a given period of time.' For firms, _____ generally refers to net-profit: what remains of revenue after expenses have been subtracted.

a. Annual report   b. Accrual

c. OIBDA   d. Income

40.   An _____ is a contract written by a seller that conveys to the buyer the right -- but not the obligation -- to buy (in the case of a call _____) or to sell (in the case of a put _____) a particular asset, such as a piece of property such as, among others, a futures contract. In return for granting the _____, the seller collects a payment (the premium) from the buyer.

For example, buying a call _____ provides the right to buy a specified quantity of a security at a set strike price at some time on or before expiration, while buying a put _____ provides the right to sell.

a. Amortization   b. AT'T Mobility LLC

c. Annuity   d. Option

41.   A _____ is the highest price that a buyer (i.e., bidder) is willing to pay for a good. It is usually referred to simply as the 'bid.'

In bid and ask, the _____ stands in contrast to the ask price or 'offer', and the difference between the two is called the bid/ask spread.

An unsolicited bid or offer is when a person or company receives a bid even though they are not looking to sell.

a. Mid price   b. Settlement date

c. Political risk   d. Bid price

42. A _____ or market-based mechanism is any of a wide variety of ways to match up buyers and sellers.

An example of a _____ uses announced bid and ask prices. Generally speaking, when two parties wish to engage in a trade, the purchaser will announce a price he is willing to pay (the bid price) and seller will announce a price he is willing to accept (the ask price).

a. 529 plan
b. 4-4-5 Calendar
c. 7-Eleven
d. Price mechanism

43. The _____ for securities is the difference between the price quoted by a market maker for an immediate sale and an immediate purchase The size of the bid-offer spread in a given commodity is a measure of the liquidity of the market.

The trader initiating the transaction is said to demand liquidity, and the other party to the transaction supplies liquidity.

a. Capital outflow
b. Trade-off
c. Defined contribution plan
d. Bid/offer spread

44. A _____ is a firm that quotes both a buy and a sell price in a financial instrument or commodity, hoping to make a profit on the bid/offer spread, or turn.

In foreign exchange trading, where most deals are conducted over-the-counter and are, therefore, completely virtual, the _____ sells to and buys from its clients. Hence, the client's loss and the spread is the _____ firm's profit, which gets thus compensated for the effort of providing liquidity in a competitive market.

a. 7-Eleven
b. 529 plan
c. 4-4-5 Calendar
d. Market maker

45. NYSE Euronext, Inc. is a Euro-American for-profit corporation that operates multiple securities exchanges, most notably Euronext, New York Stock Exchange (NYSE), and NYSE Arca (formerly known as ArcaEx.) _____ also operates NYSE Regulation, which is a non-profit Self-Regulatory Organization that oversees securities firms and companies listed on the New York Stock Exchange and NYSE Arca.

NYSE completed its acquisition of Archipelago Holdings via reverse takeover on March 7, 2006 in a 10 billion USD deal to create the _____.

a. NYSE Group
b. PlaNet Finance
c. Federal National Mortgage Association
d. Gold exchange-traded fund

46. A _____ is a member of an exchange who is an employee of a member firm and executes orders, as agent, on the floor of the exchange for clients. The _____ receives an order via teletype machine from his firm's trading department and then proceeds to the appropriate trading post on the exchange floor. There he joins other brokers and the specialist in the security being bought or sold and executes the trade at the best competitive price available.

a. Case-Shiller Home Price Indices
b. Floor broker
c. Multivariate normal distribution
d. Business valuation standards

47.   The _____ is the market for securities, where companies and governments can raise longterm funds. The _____ includes the stock market and the bond market. Financial regulators, such as the U.S. Securities and Exchange Commission, oversee the _____s in their designated countries to ensure that investors are protected against fraud.
   a. Forward market
   c. Delta neutral
   b. Spot rate
   d. Capital Market

48.   An _____ is the term used in financial circles for a type of computer system that facilitates trading of financial products outside of stock exchanges. The primary products that are traded on an _____ are stocks and currencies. They came into existence in 1998 when the SEC authorized their creation.
   a. Insider trading
   c. Open outcry
   b. Electronic communication network
   d. Intellidex

49.   A _____ is the price of a single share of a no. of saleable stocks of the company. Once the stock is purchased, the owner becomes a shareholder of the company that issued the share.
   a. Share price
   c. Whisper numbers
   b. Stock split
   d. Trading curb

1. _____ or net present worth (NPW) is defined as the total present value (PV) of a time series of cash flows. It is a standard method for using the time value of money to appraise long-term projects. Used for capital budgeting, and widely throughout economics, it measures the excess or shortfall of cash flows, in present value terms, once financing charges are met.

   a. Tax shield   b. Present value of costs
   c. Negative gearing   d. Net present value

2. In business and accounting, _____s are everything of value that is owned by a person or company. The balance sheet of a firm records the monetary value of the _____s owned by the firm. The two major _____ classes are tangible _____s and intangible _____s.

   a. Asset   b. Income
   c. Accounts payable   d. EBITDA

3. _____ is a term used to refer to how an investor distributes his or her investments among various classes of investment vehicles (e.g., stocks and bonds.)

   A large part of financial planning is finding an _____ that is appropriate for a given person in terms of their appetite for and ability to shoulder risk. This can depend on various factors; see investor profile.

   a. Asset allocation   b. Alternative investment
   c. Investment performance   d. Investing online

4. _____ is the value on a given date of a future payment or series of future payments, discounted to reflect the time value of money and other factors such as investment risk. _____ calculations are widely used in business and economics to provide a means to compare cash flows at different times on a meaningful 'like to like' basis.

   The most commonly applied model of the time value of money is compound interest.

   a. Present value   b. Net present value
   c. Present value of benefits   d. Negative gearing

5. _____ refers to the additional value of a commodity over the cost of commodities used to produce it from the previous stage of production. An example is the price of gasoline at the pump over the price of the oil in it. In national accounts used in macroeconomics, it refers to the contribution of the factors of production, i.e., land, labor, and capital goods, to raising the value of a product and corresponds to the incomes received by the owners of these factors.

   a. Supply shock   b. Deregulation
   c. Demand shock   d. Value added

6. In finance, the _____ approach describes a method of valuing a project, company, or asset using the concepts of the time value of money. All future cash flows are estimated and discounted to give their present values. The discount rate used is generally the appropriate cost of capital and may incorporate judgments of the uncertainty (riskiness) of the future cash flows.

   a. Future-oriented   b. Discounted cash flow
   c. Present value of benefits   d. Net present value

7. _____ is the balance of the amounts of cash being received and paid by a business during a defined period of time, sometimes tied to a specific project. Measurement of _____ can be used

- to evaluate the state or performance of a business or project.
- to determine problems with liquidity. Being profitable does not necessarily mean being liquid. A company can fail because of a shortage of cash, even while profitable.
- to generate project rate of returns. The time of _____s into and out of projects are used as inputs to financial models such as internal rate of return, and net present value.
- to examine income or growth of a business when it is believed that accrual accounting concepts do not represent economic realities. Alternately, _____ can be used to 'validate' the net income generated by accrual accounting.

_____ as a generic term may be used differently depending on context, and certain _____ definitions may be adapted by analysts and users for their own uses. Common terms include operating _____ and free _____.

_____s can be classified into:

1. Operational _____s: Cash received or expended as a result of the company's core business activities.
2. Investment _____s: Cash received or expended through capital expenditure, investments or acquisitions.
3. Financing _____s: Cash received or expended as a result of financial activities, such as interests and dividends.

All three together - the net _____ - are necessary to reconcile the beginning cash balance to the ending cash balance. Loan draw downs or equity injections, that is just shifting of capital but no expenditure as such, are not considered in the net _____.

a. Corporate finance
c. Shareholder value

b. Real option
d. Cash flow

8. In finance, _____ is the process of estimating the potential market value of a financial asset or liability. they can be done on assets (for example, investments in marketable securities such as stocks, options, business enterprises, or intangible assets such as patents and trademarks) or on liabilities (e.g., Bonds issued by a company.) _____s are required in many contexts including investment analysis, capital budgeting, merger and acquisition transactions, financial reporting, taxable events to determine the proper tax liability, and in litigation.

a. Share
c. Procter ' Gamble

b. Valuation
d. Margin

9. The _____ is a capital budgeting metric used by firms to decide whether they should make investments. It is an indicator of the efficiency or quality of an investment, as opposed to net present value (NPV), which indicates value or magnitude.

The IRR is the annualized effective compounded return rate which can be earned on the invested capital, i.e., the yield on the investment.

a. Internal rate of return

b. A Random Walk Down Wall Street

c. ABN Amro

d. AAB

10.   In finance, _____, also known as return on investment is the ratio of money gained or lost on an investment relative to the amount of money invested. The amount of money gained or lost may be referred to as interest, profit/loss, gain/loss, or net income/loss. The money invested may be referred to as the asset, capital, principal, or the cost basis of the investment.

a. Stock or scrip dividends

b. Doctrine of the Proper Law

c. Composiition of Creditors

d. Rate of return

11.   In finance, a _____ is a debt security, in which the authorized issuer owes the holders a debt and, depending on the terms of the _____, is obliged to pay interest (the coupon) and/or to repay the principal at a later date, termed maturity.

Thus a _____ is a loan: the issuer is the borrower, the _____ holder is the lender, and the coupon is the interest. _____s provide the borrower with external funds to finance long-term investments, or, in the case of government _____s, to finance current expenditure.

a. Bond

b. Catastrophe bonds

c. Puttable bond

d. Convertible bond

12.   In finance, the term _____ describes the amount in cash that returns to the owners of a security. Normally it does not include the price variations, at the difference of the total return. _____ applies to various stated rates of return on stocks (common and preferred, and convertible), fixed income instruments (bonds, notes, bills, strips, zero coupon), and some other investment type insurance products (e.g. annuities.)

a. Macaulay duration

b. Yield to maturity

c. 4-4-5 Calendar

d. Yield

13.   _____ in business and economics refers to the period of time required for the return on an investment to 'repay' the sum of the original investment. For example, a $1000 investment which returned $500 per year would have a two year _____. It intuitively measures how long something takes to 'pay for itself.' _____ is widely used due to its ease of use despite recognized limitations.

a. Payback period

b. Consignment stock

c. Financial Gerontology

d. Seasoned equity offering

14.   The _____ is the average project earnings after taxes and depreciation, divided by the average book value of the investment during its life.

There are three steps to calculating the _____.

First, determine the average net income of each year of the project's life. Second, determine the average investment, taking depreciation into account. Third, determine the _____ by dividing the average net income by the average investment.

a. Information ratio

b. Operating leverage

c. Assets turnover

d. Average accounting return

15. _____ are formal records of a business' financial activities.

_____ provide an overview of a business' financial condition in both short and long term. There are four basic _____:

1. **Balance sheet**: also referred to as statement of financial position or condition, reports on a company's assets, liabilities, and net equity as of a given point in time.
2. **Income statement**: also referred to as Profit and Loss statement (or a 'P'L'), reports on a company's income, expenses, and profits over a period of time.
3. **Statement of retained earnings**: explains the changes in a company's retained earnings over the reporting period.
4. **Statement of cash flows**: reports on a company's cash flow activities, particularly its operating, investing and financing activities.

a. Notes to the Financial Statements

b. Financial statements

c. Statement on Auditing Standards No. 70: Service Organizations

d. Statement of retained earnings

16. A '_____' is a 'Charge' that is paid to obtain the right to delay a payment. Essentially, the payer purchases the right to make a given payment in the future instead of in the Present. The '_____', or 'Charge' that must be paid to delay the payment, is simply the difference between what the payment amount would be if it were paid in the present and what the payment amount would be paid if it were paid in the future.

a. Discount

b. Risk aversion

c. Value at risk

d. Risk modeling

17. _____ is a financial measure used to determine the attractiveness of an investment. It is generally used as part of a capital budgeting process to rank various alternative choices. It is a modification of the Internal Rate of Return (IRR).

_____ ranks project efficiency consistently with the present worth ratio (variant of NPV/Discounted Negative Cash Flow), considered the gold standard in many finance textbooks.

MIRR is calculated as follows:

width=747 border=0>

where n is the number of (equal) periods in which the cash flows occur.

a. Current yield

b. Modified Internal Rate of Return

c. Binomial options pricing model

d. Black-Scholes

18. _____ identifies the relationship of investment to payoff of a proposed project. The ratio is calculated as follows:

- >

_____ is also known as Profit Investment Ratio, abbreviated to P.I. and Value Investment Ratio (V.I.R.). _____ is a good tool for ranking projects because it allows you to clearly identify the amount of value created per unit of investment, thus if you are capital constrained you wish to invest in those projects which create value most efficiently first.

a. Total return

b. Conditional prepayment rate

c. Profitability index

d. Capitalization rate

19. _____ is the planning process used to determine whether a firm's long term investments such as new machinery, replacement machinery, new plants, new products, and research development projects are worth pursuing. It is budget for major capital, or investment, expenditures.

Many formal methods are used in _____, including the techniques such as

- Net present value
- Profitability index
- Internal rate of return
- Modified Internal Rate of Return
- Equivalent annuity

These methods use the incremental cash flows from each potential investment, or project. Techniques based on accounting earnings and accounting rules are sometimes used - though economists consider this to be improper - such as the accounting rate of return, and 'return on investment.' Simplified and hybrid methods are used as well, such as payback period and discounted payback period.

a. Preferred stock

b. Financial distress

c. Shareholder value

d. Capital budgeting

20. An _____ is a contract written by a seller that conveys to the buyer the right -- but not the obligation -- to buy (in the case of a call _____) or to sell (in the case of a put _____) a particular asset, such as a piece of property such as, among others, a futures contract. In return for granting the _____, the seller collects a payment (the premium) from the buyer.

For example, buying a call _____ provides the right to buy a specified quantity of a security at a set strike price at some time on or before expiration, while buying a put _____ provides the right to sell.

a. Annuity

b. AT'T Mobility LLC

c. Option

d. Amortization

1. _____ is the balance of the amounts of cash being received and paid by a business during a defined period of time, sometimes tied to a specific project. Measurement of _____ can be used

- to evaluate the state or performance of a business or project.
- to determine problems with liquidity. Being profitable does not necessarily mean being liquid. A company can fail because of a shortage of cash, even while profitable.
- to generate project rate of returns. The time of _____s into and out of projects are used as inputs to financial models such as internal rate of return, and net present value.
- to examine income or growth of a business when it is believed that accrual accounting concepts do not represent economic realities. Alternately, _____ can be used to 'validate' the net income generated by accrual accounting.

_____ as a generic term may be used differently depending on context, and certain _____ definitions may be adapted by analysts and users for their own uses. Common terms include operating _____ and free _____.

_____s can be classified into:

1. Operational _____s: Cash received or expended as a result of the company's core business activities.
2. Investment _____s: Cash received or expended through capital expenditure, investments or acquisitions.
3. Financing _____s: Cash received or expended as a result of financial activities, such as interests and dividends.

All three together - the net _____ - are necessary to reconcile the beginning cash balance to the ending cash balance. Loan draw downs or equity injections, that is just shifting of capital but no expenditure as such, are not considered in the net _____.

a. Corporate finance
c. Shareholder value

b. Cash flow
d. Real option

2. _____ or net present worth (NPW) is defined as the total present value (PV) of a time series of cash flows. It is a standard method for using the time value of money to appraise long-term projects. Used for capital budgeting, and widely throughout economics, it measures the excess or shortfall of cash flows, in present value terms, once financing charges are met.

a. Negative gearing
c. Net present value

b. Present value of costs
d. Tax shield

3. _____ is the value on a given date of a future payment or series of future payments, discounted to reflect the time value of money and other factors such as investment risk. _____ calculations are widely used in business and economics to provide a means to compare cash flows at different times on a meaningful 'like to like' basis.

The most commonly applied model of the time value of money is compound interest.

a. Present value of benefits
c. Negative gearing

b. Present value
d. Net present value

4. _____ or economic opportunity loss is the value of the next best alternative foregone as the result of making a decision. _____ analysis is an important part of a company's decision-making processes but is not treated as an actual cost in any financial statement. The next best thing that a person can engage in is referred to as the _____ of doing the best thing and ignoring the next best thing to be done.

a. AAB

b. ABN Amro

c. A Random Walk Down Wall Street

d. Opportunity cost

5. In economics and business decision-making, _____ are costs that cannot be recovered once they have been incurred. _____ are sometimes contrasted with variable costs, which are the costs that will change due to the proposed course of action, and prospective costs which are costs that will be incurred if an action is taken. In microeconomic theory, only variable costs are relevant to a decision.

a. Hyperbolic discounting

b. 4-4-5 Calendar

c. Hindsight bias

d. Sunk costs

6. In economics, business, and accounting, a _____ is the value of money that has been used up to produce something, and hence is not available for use anymore. In business, the _____ may be one of acquisition, in which case the amount of money expended to acquire it is counted as _____. In this case, money is the input that is gone in order to acquire the thing.

a. Marginal cost

b. Fixed costs

c. Sliding scale fees

d. Cost

7. In economics, the concept of the _____ refers to the decision-making time frame of a firm in which at least one factor of production is fixed. Costs which are fixed in the _____ have no impact on a firms decisions. For example a firm can raise output by increasing the amount of labour through overtime.

a. Long-run

b. 529 plan

c. 4-4-5 Calendar

d. Short-run

8. _____ or financing is to provide capital (funds), which means money for a project, a person, a business or any other private or public institutions.

Those funds can be allocated for either short term or long term purposes. The health fund is a new way of _____ private healthcare centers.

a. Synthetic CDO

b. Proxy fight

c. Product life cycle

d. Funding

9. _____ is a financial metric which represents operating liquidity available to a business. Along with fixed assets such as plant and equipment, _____ is considered a part of operating capital. It is calculated as current assets minus current liabilities.

a. Working capital

b. 529 plan

c. Working capital management

d. 4-4-5 Calendar

10. The term _____ is a term applied to practices that are perfunctory, or seek to satisfy the minimum requirements or to conform to a convention or doctrine. It has different meanings in different fields.

In accounting, _____ earnings are those earnings of companies in addition to actual earnings calculated under the Generally Accepted Accounting Principles (GAAP) in their quarterly and yearly financial reports.

a. Pro forma

b. Deferred income

c. Long-term liabilities

d. Deferred financing costs

11.   _____ are formal records of a business' financial activities.

_____ provide an overview of a business' financial condition in both short and long term. There are four basic _____:

1. **Balance sheet**: also referred to as statement of financial position or condition, reports on a company's assets, liabilities, and net equity as of a given point in time.
2. **Income statement**: also referred to as Profit and Loss statement (or a 'P'L'), reports on a company's income, expenses, and profits over a period of time.
3. **Statement of retained earnings**: explains the changes in a company's retained earnings over the reporting period.
4. **Statement of cash flows**: reports on a company's cash flow activities, particularly its operating, investing and financing activities.

a. Statement of retained earnings

b. Financial statements

c. Statement on Auditing Standards No. 70: Service Organizations

d. Notes to the Financial Statements

12.   In financial accounting, _____ , cash flow provided by operations or cash flow from operating activities, refers to the amount of cash a company generates from the revenues it brings in, excluding costs associated with long-term investment on capital items or investment in securities.

_____ = Cash generated from operations less taxation and interest paid, investment income received and less dividends paid gives rise to _____s per International Financial Reporting Standards.

To calculate cash generated from operations, one must calculate cash generated from customers and cash paid to suppliers.

a. A Random Walk Down Wall Street

b. Other Comprehensive Basis of Accounting

c. Appreciation

d. Operating cash flow

13.   _____ is the planning process used to determine whether a firm's long term investments such as new machinery, replacement machinery, new plants, new products, and research development projects are worth pursuing. It is budget for major capital, or investment, expenditures.

Many formal methods are used in _____, including the techniques such as

- Net present value
- Profitability index
- Internal rate of return
- Modified Internal Rate of Return
- Equivalent annuity

These methods use the incremental cash flows from each potential investment, or project. Techniques based on accounting earnings and accounting rules are sometimes used - though economists consider this to be improper - such as the accounting rate of return, and 'return on investment.' Simplified and hybrid methods are used as well, such as payback period and discounted payback period.

a. Preferred stock

b. Financial distress

c. Shareholder value

d. Capital budgeting

14. The _____ is the current method of accelerated asset depreciation required by the United States income tax code. Under _____, all assets are divided into classes which dictate the number of years over which an asset's cost will be recovered.

Prior to the Accelerated Cost Recovery System (ACRS), most capital purchases were depreciated using a straight line technique, that allowed for the depreciation of the asset over its useful life.

a. 7-Eleven

b. 529 plan

c. 4-4-5 Calendar

d. Modified Accelerated Cost Recovery System

15. _____ is a term used in accounting, economics and finance to spread the cost of an asset over the span of several years.

In simple words we can say that _____ is the reduction in the value of an asset due to usage, passage of time, wear and tear, technological outdating or obsolescence, depletion or other such factors.

In accounting, _____ is a term used to describe any method of attributing the historical or purchase cost of an asset across its useful life, roughly corresponding to normal wear and tear.

a. Deferred financing costs

b. Bottom line

c. Matching principle

d. Depreciation

16. _____ is the price at which an asset would trade in a competitive Walrasian auction setting. _____ is often used interchangeably with open _____, fair value or fair _____, although these terms have distinct definitions in different standards, and may differ in some circumstances.

International Valuation Standards defines _____ as 'the estimated amount for which a property should exchange on the date of valuation between a willing buyer and a willing seller in an arm'e;s-length transaction after proper marketing wherein the parties had each acted knowledgeably, prudently, and without compulsion.'

_____ is a concept distinct from market price, which is 'e;the price at which one can transact'e;, while _____ is 'e;the true underlying value'e; according to theoretical standards.

a. Market value

b. Debt restructuring

c. Wrap account

d. T-Model

17.   In accounting, _____ or *Carrying value* is the value of an asset according to its balance sheet account balance. For assets, the value is based on the original cost of the asset less any depreciation, amortization or impairment costs made against the asset. A company's _____ is its total assets minus intangible assets and liabilities.

a. Pro forma

b. Current liabilities

c. Book value

d. Retained earnings

18.   A _____ is the reduction in income taxes that results from taking an allowable deduction from taxable income. For example, because interest on debt is a tax-deductible expense, taking on debt creates a _____. Since a _____ is a way to save cash flows, it increases the value of the business, and it is an important aspect of business valuation.

a. Tax shield

b. Refinancing risk

c. Present value of costs

d. Present value of benefits

19.   In finance, the _____ approach describes a method of valuing a project, company, or asset using the concepts of the time value of money. All future cash flows are estimated and discounted to give their present values. The discount rate used is generally the appropriate cost of capital and may incorporate judgments of the uncertainty (riskiness) of the future cash flows.

a. Net present value

b. Present value of benefits

c. Future-oriented

d. Discounted cash flow

20.   In finance, _____ is the process of estimating the potential market value of a financial asset or liability. they can be done on assets (for example, investments in marketable securities such as stocks, options, business enterprises, or intangible assets such as patents and trademarks) or on liabilities (e.g., Bonds issued by a company.) _____s are required in many contexts including investment analysis, capital budgeting, merger and acquisition transactions, financial reporting, taxable events to determine the proper tax liability, and in litigation.

a. Margin

b. Procter ' Gamble

c. Share

d. Valuation

21.   A _____ is the highest price that a buyer (i.e., bidder) is willing to pay for a good. It is usually referred to simply as the 'bid.'

In bid and ask, the _____ stands in contrast to the ask price or 'offer', and the difference between the two is called the bid/ask spread.

An unsolicited bid or offer is when a person or company receives a bid even though they are not looking to sell.

a. Bid price   b. Settlement date
c. Mid price   d. Political risk

22.   In finance the _____ is the cost per year of owning and operating an asset over its entire lifespan.

_____ is often used as a decision making tool in capital budgeting when comparing investment projects of unequal lifespans. For example if project A has an expected lifetime of 7 years, and project B has an expected lifetime of 11 years it would be improper to simply compare the net present values (NPVs) of the two projects, unless neither project could be repeated.

a. A Random Walk Down Wall Street   b. Indirect costs
c. AAB   d. Equivalent annual cost

23.   An _____ is a contract written by a seller that conveys to the buyer the right -- but not the obligation -- to buy (in the case of a call _____) or to sell (in the case of a put _____) a particular asset, such as a piece of property such as, among others, a futures contract. In return for granting the _____, the seller collects a payment (the premium) from the buyer.

For example, buying a call _____ provides the right to buy a specified quantity of a security at a set strike price at some time on or before expiration, while buying a put _____ provides the right to sell.

a. Annuity   b. Amortization
c. AT'T Mobility LLC   d. Option

1. _____ or net present worth (NPW) is defined as the total present value (PV) of a time series of cash flows. It is a standard method for using the time value of money to appraise long-term projects. Used for capital budgeting, and widely throughout economics, it measures the excess or shortfall of cash flows, in present value terms, once financing charges are met.

 a. Negative gearing   b. Tax shield
 c. Present value of costs   d. Net present value

2. _____ is the balance of the amounts of cash being received and paid by a business during a defined period of time, sometimes tied to a specific project. Measurement of _____ can be used

- to evaluate the state or performance of a business or project.
- to determine problems with liquidity. Being profitable does not necessarily mean being liquid. A company can fail because of a shortage of cash, even while profitable.
- to generate project rate of returns. The time of _____s into and out of projects are used as inputs to financial models such as internal rate of return, and net present value.
- to examine income or growth of a business when it is believed that accrual accounting concepts do not represent economic realities. Alternately, _____ can be used to 'validate' the net income generated by accrual accounting.

_____ as a generic term may be used differently depending on context, and certain _____ definitions may be adapted by analysts and users for their own uses. Common terms include operating _____ and free _____.

_____s can be classified into:

1. Operational _____s: Cash received or expended as a result of the company's core business activities.
2. Investment _____s: Cash received or expended through capital expenditure, investments or acquisitions.
3. Financing _____s: Cash received or expended as a result of financial activities, such as interests and dividends.

All three together - the net _____ - are necessary to reconcile the beginning cash balance to the ending cash balance. Loan draw downs or equity injections, that is just shifting of capital but no expenditure as such, are not considered in the net _____.

 a. Shareholder value   b. Real option
 c. Corporate finance   d. Cash flow

3. _____ is the value on a given date of a future payment or series of future payments, discounted to reflect the time value of money and other factors such as investment risk. _____ calculations are widely used in business and economics to provide a means to compare cash flows at different times on a meaningful 'like to like' basis.

The most commonly applied model of the time value of money is compound interest.

 a. Present value of benefits   b. Net present value
 c. Present value   d. Negative gearing

4.   A _____ is a financial contract between two parties, the buyer and the seller of this type of option. Often it is simply labeled a 'call'. The buyer of the option has the right, but not the obligation to buy an agreed quantity of a particular commodity or financial instrument (the underlying instrument) from the seller of the option at a certain time (the expiration date) for a certain price (the strike price.)

a. Bear spread
c. Bear call spread

b. Call option
d. Bull spread

5.   An _____ is a contract written by a seller that conveys to the buyer the right -- but not the obligation -- to buy (in the case of a call _____) or to sell (in the case of a put _____) a particular asset, such as a piece of property such as, among others, a futures contract. In return for granting the _____, the seller collects a payment (the premium) from the buyer.

For example, buying a call _____ provides the right to buy a specified quantity of a security at a set strike price at some time on or before expiration, while buying a put _____ provides the right to sell.

a. Annuity
c. AT'T Mobility LLC

b. Amortization
d. Option

6.   _____ is a process of analyzing possible future events by considering alternative possible outcomes (scenarios.) The analysis is designed to allow improved decision-making by allowing consideration of outcomes and their implications.

For example, in economics and finance, a financial institution might attempt to forecast several possible scenarios for the economy (e.g. rapid growth, moderate growth, slow growth) and it might also attempt to forecast financial market returns (for bonds, stocks and cash) in each of those scenarios.

a. Scenario analysis
c. Detection Risk

b. 4-4-5 Calendar
d. 529 plan

7.   _____ is the study of how the variation (uncertainty) in the output of a mathematical model can be apportioned, qualitatively or quantitatively, to different sources of variation in the input of a model .

In more general terms uncertainty and sensitivity analyses investigate the robustness of a study when the study includes some form of mathematical modelling. While uncertainty analysis studies the overall uncertainty in the conclusions of the study, _____ tries to identify what source of uncertainty weights more on the study's conclusions.

a. Proxy fight
c. Synthetic CDO

b. Golden parachute
d. Sensitivity analysis

8.   In economics and business, specifically cost accounting, the _____ is the point at which cost or expenses and revenue are equal: there is no net loss or gain, and one has 'broken even'. A profit or a loss has not been made, although opportunity costs have been paid, and capital has received the risk-adjusted, expected return.

For example, if the business sells less than 200 tables each month, it will make a loss, if it sells more, it will be a profit.

a. Market microstructure

b. Defined contribution plan

c. Fixed asset turnover

d. Break-even point

9. _____ are expenses that change in proportion to the activity of a business. In other words, _____ are the sum of marginal costs. It can also be considered normal costs. Along with fixed costs, _____ make up the two components of total cost. Direct Costs, however, are costs that can be associated with a particular cost object.

a. Cost accounting

b. Transaction cost

c. Variable costs

d. Fixed costs

10. In economics, business, and accounting, a _____ is the value of money that has been used up to produce something, and hence is not available for use anymore. In business, the _____ may be one of acquisition, in which case the amount of money expended to acquire it is counted as _____. In this case, money is the input that is gone in order to acquire the thing.

a. Fixed costs

b. Sliding scale fees

c. Cost

d. Marginal cost

11. _____ are business expenses that are not dependent on the level of production or sales. They tend to be time-related, such as salaries or rents being paid per month. This is in contrast to Variable costs, which are volume-related (and are paid per quantity.)

a. Sliding scale fees

b. Transaction cost

c. Marginal cost

d. Fixed costs

12. In economics, and cost accounting, _____ describes the total economic cost of production and is made up of variable costs, which vary according to the quantity of a good produced and include inputs such as labor and raw materials, plus fixed costs, which are independent of the quantity of a good produced and include inputs (capital) that cannot be varied in the short term, such as buildings and machinery. _____ in economics includes the total opportunity cost of each factor of production in addition to fixed and variable costs.

The rate at which _____ changes as the amount produced changes is called marginal cost.

a. 7-Eleven

b. Total cost

c. 4-4-5 Calendar

d. 529 plan

13. In economics and finance, _____ is the change in total cost that arises when the quantity produced changes by one unit. It is the cost of producing one more unit of a good. Mathematically, the _____ function is expressed as the first derivative of the total cost (TC) function with respect to quantity (Q). Note that the _____ may change with volume, and so at each level of production, the _____ is the cost of the next unit produced.

A typical _____ Curve

>

a. Marginal cost

b. Sliding scale fees

c. Fixed costs

d. Cost accounting

14. In business, _____ is income that a company receives from its normal business activities, usually from the sale of goods and services to customers. Some companies also receive _____ from interest, dividends or royalties paid to them by other companies. _____ may refer to business income in general, or it may refer to the amount, in a monetary unit, received during a period of time, as in 'Last year, Company X had _____ of $32 million.'

In many countries, including the UK, _____ is referred to as turnover.

a. Furniture, Fixtures and Equipment   b. Bottom line
c. Matching principle   d. Revenue

15. In cost-volume-profit analysis, a form of management accounting, _____ is the marginal profit per unit sale. It is a useful quantity in carrying out various calculations, and can be used as a measure of operating leverage.

The Total _____ is Total Revenue (TR, or Sales) minus Total Variable Cost (TVC):

TContribution margin = TR >− TVC

The Unit _____ (C) is Unit Revenue (Price, P) minus Unit Variable Cost (V):

C = P >− V

The _____ Ratio is the percentage of Contribution over Total Revenue, which can be calculated from the unit contribution over unit price or total contribution over Total Revenue:

For instance, if the price is $10 and the unit variable cost is $2, then the unit _____ is $8, and the _____ ratio is $8/$10 = 80%.

a. 4-4-5 Calendar   b. 529 plan
c. 7-Eleven   d. Contribution margin

16. In finance, a _____ is collateral that the holder of a position in securities, options, or futures contracts has to deposit to cover the credit risk of his counterparty (most often his broker.) This risk can arise if the holder has done any of the following:

- borrowed cash from the counterparty to buy securities or options,
- sold securities or options short, or
- entered into a futures contract.

The collateral can be in the form of cash or securities, and it is deposited in a _____ account. On U.S. futures exchanges, '_____' was formally called performance bond.

_____ buying is buying securities with cash borrowed from a broker, using other securities as collateral.

a. Procter ' Gamble   b. Share
c. Credit   d. Margin

17.   In financial accounting, _____ , cash flow provided by operations or cash flow from operating activities, refers to the amount of cash a company generates from the revenues it brings in, excluding costs associated with long-term investment on capital items or investment in securities.

_____ = Cash generated from operations less taxation and interest paid, investment income received and less dividends paid gives rise to _____s per International Financial Reporting Standards.

To calculate cash generated from operations, one must calculate cash generated from customers and cash paid to suppliers.

a. A Random Walk Down Wall Street   b. Other Comprehensive Basis of Accounting
c. Appreciation   d. Operating cash flow

18.   _____ is a measure of the ability of a debtor to pay their debts as and when they fall due. It is usually expressed as a ratio or a percentage of current liabilities.

For a corporation with a published balance sheet there are various ratios used to calculate a measure of liquidity.

a. Invested capital   b. Operating leverage
c. Operating profit margin   d. Accounting liquidity

19.   The _____ is a measure of how revenue growth translates into growth in operating income. It is a measure of leverage, and of how risky (volatile) a company's operating income is.

There are various measures of _____, which can be interpreted analogously to financial leverage.

a. Invested capital   b. Operating leverage
c. Average accounting return   d. Asset turnover

20.   In finance, _____ (or gearing) is borrowing money to supplement existing funds for investment in such a way that the potential positive or negative outcome is magnified and/or enhanced. It generally refers to using borrowed funds, or debt, so as to attempt to increase the returns to equity. Deleveraging is the action of reducing borrowings.
a. Leverage   b. Pension fund
c. Financial endowment   d. Limited partnership

1. _____ is the balance of the amounts of cash being received and paid by a business during a defined period of time, sometimes tied to a specific project. Measurement of _____ can be used

- to evaluate the state or performance of a business or project.
- to determine problems with liquidity. Being profitable does not necessarily mean being liquid. A company can fail because of a shortage of cash, even while profitable.
- to generate project rate of returns. The time of _____s into and out of projects are used as inputs to financial models such as internal rate of return, and net present value.
- to examine income or growth of a business when it is believed that accrual accounting concepts do not represent economic realities. Alternately, _____ can be used to 'validate' the net income generated by accrual accounting.

_____ as a generic term may be used differently depending on context, and certain _____ definitions may be adapted by analysts and users for their own uses. Common terms include operating _____ and free _____.

_____s can be classified into:

1. Operational _____s: Cash received or expended as a result of the company's core business activities.
2. Investment _____s: Cash received or expended through capital expenditure, investments or acquisitions.
3. Financing _____s: Cash received or expended as a result of financial activities, such as interests and dividends.

All three together - the net _____ - are necessary to reconcile the beginning cash balance to the ending cash balance. Loan draw downs or equity injections, that is just shifting of capital but no expenditure as such, are not considered in the net _____.

a. Corporate finance	b. Shareholder value
c. Real option	d. Cash flow

2. In finance, the _____ approach describes a method of valuing a project, company, or asset using the concepts of the time value of money. All future cash flows are estimated and discounted to give their present values. The discount rate used is generally the appropriate cost of capital and may incorporate judgments of the uncertainty (riskiness) of the future cash flows.

a. Net present value	b. Future-oriented
c. Present value of benefits	d. Discounted cash flow

3. _____ are made by investors and investment managers.

Investors commonly perform investment analysis by making use of fundamental analysis, technical analysis and gut feel.

_____ are often supported by decision tools.

a. Asset allocation   b. Investing online
c. Investment performance   d. Investment decisions

4. _____ is a risk-adjusted measure of the so-called active return on an investment. It is the return in excess of the compensation for the risk borne, and thus commonly used to assess active managers' performances. Often, the return of a benchmark is subtracted in order to consider relative performance, which yields Jensen's _____.
   a. Option   b. Annuity
   c. Amortization   d. Alpha

5.

In finance, the _____ can be the expected rate of return above the risk-free interest rate. When measuring risk, a common sense approach is to compare the risk-free return on T-bills and the very risky return on other investments. The difference between these two returns can be interpreted as a measure of the excess return on the average risky asset. This excess return is known as the _____.

   a. Risk modeling   b. Risk adjusted return on capital
   c. Risk aversion   d. Risk premium

6. In statistics, a _____ is a tabulation of the values that one or more variables take in a sample.

Univariate _____s are often presented as lists ordered by quantity showing the number of times each value appears. For example, if 100 people rate a five-point Likert scale assessing their agreement with a statement on a scale on which 1 denotes strong agreement and 5 strong disagreement, the _____ of their responses might look like:

This simple tabulation has two drawbacks.

   a. Frequency distribution   b. Random variables
   c. Variance   d. Covariance

7. In probability and statistics, the _____ of a collection of numbers is a measure of the dispersion of the numbers from their expected (mean) value. It can apply to a probability distribution, a random variable, a population or a data set. The _____ is usually denoted with the letter σ (lowercase sigma.)
   a. Kurtosis   b. Mean
   c. Standard deviation   d. Sample size

8. In probability theory and statistics, the _____ of a random variable, probability distribution averaging the squared distance of its possible values from the expected value (mean.) Whereas the mean is a way to describe the location of a distribution, the _____ is a way to capture its scale or degree of being spread out. The unit of _____ is the square of the unit of the original variable.
   a. Monte Carlo methods   b. Variance
   c. Semivariance   d. Harmonic mean

9. The _____ is an important family of continuous probability distributions, applicable in many fields. Each member of the family may be defined by two parameters, location and scale: the mean and variance respectively. The standard _____ is the _____ with a mean of zero and a variance of one

  a. Random variables   b. Correlation

  c. Probability distribution   d. Normal distribution

10. The _____ is the market for securities, where companies and governments can raise longterm funds. The _____ includes the stock market and the bond market. Financial regulators, such as the U.S. Securities and Exchange Commission, oversee the _____s in their designated countries to ensure that investors are protected against fraud.

  a. Forward market   b. Delta neutral

  c. Capital market   d. Spot rate

11. In finance, _____ are stocks that appreciate in value and yield a high return on equity (ROE.) Analysts compute ROE by taking the company's net income and dividing it by the company's equity. To be classified as a growth stock, analysts expect to see at least 15 percent return on equity.

  a. 4-4-5 Calendar   b. Stock valuation

  c. Growth stocks   d. Security Analysis

12. In business and finance, a _____ (also referred to as equity _____) of stock means a _____ of ownership in a corporation (company.) In the plural, stocks is often used as a synonym for _____s especially in the United States, but it is less commonly used that way outside of North America.

In the United Kingdom, South Africa, and Australia, stock can also refer to completely different financial instruments such as government bonds or, less commonly, to all kinds of marketable securities.

  a. Bucket shop   b. Share

  c. Margin   d. Procter ' Gamble

13. _____ is an economic concept with commonplace familiarity. It is the price that a good or service is offered at, or will fetch, in the marketplace. It is of interest mainly in the study of microeconomics.

  a. Delta hedging   b. Central Securities Depository

  c. Market price   d. Convertible arbitrage

14. In finance, a _____ is a debt security, in which the authorized issuer owes the holders a debt and, depending on the terms of the _____, is obliged to pay interest (the coupon) and/or to repay the principal at a later date, termed maturity.

Thus a _____ is a loan: the issuer is the borrower, the _____ holder is the lender, and the coupon is the interest. _____s provide the borrower with external funds to finance long-term investments, or, in the case of government _____s, to finance current expenditure.

  a. Convertible bond   b. Catastrophe bonds

  c. Bond   d. Puttable bond

15.   In economics, _____ describes the state of a market with respect to competition.

- Perfect competition, in which the market consists of a very large number of firms producing a homogeneous product.
- Monopolistic competition where there are a large number of independent firms which have a very small proportion of the market share.
- Oligopoly, in which a market is dominated by a small number of firms which own more than 40% of the market share.
- Oligopsony, a market dominated by many sellers and a few buyers.
- Monopoly, where there is only one provider of a product or service.
- Natural monopoly, a monopoly in which economies of scale cause efficiency to increase continuously with the size of the firm. A firm is a natural monopoly if it is able to serve the entire market demand at a lower cost than any combination of two or more smaller, more specialized firms.
- Monopsony, when there is only one buyer in a market.

The imperfectly competitive structure is quite identical to the realistic market conditions where some monopolistic competitors, monopolists, oligopolists, and duopolists exist and dominate the market conditions. The elements of _____ include the number and size distribution of firms, entry conditions, and the extent of differentiation.

These somewhat abstract concerns tend to determine some but not all details of a specific concrete market system where buyers and sellers actually meet and commit to trade.

a. Human capital   b. Market structure
c. Gross domestic product   d. Fixed exchange rate

16.   In finance, a _____ is a type of bond that can be converted into shares of stock in the issuing company, usually at some pre-announced ratio. It is a hybrid security with debt- and equity-like features. Although it typically has a low coupon rate, the holder is compensated with the ability to convert the bond to common stock, usually at a substantial discount to the stock's market value.

a. Corporate bond   b. Gilts
c. Bond fund   d. Convertible bond

1.

In finance, the _____ can be the expected rate of return above the risk-free interest rate. When measuring risk, a common sense approach is to compare the risk-free return on T-bills and the very risky return on other investments. The difference between these two returns can be interpreted as a measure of the excess return on the average risky asset. This excess return is known as the _____.

a. Risk aversion

b. Risk adjusted return on capital

c. Risk modeling

d. Risk premium

2. A _____ is a fungible, negotiable instrument representing financial value. They are broadly categorized into debt securities (such as banknotes, bonds and debentures), and equity securities; e.g., common stocks. The company or other entity issuing the _____ is called the issuer.

a. Security

b. Book entry

c. Tracking stock

d. Securities lending

3.   In Modern Portfolio Theory, the _____ is the graphical representation of the Capital Asset Pricing Model. It displays the expected rate of return for an overall market as a function of systematic (non-diversifiable) risk (beta.)

The Y-Intercept (beta=0) of the _____ is equal to the risk-free interest rate.

a. Rebalancing

b. Security market line

c. Certificate in Investment Performance Measurement

d. Divestment

4.   In finance, _____ is that risk which is common to an entire market and not to any individual entity or component thereof. It should be distinguished from systemic risk which is the risk that the entire financial system will collapse as a result of some catastrophic event.

Risks can be reduced in four main ways: Avoidance, Reduction, Retention and Transfer.

a. Systematic risk

b. Capital surplus

c. Conglomerate merger

d. Primary market

5.   The _____ is the weighted-average most likely outcome in gambling, probability theory, economics or finance.

In gambling and probability theory, there is usually a discrete set of possible outcomes. In this case, _____ is a measure of the relative balance of win or loss weighted by their chances of occurring.

a. AAB

b. A Random Walk Down Wall Street

c. ABN Amro

d. Expected return

6.   In probability theory and statistics, the _____ of a random variable, probability distribution averaging the squared distance of its possible values from the expected value (mean.) Whereas the mean is a way to describe the location of a distribution, the _____ is a way to capture its scale or degree of being spread out. The unit of _____ is the square of the unit of the original variable.

a. Monte Carlo methods

b. Harmonic mean

c. Semivariance

d. Variance

7.   In probability and statistics, the _____ of a collection of numbers is a measure of the dispersion of the numbers from their expected (mean) value. It can apply to a probability distribution, a random variable, a population or a data set. The _____ is usually denoted with the letter σ (lowercase sigma.)

a. Standard deviation

b. Sample size

c. Kurtosis

d. Mean

8.   _____ in finance is a risk management technique, related to hedging, that mixes a wide variety of investments within a portfolio. Because the fluctuations of a single security have less impact on a diverse portfolio, _____ minimizes the risk from any one investment.

A simple example of _____ is the following: On a particular island the entire economy consists of two companies: one that sells umbrellas and another that sells sunscreen.

a. 4-4-5 Calendar

b. 7-Eleven

c. 529 plan

d. Diversification

9.   A '_____' is a 'Charge' that is paid to obtain the right to delay a payment. Essentially, the payer purchases the right to make a given payment in the future instead of in the Present. The '_____', or 'Charge' that must be paid to delay the payment, is simply the difference between what the payment amount would be if it were paid in the present and what the payment amount would be paid if it were paid in the future.

a. Risk aversion

b. Value at risk

c. Risk modeling

d. Discount

10.   _____ is the risk that the value of an investment will decrease due to moves in market factors. The five standard _____ factors are:

- Equity risk, the risk that stock prices will change.
- Interest rate risk, the risk that interest rates will change.
- Currency risk, the risk that foreign exchange rates will change.
- Commodity risk, the risk that commodity prices (e.g. grains, metals) will change.

As with other forms of risk, _____ may be measured in a number of ways. Traditionally, this is done using a Value at Risk methodology. Value at risk is well established as a risk management technique, but it contains a number of limiting assumptions that constrain its accuracy.

a. Tracking error

b. Currency risk

c. Transaction risk

d. Market risk

11.   The _____, in terms of finance and investing, describes how the expected return of a stock or portfolio is correlated to the return of the financial market as a whole.

An asset with a beta of 0 means that its price is not at all correlated with the market; that asset is independent. A positive beta means that the asset generally follows the market.

a. Perpetuity

b. Current yield

c. LIBOR market model

d. Beta coefficient

12. In economics, the concept of the _____ refers to the decision-making time frame of a firm in which at least one factor of production is fixed. Costs which are fixed in the _____ have no impact on a firms decisions. For example a firm can raise output by increasing the amount of labour through overtime.

a. 4-4-5 Calendar

b. Long-run

c. 529 plan

d. Short-run

13. _____ are costs incurred on the purchase of land, buildings, construction and equipment to be used in the production of goods or the rendering of services. In other words, the total cost needed to bring a project to a commercially operable status. However, _____ are not limited to the initial construction of a factory or other business.

a. Defined contribution plan

b. Capital costs

c. Trade-off

d. Capital outflow

14. In business and accounting, _____s are everything of value that is owned by a person or company. The balance sheet of a firm records the monetary value of the _____s owned by the firm. The two major _____ classes are tangible _____s and intangible _____s.

a. Accounts payable

b. EBITDA

c. Income

d. Asset

15. In finance, _____ is the process of estimating the potential market value of a financial asset or liability. they can be done on assets (for example, investments in marketable securities such as stocks, options, business enterprises, or intangible assets such as patents and trademarks) or on liabilities (e.g., Bonds issued by a company.) _____s are required in many contexts including investment analysis, capital budgeting, merger and acquisition transactions, financial reporting, taxable events to determine the proper tax liability, and in litigation.

a. Share

b. Procter ' Gamble

c. Margin

d. Valuation

16.   The term _____ has three unrelated technical definitions, and is also used in a variety of non-technical ways.

- In financial economics, it refers to any asset used to make money, as opposed to assets used for personal enjoyment or consumption. This is an important distinction because two people can disagree sharply about the value of personal assets, one person might think a sports car is more valuable than a pickup truck, another person might have the opposite taste. But if an asset is held for the purpose of making money, taste has nothing to do with it, only differences of opinion about how much money the asset will produce. With the further assumption that people agree on the probability distribution of future cash flows, it is possible to have an objective _____ pricing model. Even without the assumption of agreement, it is possible to set rational limits on _____ value.
- In governmental accounting, it is defined as any asset used in operations with an initial useful life extending beyond one reporting period. Generally, government managers have a 'stewardship' duty to maintain _____s under their control. See International Public Sector Accounting Standards for details.
- In US tax accounting, it is defined as any property other than a list of exceptions. The main exceptions are anything held for sale, and any real estate or depreciable property used in business. Almost everything you own and use for personal purposes, pleasure or investment is a _____. If something is a _____ for tax purposes, gains or losses on sale or disposition are capital gains or capital losses. For individuals, however, capital losses on property held for personal use are generally not deductible. See the IRS publication Tax Facts about Capital Gains and Losses for details.

A well-known financial accounting textbook advises that the term be avoided except in tax accounting because it is used in so many different senses, not all of them well-defined. For example it is often used as a synonym for fixed assets or for investments in securities.

A common non-technical usage occurs when people ask that employees or the environment or something else be treated as a _____.

a. Settlement date
c. Political risk

b. Solvency
d. Capital asset

17.   In finance, the _____ is used to determine a theoretically appropriate required rate of return of an asset, if that asset is to be added to an already well-diversified portfolio, given that asset's non-diversifiable risk. The model takes into account the asset's sensitivity to non-diversifiable risk (also known as systemic risk or market risk), often represented by the quantity beta (β) in the financial industry, as well as the expected return of the market and the expected return of a theoretical risk-free asset.

The model was introduced by Jack Treynor (1961, 1962), William Sharpe (1964), John Lintner (1965a,b) and Jan Mossin (1966) independently, building on the earlier work of Harry Markowitz on diversification and modern portfolio theory.

a. Cox-Ingersoll-Ross model
c. Random walk hypothesis

b. Hull-White model
d. Capital asset pricing model

18.   In economics, business, and accounting, a _____ is the value of money that has been used up to produce something, and hence is not available for use anymore. In business, the _____ may be one of acquisition, in which case the amount of money expended to acquire it is counted as _____. In this case, money is the input that is gone in order to acquire the thing.

a. Sliding scale fees

b. Fixed costs

c. Marginal cost

d. Cost

19.   A _____ is a portfolio consisting of a weighted sum of every asset in the market, with weights in the proportions that they exist in the market (with the necessary assumption that these assets are infinitely divisible.)

Neha Tyagi's critique (1977) states that this is only a theoretical concept, as to create a _____ for investment purposes in practice would necessarily include every single possible available asset, including real estate, precious metals, stamp collections, jewelry, and anything with any worth, as the theoretical market being referred to would be the world market. As a result, proxies for the market are used in practice by investors.

a. Market price

b. Delta neutral

c. Central Securities Depository

d. Market Portfolio

20.   The _____ is an expected return that the provider of capital plans to earn on their investment.

Capital (money) used for funding a business should earn returns for the capital providers who risk their capital. For an investment to be worthwhile, the expected return on capital must be greater than the _____.

a. Weighted average cost of capital

b. 4-4-5 Calendar

c. Capital intensity

d. Cost of capital

1.   An _____ is a contract written by a seller that conveys to the buyer the right -- but not the obligation -- to buy (in the case of a call _____) or to sell (in the case of a put _____) a particular asset, such as a piece of property such as, among others, a futures contract. In return for granting the _____, the seller collects a payment (the premium) from the buyer.

For example, buying a call _____ provides the right to buy a specified quantity of a security at a set strike price at some time on or before expiration, while buying a put _____ provides the right to sell.

   a. Option   b. Amortization
   c. AT'T Mobility LLC   d. Annuity

2.   A _____ is a financial contract between two parties, the buyer and the seller of this type of option. Often it is simply labeled a 'call'. The buyer of the option has the right, but not the obligation to buy an agreed quantity of a particular commodity or financial instrument (the underlying instrument) from the seller of the option at a certain time (the expiration date) for a certain price (the strike price.)
   a. Bear spread   b. Bull spread
   c. Bear call spread   d. Call Option

3.   In finance, _____ is the process of estimating the potential market value of a financial asset or liability. they can be done on assets (for example, investments in marketable securities such as stocks, options, business enterprises, or intangible assets such as patents and trademarks) or on liabilities (e.g., Bonds issued by a company.) _____s are required in many contexts including investment analysis, capital budgeting, merger and acquisition transactions, financial reporting, taxable events to determine the proper tax liability, and in litigation.
   a. Margin   b. Valuation
   c. Share   d. Procter ' Gamble

4.   In options, the _____ is a key variable in a derivatives contract between two parties. Where the contract requires delivery of the underlying instrument, the trade will be at the _____, regardless of the spot price (market price) of the underlying instrument at that time.

Definition - The fixed price at which the owner of an option can purchase, in the case of a call in the case of a put, the underlying security or commodity.

   a. Naked put   b. Swaption
   c. Strike price   d. Moneyness

5.   A _____ is a financial contract between two parties, the seller (writer) and the buyer of the option. The put allows its buyer the right but not the obligation to sell a commodity or financial instrument (the underlying instrument) to the writer (seller) of the option at a certain time for a certain price (the strike price.) The writer (seller) has the obligation to purchase the underlying asset at that strike price, if the buyer exercises the option.
   a. Bear call spread   b. Bear spread
   c. Debit spread   d. Put option

6.   In finance, a _____ is a debt security, in which the authorized issuer owes the holders a debt and, depending on the terms of the _____, is obliged to pay interest (the coupon) and/or to repay the principal at a later date, termed maturity.

Thus a _____ is a loan: the issuer is the borrower, the _____ holder is the lender, and the coupon is the interest. _____s provide the borrower with external funds to finance long-term investments, or, in the case of government _____s, to finance current expenditure.

a. Bond

b. Convertible bond

c. Catastrophe bonds

d. Puttable bond

7.   In economics and finance, _____ is the practice of taking advantage of a price differential between two or more markets: striking a combination of matching deals that capitalize upon the imbalance, the profit being the difference between the market prices. When used by academics, an _____ is a transaction that involves no negative cash flow at any probabilistic or temporal state and a positive cash flow in at least one state; in simple terms, a risk-free profit.

a. Arbitrage

b. Efficient-market hypothesis

c. Initial margin

d. Issuer

8.   In finance, _____ refers to the value of a security which is intrinsic to or contained in the security itself. It is also frequently called fundamental value. It is ordinarily calculated by summing the future income generated by the asset, and discounting it to the present value.

a. Amortization

b. Accretion

c. Alpha

d. Intrinsic value

9.   A _____ is the price of a single share of a no. of saleable stocks of the company. Once the stock is purchased, the owner becomes a shareholder of the company that issued the share.

a. Whisper numbers

b. Trading curb

c. Stock split

d. Share price

10.   In business and accounting, _____s are everything of value that is owned by a person or company. The balance sheet of a firm records the monetary value of the _____s owned by the firm. The two major _____ classes are tangible _____s and intangible _____s.

a. Asset

b. Income

c. Accounts payable

d. EBITDA

11.   In finance, the _____ of a derivative is an asset, basket of assets, index, or even another derivative, such that the cash flows of the (former) derivative depend on the value of this _____. There must be an independent way to observe this value to avoid conflicts of interest.

For example, in a stock option to buy 100 shares of Nokia at EUR 50 in September 2006, the _____ is a Nokia share.

a. AAB

b. A Random Walk Down Wall Street

c. ABN Amro

d. Underlying

12.   In probability theory and statistics, the _____ of a random variable, probability distribution averaging the squared distance of its possible values from the expected value (mean.) Whereas the mean is a way to describe the location of a distribution, the _____ is a way to capture its scale or degree of being spread out. The unit of _____ is the square of the unit of the original variable.

a. Semivariance

b. Monte Carlo methods

c. Harmonic mean

d. Variance

13.   The term _____ refers to three closely related concepts:

- The _____ model is a mathematical model of the market for an equity, in which the equity's price is a stochastic process.
- The _____ PDE is a partial differential equation which (in the model) must be satisfied by the price of a derivative on the equity.
- The _____ formula is the result obtained by solving the _____ PDE for a European call option.

Fischer Black and Myron Scholes first articulated the _____ formula in their 1973 paper, 'The Pricing of Options and Corporate Liabilities.' The foundation for their research relied on work developed by scholars such as Jack L. Treynor, Paul Samuelson, A. James Boness, Sheen T. Kassouf, and Edward O. Thorp. The fundamental insight of _____ is that the option is implicitly priced if the stock is traded.

Robert C. Merton was the first to publish a paper expanding the mathematical understanding of the options pricing model and coined the term '_____' options pricing model.

a. Black-Scholes

b. Modified Internal Rate of Return

c. Stochastic volatility

d. Perpetuity

14.   An _____ is a call option on the common stock of a company, issued as a form of non-cash compensation. Restrictions on the option (such as vesting and limited transferability) attempt to align the holder's interest with those of the business' shareholders. If the company's stock rises, holders of options experience a direct financial benefit.

a. Internal financing

b. Underwriting contract

c. Employee stock option

d. Operating ratio

15.   The _____ of 2002 (Pub.L. 107-204, 116 Stat. 745, enacted July 30, 2002), also known as the Public Company Accounting Reform and Investor Protection Act of 2002 and commonly called Sarbanes-Oxley, Sarbox or SOX, is a United States federal law enacted on July 30, 2002 in response to a number of major corporate and accounting scandals including those affecting Enron, Tyco International, Adelphia, Peregrine Systems and WorldCom.

a. Duty of loyalty

b. Sarbanes-Oxley Act

c. Blue sky law

d. Foreign Corrupt Practices Act

16.   _____ is that which is owed; usually referencing assets owed, but the term can cover other obligations. In the case of assets, _____ is a means of using future purchasing power in the present before a summation has been earned. Some companies and corporations use _____ as a part of their overall corporate finance strategy.

a. Credit cycle

b. Cross-collateralization

c. Debt

d. Partial Payment

17.   In economics, business, and accounting, a _____ is the value of money that has been used up to produce something, and hence is not available for use anymore. In business, the _____ may be one of acquisition, in which case the amount of money expended to acquire it is counted as _____. In this case, money is the input that is gone in order to acquire the thing.

a. Sliding scale fees

c. Marginal cost

b. Cost

d. Fixed costs

18. _____ is the planning process used to determine whether a firm's long term investments such as new machinery, replacement machinery, new plants, new products, and research development projects are worth pursuing. It is budget for major capital, or investment, expenditures.

Many formal methods are used in _____, including the techniques such as

- Net present value
- Profitability index
- Internal rate of return
- Modified Internal Rate of Return
- Equivalent annuity

These methods use the incremental cash flows from each potential investment, or project. Techniques based on accounting earnings and accounting rules are sometimes used - though economists consider this to be improper - such as the accounting rate of return, and 'return on investment.' Simplified and hybrid methods are used as well, such as payback period and discounted payback period.

a. Capital budgeting

c. Shareholder value

b. Preferred stock

d. Financial distress

19. In corporate finance, _____ analysis applies put option and call option valuation techniques to capital budgeting decisions. A _____ itself, is the right--but not the obligation--to undertake some business decision; typically the option to make, or abandon, a capital investment. For example, the opportunity to invest in the expansion of a firm's factory, or alternatively to sell the factory, is a _____.

a. Capital budgeting

c. Cash flow

b. Book building

d. Real option

20. A _____ is an exchange of promises between two or more parties to do an act which is enforceable in a court of law. It is where an unqualified offer meets a qualified acceptance and the parties reach Consensus ad Idem. The parties must have the necessary capacity to _____ and the _____ must not be either trifling, indeterminate, impossible or illegal.

a. 7-Eleven

c. 529 plan

b. 4-4-5 Calendar

d. Contract

21. In finance, a _____ is a security that entitles the holder to buy stock of the company that issued it at a specified price, which is usually higher than the stock price at time of issue.

_____s are frequently attached to bonds or preferred stock as a sweetener, allowing the issuer to pay lower interest rates or dividends. They can be used to enhance the yield of the bond, and make them more attractive to potential buyers.

a. Warrant
c. Clearing

b. Clearing house
d. Credit

22. In financial accounting, _____s are precautions for which the amount or probability of occurrence are not known. Typical examples are _____s for warranty costs and _____ for taxes the term reserve is used instead of term _____; such a use, however, is inconsistent with the terminology suggested by International Accounting Standards Board.

a. Money measurement concept
c. Momentum Accounting and Triple-Entry Bookkeeping

b. Petty cash
d. Provision

23. A _____ is a fungible, negotiable instrument representing financial value. They are broadly categorized into debt securities (such as banknotes, bonds and debentures), and equity securities; e.g., common stocks. The company or other entity issuing the _____ is called the issuer.

a. Book entry
c. Tracking stock

b. Securities lending
d. Security

24. In finance, a _____ is a type of bond that can be converted into shares of stock in the issuing company, usually at some pre-announced ratio. It is a hybrid security with debt- and equity-like features. Although it typically has a low coupon rate, the holder is compensated with the ability to convert the bond to common stock, usually at a substantial discount to the stock's market value.

a. Gilts
c. Convertible bond

b. Corporate bond
d. Bond fund

25. _____ is a combination of straight bond and embedded put option. The holder of the _____ has the right, but not the obligation, to demand early repayment of the principal. The put option is usually exercisable on specified dates.

a. Convertible bond
c. Callable bond

b. Brady bonds
d. Puttable bond

26. In finance, the term _____ describes the amount in cash that returns to the owners of a security. Normally it does not include the price variations, at the difference of the total return. _____ applies to various stated rates of return on stocks (common and preferred, and convertible), fixed income instruments (bonds, notes, bills, strips, zero coupon), and some other investment type insurance products (e.g. annuities.)

a. Yield to maturity
c. Yield

b. Macaulay duration
d. 4-4-5 Calendar

1. In economics, business, and accounting, a _____ is the value of money that has been used up to produce something, and hence is not available for use anymore. In business, the _____ may be one of acquisition, in which case the amount of money expended to acquire it is counted as _____. In this case, money is the input that is gone in order to acquire the thing.

  a. Cost
                                     b. Sliding scale fees
  c. Fixed costs
                                    d. Marginal cost

2. The _____ is an expected return that the provider of capital plans to earn on their investment.

Capital (money) used for funding a business should earn returns for the capital providers who risk their capital. For an investment to be worthwhile, the expected return on capital must be greater than the _____.

  a. Capital intensity
                                     b. Weighted average cost of capital
  c. 4-4-5 Calendar
                                   d. Cost of capital

3. The _____ is the rate that a company is expected to pay to finance its assets. WACC is the minimum return that a company must earn on existing asset base to satisfy its creditors, owners, and other providers of capital.

Companies raise money from a number of sources: common equity, preferred equity, straight debt, convertible debt, exchangeable debt, warrants, options, pension liabilities, executive stock options, governmental subsidies, and so on.

  a. Cost of capital
                                     b. Capital intensity
  c. 4-4-5 Calendar
                                   d. Weighted average cost of capital

4. In finance, _____ refers to the way a corporation finances its assets through some combination of equity, debt, or hybrid securities. A firm's _____ is then the composition or 'structure' of its liabilities. For example, a firm that sells $20 billion in equity and $80 billion in debt is said to be 20% equity-financed and 80% debt-financed.

  a. Book building
                                     b. Market for corporate control
  c. Rights issue
                                     d. Capital structure

5. A '_____' is a 'Charge' that is paid to obtain the right to delay a payment. Essentially, the payer purchases the right to make a given payment in the future instead of in the Present. The '_____', or 'Charge' that must be paid to delay the payment, is simply the difference between what the payment amount would be if it were paid in the present and what the payment amount would be paid if it were paid in the future.

  a. Risk modeling
                                     b. Value at risk
  c. Risk aversion
                                    d. Discount

6. The _____ is an interest rate a central bank charges depository institutions that borrow reserves from it.

The term _____ has two meanings:

- the same as interest rate; the term 'discount' does not refer to the meaning of the word, but to the purpose of using the quantity, such as computations of present value, e.g. net present value / discounted cash flow

- the annual effective _____, which is the annual interest divided by the capital including that interest; this rate is lower than the interest rate; it corresponds to using the value after a year as the nominal value, and seeing the initial value as the nominal value minus a discount; it is used for Treasury Bills and similar financial instruments

The annual effective _____ is the annual interest divided by the capital including that interest, which is the interest rate divided by 100% plus the interest rate. It is the annual discount factor to be applied to the future cash flow, to find the discount, subtracted from a future value to find the value one year earlier.

For example, suppose there is a government bond that sells for $95 and pays $100 in a year's time.

a. Stochastic volatility   b. Black-Scholes
c. Fisher equation   d. Discount rate

7.   _____ is a legally declared inability or impairment of ability of an individual or organization to pay their creditors. Creditors may file a _____ petition against a debtor ('involuntary _____') in an effort to recoup a portion of what they are owed or initiate a restructuring. In the majority of cases, however, _____ is initiated by the debtor (a 'voluntary _____' that is filed by the bankrupt individual or organization.)

a. Debt settlement   b. 4-4-5 Calendar
c. 529 plan   d. Bankruptcy

8.   In finance, the _____ is the minimum rate of return a firm must offer shareholders to compensate for waiting for their returns, and for bearing some risk.

The _____ capital for a particular company is the rate of return on investment that is required by the company's ordinary shareholders. The return consists both of dividend and capital gains, e.g. increases in the share price.

a. Round-tripping   b. Residual value
c. Net pay   d. Cost of equity

9.   A _____ is a payment made by a corporation to its shareholder members. When a corporation earns a profit or surplus, that money can be put to two uses: it can either be re-invested in the business (called retained earnings), or it can be paid to the shareholders as a _____. Many corporations retain a portion of their earnings and pay the remainder as a _____.

a. Dividend yield   b. Special dividend
c. Dividend puzzle   d. Dividend

10.   A _____ is a fungible, negotiable instrument representing financial value. They are broadly categorized into debt securities (such as banknotes, bonds and debentures), and equity securities; e.g., common stocks. The company or other entity issuing the _____ is called the issuer.

  a. Security

  c. Book entry

                    b. Tracking stock

                    d. Securities lending

11.   In Modern Portfolio Theory, the _____ is the graphical representation of the Capital Asset Pricing Model. It displays the expected rate of return for an overall market as a function of systematic (non-diversifiable) risk (beta.)

The Y-Intercept (beta=0) of the _____ is equal to the risk-free interest rate.

  a. Security market line

  c. Rebalancing

                    b. Certificate in Investment Performance Measurement

                    d. Divestment

12.   In finance, a _____ is a debt security, in which the authorized issuer owes the holders a debt and, depending on the terms of the _____, is obliged to pay interest (the coupon) and/or to repay the principal at a later date, termed maturity.

Thus a _____ is a loan: the issuer is the borrower, the _____ holder is the lender, and the coupon is the interest. _____s provide the borrower with external funds to finance long-term investments, or, in the case of government _____s, to finance current expenditure.

  a. Convertible bond

  c. Catastrophe bonds

                    b. Bond

                    d. Puttable bond

13.   _____ is that which is owed; usually referencing assets owed, but the term can cover other obligations. In the case of assets, _____ is a means of using future purchasing power in the present before a summation has been earned. Some companies and corporations use _____ as a part of their overall corporate finance strategy.

  a. Partial Payment

  c. Cross-collateralization

                    b. Credit cycle

                    d. Debt

14.   _____ is typically a higher ranking stock than voting shares, and its terms are negotiated between the corporation and the investor.

_____ usually carry no voting rights, but may carry superior priority over common stock in the payment of dividends and upon liquidation. _____ may carry a dividend that is paid out prior to any dividends to common stock holders.

  a. Second lien loan

  c. Follow-on offering

                    b. Trade-off theory

                    d. Preferred stock

15.   _____ is the planning process used to determine whether a firm's long term investments such as new machinery, replacement machinery, new plants, new products, and research development projects are worth pursuing. It is budget for major capital, or investment, expenditures.

Many formal methods are used in _____, including the techniques such as

- Net present value
- Profitability index
- Internal rate of return
- Modified Internal Rate of Return
- Equivalent annuity

These methods use the incremental cash flows from each potential investment, or project. Techniques based on accounting earnings and accounting rules are sometimes used - though economists consider this to be improper - such as the accounting rate of return, and 'return on investment.' Simplified and hybrid methods are used as well, such as payback period and discounted payback period.

a. Financial distress	b. Shareholder value
c. Preferred stock	d. Capital budgeting

16.   In corporate finance, _____ is an estimate of true economic profit after making corrective adjustments to GAAP accounting, including deducting the opportunity cost of equity capital. GAAP is estimated to ignore US$300 billion in shareholder opportunity costs. _____ can be measured as Net Operating Profit After Taxes(or NOPAT) less the money cost of capital.

a. Economic value added	b. A Random Walk Down Wall Street
c. AAB	d. ABN Amro

17.   _____ is the price at which an asset would trade in a competitive Walrasian auction setting. _____ is often used interchangeably with open _____, fair value or fair _____, although these terms have distinct definitions in different standards, and may differ in some circumstances.

International Valuation Standards defines _____ as 'the estimated amount for which a property should exchange on the date of valuation between a willing buyer and a willing seller in an arm'e;s-length transaction after proper marketing wherein the parties had each acted knowledgeably, prudently, and without compulsion.'

_____ is a concept distinct from market price, which is 'e;the price at which one can transact'e;, while _____ is 'e;the true underlying value'e; according to theoretical standards.

a. T-Model	b. Wrap account
c. Debt restructuring	d. Market value

18.   _____ is the difference between the current market value of a firm and the capital contributed by investors. If _____ is positive, the firm has added value. If it is negative, the firm has destroyed value.

a. Decision process tool	b. Market value added
c. Monetary system	d. Wrap account

19. _____ is a business buzz term, which implies that the ultimate measure of a company's success is to enrich shareholders. It became popular during the 1980s, and is particularly associated with former CEO of General Electric, Jack Welch. In March 2009, Welch openly turned his back on the concept, calling _____ 'the dumbest idea in the world'.

For a publicly traded company, _____ is the part of its capitalization that is equity as opposed to long-term debt. In the case of only one type of stock, this would roughly be the number of outstanding shares times current shareprice. Things like dividends augment _____ while issuing of shares (stock options) lower it. This _____ added should be compared to average/required increase in value, aka cost of capital.

For a privately held company, the value of the firm after debt must be estimated using one of several valuation methods, s.a. discounted cash flow or others.

a. Shareholder value
c. Commercial paper

b. Restricted stock
d. Cash flow

20. _____ refers to the additional value of a commodity over the cost of commodities used to produce it from the previous stage of production. An example is the price of gasoline at the pump over the price of the oil in it. In national accounts used in macroeconomics, it refers to the contribution of the factors of production, i.e., land, labor, and capital goods, to raising the value of a product and corresponds to the incomes received by the owners of these factors.

a. Supply shock
c. Demand shock

b. Deregulation
d. Value added

21. In e-business terms, a _____ is an organization that originated and does business purely through the internet, they have no physical store (brick and mortar) where customers can shop. Examples of large _____ companies include Amazon.com and Netflix.com. There are also many smaller, niche oriented _____ mail order companies such as women's travel accessories company Christine Columbus and fashion jewelry merchant Jewels of Denial.

a. Pure play
c. 529 plan

b. The Dogs of the Dow
d. 4-4-5 Calendar

22. A _____, also known by its legal title as an 'over-allotment option' (the only way it can be referred to in a prospectus), gives underwriters the right to sell additional shares in a registered securities offering if demand for the securities is in excess of the original amount offered. The _____ can vary in size up to 15% of the original number of shares offered.

The _____ option is popular because it is the only SEC-permitted means for an underwriter to stabilize the price of a new issue post-pricing.

a. Supply and demand
c. Foreign Language and Area Studies

b. Business valuation standards
d. Green Shoe

23. An _____ is a contract written by a seller that conveys to the buyer the right -- but not the obligation -- to buy (in the case of a call _____) or to sell (in the case of a put _____) a particular asset, such as a piece of property such as, among others, a futures contract. In return for granting the _____, the seller collects a payment (the premium) from the buyer.

For example, buying a call _____ provides the right to buy a specified quantity of a security at a set strike price at some time on or before expiration, while buying a put _____ provides the right to sell.

    a. AT'T Mobility LLC   b. Amortization
    c. Option   d. Annuity

24.   _____ or net present worth (NPW) is defined as the total present value (PV) of a time series of cash flows. It is a standard method for using the time value of money to appraise long-term projects. Used for capital budgeting, and widely throughout economics, it measures the excess or shortfall of cash flows, in present value terms, once financing charges are met.

    a. Present value of costs   b. Tax shield
    c. Negative gearing   d. Net present value

25.   _____ is the value on a given date of a future payment or series of future payments, discounted to reflect the time value of money and other factors such as investment risk. _____ calculations are widely used in business and economics to provide a means to compare cash flows at different times on a meaningful 'like to like' basis.

The most commonly applied model of the time value of money is compound interest.

    a. Net present value   b. Negative gearing
    c. Present value   d. Present value of benefits

1.   In finance, _____ is an asset class consisting of equity securities in operating companies that are not publicly traded on a stock exchange. Investments in _____ most often involve either an investment of capital into an operating company or the acquisition of an operating company. Capital for _____ is raised primarily from institutional investors.
   a. Private equity
   c. Currency swap
   b. Stock valuation
   d. Pecking order theory

2.   _____ is a type of private equity capital typically provided to early-stage, high-potential, growth companies in the interest of generating a return through an eventual realization event such as an IPO or trade sale of the company. _____ investments are generally made as cash in exchange for shares in the invested company. It is typical for _____ investors to identify and back companies in high technology industries such as biotechnology and ICT.
   a. Treasury Inflation-Protected Securities
   c. Tail risk
   b. Venture capital
   d. Probability distribution

3.   _____ or financing is to provide capital (funds), which means money for a project, a person, a business or any other private or public institutions.

Those funds can be allocated for either short term or long term purposes. The health fund is a new way of _____ private healthcare centers.

   a. Product life cycle
   c. Proxy fight
   b. Synthetic CDO
   d. Funding

4.   The U.S. _____ is an independent agency of the United States government which holds primary responsibility for enforcing the federal securities laws and regulating the securities industry, the nation's stock and options exchanges, and other electronic securities markets. The SEC was created by section 4 of the SEC of 1934 (now codified as 15 U.S.C. Â§ 78d and commonly referred to as the 1934 Act.)
   a. 4-4-5 Calendar
   c. 7-Eleven
   b. 529 plan
   d. Securities and Exchange Commission

5.   A _____ is a fungible, negotiable instrument representing financial value. They are broadly categorized into debt securities (such as banknotes, bonds and debentures), and equity securities; e.g., common stocks. The company or other entity issuing the _____ is called the issuer.
   a. Tracking stock
   c. Securities lending
   b. Book entry
   d. Security

6.   Congress enacted the _____, in the aftermath of the stock market crash of 1929 and during the ensuing Great Depression. It requires that any offer or sale of securities using the means and instrumentalities of interstate commerce be registered pursuant to the 1933 Act, unless an exemption from registration exists under the law.
   a. 7-Eleven
   c. 529 plan
   b. 4-4-5 Calendar
   d. Securities Act of 1933

7.   The _____ of 1934 is a law governing the secondary trading of securities (stocks, bonds, and debentures) in the United States of America. The Act, 48 Stat. 881 (enacted June 6, 1934), codified at 15 U.S.C. Â§ 78a et seq., was a sweeping piece of legislation. The Act and related statutes form the basis of regulation of the financial markets and their participants in the United States.

a. 529 plan   b. 7-Eleven
c. 4-4-5 Calendar   d. Securities Exchange Act

8. _____, is when a company issues common stock or shares to the public for the first time. They are often issued by smaller, younger companies seeking capital to expand, but can also be done by large privately-owned companies looking to become publicly traded.

In an _____ the issuer may obtain the assistance of an underwriting firm, which helps it determine what type of security to issue (common or preferred), best offering price and time to bring it to market.

a. Asian Financial Crisis   b. Insolvency
c. Interest   d. Initial public offering

9. Under a secondary market offering or seasoned equity offering of shares to raise money, a company can opt for a _____ to raise capital. The _____ is a special form of shelf offering or shelf registration. With the issued rights, existing shareholders have the privilege to buy a specified number of new shares from the firm at a specified price within a specified time.
a. Tender offer   b. Corporate finance
c. Rights issue   d. Market for corporate control

10. A _____, also known by its legal title as an 'over-allotment option' (the only way it can be referred to in a prospectus), gives underwriters the right to sell additional shares in a registered securities offering if demand for the securities is in excess of the original amount offered. The _____ can vary in size up to 15% of the original number of shares offered.

The _____ option is popular because it is the only SEC-permitted means for an underwriter to stabilize the price of a new issue post-pricing.

a. Foreign Language and Area Studies   b. Business valuation standards
c. Supply and demand   d. Green Shoe

11. A _____ or Capital increase is a new equity issue by a company after its IPO. It differs from a secondary equity offering, in which owners (not the company) sell their shares. In the latter case, the company gets no money and no ownership dilution happens, for the company does not issue new shares.
a. FATF Blacklist   b. Debt-for-equity swap
c. Sinking fund   d. Seasoned equity offering

12. Unemployment occurs when a person is available to work and currently seeking work, but the person is without work. The prevalence of unemployment is usually measured using the _____, which is defined as the percentage of those in the labor force who are unemployed. The _____ is also used in economic studies and economic indexes such as the United States' Conference Board's Index of Leading Indicators as a measure of the state of the macroeconomics.
a. ABN Amro   b. Unemployment rate
c. A Random Walk Down Wall Street   d. AAB

13. In financial accounting, _____s are precautions for which the amount or probability of occurrence are not known. Typical examples are _____s for warranty costs and _____ for taxes the term reserve is used instead of term _____; such a use, however, is inconsistent with the terminology suggested by International Accounting Standards Board.

a. Money measurement concept
b. Provision
c. Petty cash
d. Momentum Accounting and Triple-Entry Bookkeeping

14. In the _____ contract the underwriter agrees to sell as many shares as possible at the agreed-upon price.

Under the all-or-none contract the underwriter agrees either to sell the entire offering or to cancel the deal.

Stand-by underwriting, also known as strict underwriting or old-fashioned underwriting is a form of stock insurance: the issuer contracts the underwriter for the latter to purchase the shares the issuer failed to sell under stockholders' subscription and applications.

a. Real option
b. Book building
c. Follow-on offering
d. Best efforts

15. A _____ is a type of auction where the auctioneer begins with a high asking price which is lowered until some participant is willing to accept the auctioneer's price, or a predetermined reserve price (the seller's minimum acceptable price) is reached. The winning participant pays the last announced price. This is also known as a 'clock auction' or an open-outcry descending-price auction.

a. Dutch auction
b. 529 plan
c. 7-Eleven
d. 4-4-5 Calendar

16. In the _____ contract the underwriter guarantees the sale of the issued stock at the agreed-upon price. For the issuer, it is the safest but the most expensive type of the contracts, since the underwriter takes the risk of sale.

In the best efforts contract the underwriter agrees to sell as many shares as possible at the agreed-upon price.

a. Special purpose entity
b. Rights issue
c. Participating preferred stock
d. Firm commitment

17. _____ refers to the fees that underwriters receive for arranging and underwriting an offering of debt or equity securities. The _____ for an initial public offering (IPO) can be higher than 10% while the _____ on a debt offering can be as low as 0.05%.

For example, if a company sells $100 million of shares in an IPO and the _____ is 7%, the underwriting syndicate will receive fees of $7 million.

a. Gross spread
b. Capital guarantee
c. Redemption value
d. Package loan

18. In finance, a _____ is a security that entitles the holder to buy stock of the company that issued it at a specified price, which is usually higher than the stock price at time of issue.

_____s are frequently attached to bonds or preferred stock as a sweetener, allowing the issuer to pay lower interest rates or dividends. They can be used to enhance the yield of the bond, and make them more attractive to potential buyers.

a. Credit

c. Clearing

b. Warrant

d. Clearing house

19. The _____ is the financial market where previously issued securities and financial instruments such as stock, bonds, options, and futures are bought and sold. The term '_____' is also used refer to the market for any used goods or assets, or an alternative use for an existing product or asset where the customer base is the second market

With primary issuances of securities or financial instruments, or the primary market, investors purchase these securities directly from issuers such as corporations issuing shares in an IPO or private placement, or directly from the federal government in the case of treasuries.

a. Performance attribution

c. Delta neutral

b. Secondary market

d. Financial market

20. The term _____, also known as a waiting period is a period extended from the time a company files a registration statement with the SEC until SEC staff declared the registration statement effective. During that period, the federal securities laws limited what information a company and related parties can release to the public.'

Under the rules of the Securities Act of 1933, as modified June 29, 2005, electronic communications, including electronic road shows and information located on or hyperlinked to an issuer's website are also governed. The rules changes of June 29, 2005 also included various changes which 'liberalize permitted offering activity and communications to allow more information' for certain qualifying organizations.

a. Duty of loyalty

c. Lien

b. Quiet period

d. Leasing

21. In finance, a _____ is a debt security, in which the authorized issuer owes the holders a debt and, depending on the terms of the _____, is obliged to pay interest (the coupon) and/or to repay the principal at a later date, termed maturity.

Thus a _____ is a loan: the issuer is the borrower, the _____ holder is the lender, and the coupon is the interest. _____s provide the borrower with external funds to finance long-term investments, or, in the case of government _____s, to finance current expenditure.

a. Bond

c. Puttable bond

b. Convertible bond

d. Catastrophe bonds

22. A '_____' is a 'Charge' that is paid to obtain the right to delay a payment. Essentially, the payer purchases the right to make a given payment in the future instead of in the Present. The '_____', or 'Charge' that must be paid to delay the payment, is simply the difference between what the payment amount would be if it were paid in the present and what the payment amount would be paid if it were paid in the future.

a. Risk aversion

b. Discount

c. Value at risk

d. Risk modeling

23. A _____ is a bond bought at a price lower than its face value, with the face value repaid at the time of maturity. It does not make periodic interest payments, or so-called 'coupons,' hence the term zero-coupon bond. Investors earn return from the compounded interest all paid at maturity plus the difference between the discounted price of the bond and its par value.

a. Callable bond

b. Zero coupon bond

c. Bowie bonds

d. Municipal bond

24. An _____ is a contract written by a seller that conveys to the buyer the right -- but not the obligation -- to buy (in the case of a call _____) or to sell (in the case of a put _____) a particular asset, such as a piece of property such as, among others, a futures contract. In return for granting the _____, the seller collects a payment (the premium) from the buyer.

For example, buying a call _____ provides the right to buy a specified quantity of a security at a set strike price at some time on or before expiration, while buying a put _____ provides the right to sell.

a. Amortization

b. Option

c. AT'T Mobility LLC

d. Annuity

25. _____ is a life of security. It may also refer to the final payment date of a loan or other financial instrument, at which point all remaining interest and principal is due to be paid.

1, 3, 6 months _____ band can be calculated by using 30-day per month periods.

a. Primary market

b. Replacement cost

c. Maturity

d. False billing

26.

In finance, the _____ can be the expected rate of return above the risk-free interest rate. When measuring risk, a common sense approach is to compare the risk-free return on T-bills and the very risky return on other investments. The difference between these two returns can be interpreted as a measure of the excess return on the average risky asset. This excess return is known as the _____.

a. Risk modeling

b. Risk premium

c. Risk aversion

d. Risk adjusted return on capital

27. In finance, an _____ is the difference between the expected return of a security and the actual return. _____s are sometimes triggered by 'events.' Events can include mergers, dividend announcements, company earning announcements, interest rate increases, lawsuits, etc. all which can contribute to an _____.

a. AAB   b. A Random Walk Down Wall Street
c. Abnormal return   d. ABN Amro

28.   In economics, business, and accounting, a _____ is the value of money that has been used up to produce something, and hence is not available for use anymore. In business, the _____ may be one of acquisition, in which case the amount of money expended to acquire it is counted as _____. In this case, money is the input that is gone in order to acquire the thing.
   a. Sliding scale fees   b. Marginal cost
   c. Cost   d. Fixed costs

29.   In business and finance, a _____ (also referred to as equity _____) of stock means a _____ of ownership in a corporation (company.) In the plural, stocks is often used as a synonym for _____s especially in the United States, but it is less commonly used that way outside of North America.

In the United Kingdom, South Africa, and Australia, stock can also refer to completely different financial instruments such as government bonds or, less commonly, to all kinds of marketable securities.

   a. Procter ' Gamble   b. Share
   c. Margin   d. Bucket shop

30.   _____ is the price at which an asset would trade in a competitive Walrasian auction setting. _____ is often used interchangeably with open _____, fair value or fair _____, although these terms have distinct definitions in different standards, and may differ in some circumstances.

International Valuation Standards defines _____ as 'the estimated amount for which a property should exchange on the date of valuation between a willing buyer and a willing seller in an arm'e;s-length transaction after proper marketing wherein the parties had each acted knowledgeably, prudently, and without compulsion.'

_____ is a concept distinct from market price, which is 'e;the price at which one can transact'e;, while _____ is 'e;the true underlying value'e; according to theoretical standards.

   a. Wrap account   b. T-Model
   c. Market value   d. Debt restructuring

31.   In economics, the _____ is the proposition by Irving Fisher that the real interest rate is independent of monetary measures, especially the nominal interest rate. The Fisher equation is

$$r_r = r_n >- >\pi^e.$$

This means, the real interest rate (r_r) equals the nominal interest rate (r_n) minus expected rate of inflation ($>\pi^e$.) Here all the rates are continuously compounded.

   a. 529 plan   b. 4-4-5 Calendar
   c. 7-Eleven   d. Fisher hypothesis

32.   In the United States, a _____ is an offering of securities that are not registered with the Securities and Exchange Commission (SEC.) Such offerings exploit an exemption offered by the Securities Act of 1933 that comes with several restrictions, including a prohibition against general solicitation. This exemption allows companies to avoid quarterly reporting requirements and many of the legal liabilities associated with the Sarbanes-Oxley Act.
   a. 7-Eleven   b. 4-4-5 Calendar
   c. 529 plan   d. Private placement

33.   _____ is that which is owed; usually referencing assets owed, but the term can cover other obligations. In the case of assets, _____ is a means of using future purchasing power in the present before a summation has been earned. Some companies and corporations use _____ as a part of their overall corporate finance strategy.
   a. Cross-collateralization   b. Partial Payment
   c. Credit cycle   d. Debt

34.   In economic models, the _____ time frame assumes no fixed factors of production. Firms can enter or leave the marketplace, and the cost (and availability) of land, labor, raw materials, and capital goods can be assumed to vary. In contrast, in the short-run time frame, certain factors are assumed to be fixed, because there is not sufficient time for them to change.
   a. 529 plan   b. 4-4-5 Calendar
   c. Short-run   d. Long-run

35.   _____ is an arrangement with the U.S. Securities and Exchange Commission that allows a single registration document to be filed that permits the issuance of multiple securities.

_____ is a registration of a new issue which can be prepared up to two years in advance, so that the issue can be offered quickly as soon as funds are needed or market conditions are favorable.

For example, current market conditions in the housing market are not favorable for a specific firm to issue a public offering.

   a. Black Sea Trade and Development Bank   b. Bought deal
   c. Shelf registration   d. 4-4-5 Calendar

36.   In finance, a _____ is a type of bond that can be converted into shares of stock in the issuing company, usually at some pre-announced ratio. It is a hybrid security with debt- and equity-like features. Although it typically has a low coupon rate, the holder is compensated with the ability to convert the bond to common stock, usually at a substantial discount to the stock's market value.
   a. Bond fund   b. Corporate bond
   c. Convertible bond   d. Gilts

1. In finance, _____ refers to the way a corporation finances its assets through some combination of equity, debt, or hybrid securities. A firm's _____ is then the composition or 'structure' of its liabilities. For example, a firm that sells $20 billion in equity and $80 billion in debt is said to be 20% equity-financed and 80% debt-financed.
   a. Rights issue   b. Market for corporate control
   c. Book building   d. Capital structure

2. _____ is the corporate management term for the act of reorganizing the legal, ownership, operational, or other structures of a company for the purpose of making it more profitable or better organized for its present needs. Alternate reasons for restructing include a change of ownership or ownership structure, demerger repositioning debt _____ and financial _____.
   a. Restructuring   b. Day trading
   c. Cross-border leasing   d. Concentrated stock

3. In finance, _____ is the process of estimating the potential market value of a financial asset or liability. they can be done on assets (for example, investments in marketable securities such as stocks, options, business enterprises, or intangible assets such as patents and trademarks) or on liabilities (e.g., Bonds issued by a company.) _____s are required in many contexts including investment analysis, capital budgeting, merger and acquisition transactions, financial reporting, taxable events to determine the proper tax liability, and in litigation.
   a. Margin   b. Procter ' Gamble
   c. Share   d. Valuation

4. _____ is an estimate of the fair value of corporations and their stocks, by using fundamental economic criteria. This theoretical valuation has to be perfected with market criteria, as the final purpose is to determine potential market prices.
   a. 4-4-5 Calendar   b. Growth stocks
   c. Security Analysis   d. Stock valuation

5. A _____ is a financial contract between two parties, the buyer and the seller of this type of option. Often it is simply labeled a 'call'. The buyer of the option has the right, but not the obligation to buy an agreed quantity of a particular commodity or financial instrument (the underlying instrument) from the seller of the option at a certain time (the expiration date) for a certain price (the strike price.)
   a. Call option   b. Bear spread
   c. Bear call spread   d. Bull spread

6. In finance, _____ (or gearing) is borrowing money to supplement existing funds for investment in such a way that the potential positive or negative outcome is magnified and/or enhanced. It generally refers to using borrowed funds, or debt, so as to attempt to increase the returns to equity. Deleveraging is the action of reducing borrowings.
   a. Financial endowment   b. Leverage
   c. Pension fund   d. Limited partnership

7. An _____ is a contract written by a seller that conveys to the buyer the right -- but not the obligation -- to buy (in the case of a call _____) or to sell (in the case of a put _____) a particular asset, such as a piece of property such as, among others, a futures contract. In return for granting the _____, the seller collects a payment (the premium) from the buyer.

For example, buying a call _____ provides the right to buy a specified quantity of a security at a set strike price at some time on or before expiration, while buying a put _____ provides the right to sell.

a. AT'T Mobility LLC
c. Amortization

b. Option
d. Annuity

8.   In economics, business, and accounting, a _____ is the value of money that has been used up to produce something, and hence is not available for use anymore. In business, the _____ may be one of acquisition, in which case the amount of money expended to acquire it is counted as _____. In this case, money is the input that is gone in order to acquire the thing.

a. Cost
c. Marginal cost

b. Fixed costs
d. Sliding scale fees

9.   The _____ is an expected return that the provider of capital plans to earn on their investment.

Capital (money) used for funding a business should earn returns for the capital providers who risk their capital. For an investment to be worthwhile, the expected return on capital must be greater than the _____.

a. Weighted average cost of capital
c. 4-4-5 Calendar

b. Cost of capital
d. Capital intensity

10.   The _____ is the rate that a company is expected to pay to finance its assets. WACC is the minimum return that a company must earn on existing asset base to satisfy its creditors, owners, and other providers of capital.

Companies raise money from a number of sources: common equity, preferred equity, straight debt, convertible debt, exchangeable debt, warrants, options, pension liabilities, executive stock options, governmental subsidies, and so on.

a. 4-4-5 Calendar
c. Capital intensity

b. Cost of capital
d. Weighted average cost of capital

11.   _____ is a legally declared inability or impairment of ability of an individual or organization to pay their creditors. Creditors may file a _____ petition against a debtor ('involuntary _____') in an effort to recoup a portion of what they are owed or initiate a restructuring. In the majority of cases, however, _____ is initiated by the debtor (a 'voluntary _____' that is filed by the bankrupt individual or organization.)

a. 529 plan
c. Debt settlement

b. 4-4-5 Calendar
d. Bankruptcy

12.   In financial and business accounting, _____ is a measure of a firm's profitability that excludes interest and income tax expenses.

EBIT = Operating Revenue - Operating Expenses (OPEX) + Non-operating Income

Operating Income = Operating Revenue - Operating Expenses

Operating income is the difference between operating revenues and operating expenses, but it is also sometimes used as a synonym for EBIT and operating profit. This is true if the firm has no non-operating income.

a. AAB

b. ABN Amro

c. A Random Walk Down Wall Street

d. Earnings before interest and taxes

13. _____ are the earnings returned on the initial investment amount.

In the US, the Financial Accounting Standards Board (FASB) requires companies' income statements to report _____ for each of the major categories of the income statement: continuing operations, discontinued operations, extraordinary items, and net income.

The _____ formula does not include preferred dividends for categories outside of continued operations and net income.

a. Inventory turnover

b. Assets turnover

c. Average accounting return

d. Earnings per share

14. _____ measures the rate of return on the ownership interest (shareholders' equity) of the common stock owners. _____ is viewed as one of the most important financial ratios. It measures a firm's efficiency at generating profits from every dollar of shareholders' equity (also known as net assets or assets minus liabilities.)

a. Return on equity

b. Return on sales

c. Diluted Earnings Per Share

d. Return of capital

15. In business and finance, a _____ (also referred to as equity _____) of stock means a _____ of ownership in a corporation (company.) In the plural, stocks is often used as a synonym for _____s especially in the United States, but it is less commonly used that way outside of North America.

In the United Kingdom, South Africa, and Australia, stock can also refer to completely different financial instruments such as government bonds or, less commonly, to all kinds of marketable securities.

a. Bucket shop

b. Margin

c. Procter ' Gamble

d. Share

16. _____ is a fee paid on borrowed assets. It is the price paid for the use of borrowed money , or, money earned by deposited funds . Assets that are sometimes lent with _____ include money, shares, consumer goods through hire purchase, major assets such as aircraft, and even entire factories in finance lease arrangements.

a. Interest

b. Insolvency

c. AAB

d. A Random Walk Down Wall Street

17. In economics and business, specifically cost accounting, the _____ is the point at which cost or expenses and revenue are equal: there is no net loss or gain, and one has 'broken even'. A profit or a loss has not been made, although opportunity costs have been paid, and capital has received the risk-adjusted, expected return.

For example, if the business sells less than 200 tables each month, it will make a loss, if it sells more, it will be a profit.

a. Fixed asset turnover
c. Defined contribution plan

b. Market microstructure
d. Break-even point

18. _____ is an area of finance dealing with the financial decisions corporations make and the tools and analysis used to make these decisions. The primary goal of _____ is to maximize corporate value while managing the firm's financial risks. Although it is in principle different from managerial finance which studies the financial decisions of all firms, rather than corporations alone, the main concepts in the study of _____ are applicable to the financial problems of all kinds of firms.

a. Special purpose entity
c. Cash flow

b. Gross profit
d. Corporate finance

19. In finance, the _____ is the minimum rate of return a firm must offer shareholders to compensate for waiting for their returns, and for bearing some risk.

The _____ capital for a particular company is the rate of return on investment that is required by the company's ordinary shareholders. The return consists both of dividend and capital gains, e.g. increases in the share price.

a. Residual value
c. Round-tripping

b. Net pay
d. Cost of equity

20. _____ is normally any risk associated with any form of financing.

Depending on the nature of the investment, the type of 'investment' risk will vary. High risk investments have greater potential rewards, but you may lose your money instead by taking the risk for more money.

a. Liquidating dividend
c. Stock market index option

b. Revaluation
d. Financial risk

21. A _____ is the reduction in income taxes that results from taking an allowable deduction from taxable income. For example, because interest on debt is a tax-deductible expense, taking on debt creates a _____. Since a _____ is a way to save cash flows, it increases the value of the business, and it is an important aspect of business valuation.

a. Present value of benefits
c. Refinancing risk

b. Present value of costs
d. Tax shield

22. _____ is a form of corporation equity ownership represented in the securities. It is dangerous in comparison to preferred shares and some other investment options, in that in the event of bankruptcy, _____ investors receive their funds after preferred stockholders, bondholders, creditors, etc. On the other hand, common shares on average perform better than preferred shares or bonds over time.

a. Stock market bubble
c. Common stock

b. Stop-limit order
d. Stock split

23. _____ is a term in Corporate Finance used to indicate a condition when promises to creditors of a company are broken or honored with difficulty. Sometimes _____ can lead to bankruptcy. _____ is usually associated with some costs to the company and these are known as Costs of _____.

a. Cashflow matching
b. Financial distress
c. Capital structure
d. Commercial paper

24. _____ or financing is to provide capital (funds), which means money for a project, a person, a business or any other private or public institutions.

Those funds can be allocated for either short term or long term purposes. The health fund is a new way of _____ private healthcare centers.

a. Synthetic CDO
b. Funding
c. Proxy fight
d. Product life cycle

25. In the theory of capital structure _____ is the name for a firm using its profits as a source of capital for new investment, rather than a) distributing them to firm's owners or other investors and b) obtaining capital elsewhere. It is to be contrasted with external financing which consists of new money from outside of the firm brought in for investment. _____ is generally thought to be less expensive for the firm than external financing because the firm does not have to incur transaction costs to obtain it, nor does it have to pay the taxes associated with paying dividends.

a. Internal financing
b. Underwriting contract
c. Operating ratio
d. Employee stock option

26. In economics, the concept of the _____ refers to the decision-making time frame of a firm in which at least one factor of production is fixed. Costs which are fixed in the _____ have no impact on a firms decisions. For example a firm can raise output by increasing the amount of labour through overtime.

a. Short-run
b. 529 plan
c. Long-run
d. 4-4-5 Calendar

27. The _____, was a law enacting several significant changes to the U.S. Bankruptcy Code. Referred to colloquially as the 'New Bankruptcy Law', the Act of Congress attempts to, among other things, make it more difficult for some consumers to file bankruptcy under Chapter 7; some of these consumers may instead utilize Chapter 13.

a. Covenant
b. Foreclosure
c. Personal property
d. Bankruptcy Abuse Prevention and Consumer Protection Act of 2005

28. In law, _____ refers to the process by which a company (or part of a company) is brought to an end, and the assets and property of the company redistributed. _____ can also be referred to as winding-up or dissolution, although dissolution technically refers to the last stage of _____. The process of _____ also arises when customs, an authority or agency in a country responsible for collecting and safeguarding customs duties, determines the final computation or ascertainment of the duties or drawback accruing on an entry.

a. Liquidation
b. Debt settlement
c. 529 plan
d. 4-4-5 Calendar

29. _____ means the inability to pay one's debts as they fall due. Usually used in Business terms, _____ refers to the inability for a 'limited liability' company to pay off debts.

This is defined in two different ways:

Cash flow _____ -
> Unable to pay debts as they fall due.

Balance sheet _____ -
> Having negative net assets: liabilities exceed assets; or net liabilities.

a. A Random Walk Down Wall Street   b. Interest

c. AAB   d. Insolvency

1. A _____ is a payment made by a corporation to its shareholder members. When a corporation earns a profit or surplus, that money can be put to two uses: it can either be re-invested in the business (called retained earnings), or it can be paid to the shareholders as a _____. Many corporations retain a portion of their earnings and pay the remainder as a _____.

   a. Special dividend

   c. Dividend puzzle

   b. Dividend

   d. Dividend yield

2. _____ is a payment of a dividend to stockholders that exceeds the company's retained earnings. Once retained earnings is depleted, capital accounts such as additional paid-in capital are decreased to make up for the remaining dividend to be paid to stockholders. When a _____ occurs, it is considered to be a return of investment instead of profits.

   a. Securities offering

   c. Stock market index option

   b. Liquidating dividend

   d. Revolving credit

3. A _____ is a payment made by a company to its shareholders that is separate from the typical recurring dividend cycle, if any, for the company. The difference may be the result of the date of issue, the amount, the type of payment, or a combination of these factors.

The amount of the dividend is declared special or significant in relation to the stock price. For this reason, the ex-dividend date is set one stock trading day after the payment date. The stock will trade on an ex-distribution basis, adjusted for the amount of the dividend paid one trading day after the payment date.

   a. Dividend decision

   c. Dividend imputation

   b. Special dividend

   d. Dividend puzzle

4. The _____ on a company stock is the company's annual dividend payments divided by its market cap, or the dividend per share divided by the price per share. It is often expressed as a percentage.

Dividend payments on preferred shares are stipulated by the prospectus.

   a. Dividend reinvestment plan

   c. Dividend imputation

   b. Special dividend

   d. Dividend yield

5. The key date to remember for dividend paying stocks is the _____. The _____ is different from the record date. The _____ is typically two trading days before the record date.

In order to receive the upcoming dividend payment payout, you must already own or you must purchase the stock prior to the _____. It is important to note that in most countries, when you buy or sell any stock, there is a three trading-day settlement period on your order.

   a. Ex-dividend date

   c. Asian Financial Crisis

   b. Index number

   d. Insolvency

6. In business and finance, a _____ (also referred to as equity _____) of stock means a _____ of ownership in a corporation (company.) In the plural, stocks is often used as a synonym for _____s especially in the United States, but it is less commonly used that way outside of North America.

In the United Kingdom, South Africa, and Australia, stock can also refer to completely different financial instruments such as government bonds or, less commonly, to all kinds of marketable securities.

a. Bucket shop

b. Margin

c. Procter ' Gamble

d. Share

7. In finance, the term _____ describes the amount in cash that returns to the owners of a security. Normally it does not include the price variations, at the difference of the total return. _____ applies to various stated rates of return on stocks (common and preferred, and convertible), fixed income instruments (bonds, notes, bills, strips, zero coupon), and some other investment type insurance products (e.g. annuities.)

a. Yield to maturity

b. 4-4-5 Calendar

c. Macaulay duration

d. Yield

8. _____ is the balance of the amounts of cash being received and paid by a business during a defined period of time, sometimes tied to a specific project. Measurement of _____ can be used

- to evaluate the state or performance of a business or project.
- to determine problems with liquidity. Being profitable does not necessarily mean being liquid. A company can fail because of a shortage of cash, even while profitable.
- to generate project rate of returns. The time of _____s into and out of projects are used as inputs to financial models such as internal rate of return, and net present value.
- to examine income or growth of a business when it is believed that accrual accounting concepts do not represent economic realities. Alternately, _____ can be used to 'validate' the net income generated by accrual accounting.

_____ as a generic term may be used differently depending on context, and certain _____ definitions may be adapted by analysts and users for their own uses. Common terms include operating _____ and free _____.

_____s can be classified into:

1. Operational _____s: Cash received or expended as a result of the company's core business activities.
2. Investment _____s: Cash received or expended through capital expenditure, investments or acquisitions.
3. Financing _____s: Cash received or expended as a result of financial activities, such as interests and dividends.

All three together - the net _____ - are necessary to reconcile the beginning cash balance to the ending cash balance. Loan draw downs or equity injections, that is just shifting of capital but no expenditure as such, are not considered in the net _____.

a. Shareholder value

b. Cash flow

c. Real option

d. Corporate finance

9. In finance, the _____ approach describes a method of valuing a project, company, or asset using the concepts of the time value of money. All future cash flows are estimated and discounted to give their present values. The discount rate used is generally the appropriate cost of capital and may incorporate judgments of the uncertainty (riskiness) of the future cash flows.
  a. Present value of benefits   b. Future-oriented
  c. Discounted Cash flow   d. Net present value

10. A _____ is an equity investment option offered directly from the underlying company. The investor does not receive quarterly dividends directly as cash; instead, the investor's dividends are directly reinvested in the underlying equity. It should be noted that the investor still must pay tax annually on his or her dividend income, whether it is received or reinvested.
  a. Dividend payout ratio   b. Dividend puzzle
  c. Dividend decision   d. Dividend reinvestment plan

11. In corporate finance, _____ is a cash flow available for distribution among all the security holders of a company. They include equity holders, debt holders, preferred stock holders, convertible security holders, and so on.

Note that the first three lines above are calculated for you on the standard Statement of Cash Flows.

  a. Funding   b. Forfaiting
  c. Safety stock   d. Free cash flow

12. _____ are formal records of a business' financial activities.

_____ provide an overview of a business' financial condition in both short and long term. There are four basic _____:

  1. **Balance sheet**: also referred to as statement of financial position or condition, reports on a company's assets, liabilities, and net equity as of a given point in time.
  2. **Income statement**: also referred to as Profit and Loss statement (or a 'P'L'), reports on a company's income, expenses, and profits over a period of time.
  3. **Statement of retained earnings**: explains the changes in a company's retained earnings over the reporting period.
  4. **Statement of cash flows**: reports on a company's cash flow activities, particularly its operating, investing and financing activities.

  a. Statement on Auditing Standards No. 70: Service
  Organizations   b. Statement of retained earnings
  c. Notes to the Financial Statements   d. Financial statements

13. The _____ is the weighted-average most likely outcome in gambling, probability theory, economics or finance.

In gambling and probability theory, there is usually a discrete set of possible outcomes. In this case, _____ is a measure of the relative balance of win or loss weighted by their chances of occurring.

a. A Random Walk Down Wall Street

b. Expected return

c. ABN Amro

d. AAB

14. _____, is when a company issues common stock or shares to the public for the first time. They are often issued by smaller, younger companies seeking capital to expand, but can also be done by large privately-owned companies looking to become publicly traded.

In an _____ the issuer may obtain the assistance of an underwriting firm, which helps it determine what type of security to issue (common or preferred), best offering price and time to bring it to market.

a. Interest

b. Initial public offering

c. Insolvency

d. Asian Financial Crisis

15. In economics, business, and accounting, a _____ is the value of money that has been used up to produce something, and hence is not available for use anymore. In business, the _____ may be one of acquisition, in which case the amount of money expended to acquire it is counted as _____. In this case, money is the input that is gone in order to acquire the thing.

a. Fixed costs

b. Marginal cost

c. Sliding scale fees

d. Cost

16. _____, refers to consumption opportunity gained by an entity within a specified time frame, which is generally expressed in monetary terms. However, for households and individuals, '_____ is the sum of all the wages, salaries, profits, interests payments, rents and other forms of earnings received... in a given period of time.' For firms, _____ generally refers to net-profit: what remains of revenue after expenses have been subtracted.

a. Accrual

b. OIBDA

c. Annual report

d. Income

17. The _____ duty is a legal relationship of confidence or trust between two or more parties, most commonly a _____ or trustee and a principal or beneficiary. One party, for example a corporate trust company or the trust department of a bank, holds a _____ relation or acts in a _____ capacity to another, such as one whose funds are entrusted to it for investment. In a _____ relation one person justifiably reposes confidence, good faith, reliance and trust in another whose aid, advice or protection is sought in some matter.

a. Legal tender

b. Financial Institutions Reform Recovery and Enforcement Act

c. General obligation

d. Fiduciary

18. The institution most often referenced by the word '_____' is a public or publicly traded _____, the shares of which are traded on a public stock exchange (e.g., the New York Stock Exchange or Nasdaq in the United States) where shares of stock of _____s are bought and sold by and to the general public. Most of the largest businesses in the world are publicly traded _____s. However, the majority of _____s are said to be closely held, privately held or close _____s, meaning that no ready market exists for the trading of shares.

a. Corporation

b. Protect

c. Federal Home Loan Mortgage Corporation

d. Depository Trust Company

19. _____ represents the impact on the stock price that investors would cause in reaction to a change in policy of a company.

a. Clientele effect   b. Trade date

c. Bonus share   d. Volatility clustering

20. _____ is the fraction of net income a firm pays to its stockholders in dividends:

The part of the earnings not paid to investors is left for investment to provide for future earnings growth. Investors seeking high current income and limited capital growth prefer companies with high _____. However investors seeking capital growth may prefer lower payout ratio because capital gains are taxed at a lower rate.

a. Dividend payout ratio   b. Dividend puzzle

c. Dividend yield   d. Dividend imputation

21. _____ are those dividends paid out in form of additional stock shares of the issuing corporation or other corporation They are usually issued in proportion to shares owned (for example for every 100 shares of stock owned, 5% stock dividend will yield 5 extra shares). If this payment involves the issue of new shares, this is very similar to a stock split in that it increases the total number of shares while lowering the price of each share and does not change the market capitalization or the total value of the shares held

a. The Hong Kong Securities Institute   b. Time-based currency

c. Database auditing   d. Stock or scrip dividends

22. In some countries, including the United States and the United Kingdom, corporations can buy back their own stock in a share repurchase, also known as a _____ or share buyback. There has been a meteoric rise in the use of share repurchases in the U.S. in the past twenty years, from $5b in 1980 to $349b in 2005. A share repurchase distributes cash to existing shareholders in exchange for a fraction of the firm's outstanding equity.

a. Stock repurchase   b. Trading curb

c. Stockholder   d. Common stock

23. In financial and business accounting, _____ is a measure of a firm's profitability that excludes interest and income tax expenses.

EBIT = Operating Revenue - Operating Expenses (OPEX) + Non-operating Income

Operating Income = Operating Revenue - Operating Expenses

Operating income is the difference between operating revenues and operating expenses, but it is also sometimes used as a synonym for EBIT and operating profit. This is true if the firm has no non-operating income.

a. A Random Walk Down Wall Street   b. AAB

c. ABN Amro   d. Earnings before interest and taxes

24. A _____ or stock divide increases or decreases the number of shares in a public company. The price is adjusted such that the before and after market capitalization of the company remains the same and dilution does not occur. Options and warrants are included.

a. Contract for difference

b. Stop order

c. Stock split

d. Stop price

25. _____ are the earnings returned on the initial investment amount.

In the US, the Financial Accounting Standards Board (FASB) requires companies' income statements to report _____ for each of the major categories of the income statement: continuing operations, discontinued operations, extraordinary items, and net income.

The _____ formula does not include preferred dividends for categories outside of continued operations and net income.

a. Assets turnover

b. Inventory turnover

c. Average accounting return

d. Earnings per share

26. On a stock exchange, a _____ is the opposite of a stock split, i.e. a stock merge - a reduction in the number of shares and an accompanying increase in the share price. The ratio is also reversed: 1-for-2, 1-for-3 and so on.

There is a stigma attached to doing this so it is not initiated without very good reason.

a. Correlation trading

b. Conglomerate merger

c. Reverse stock split

d. Trade date

1.   In economics, the concept of the _____ refers to the decision-making time frame of a firm in which at least one factor of production is fixed. Costs which are fixed in the _____ have no impact on a firms decisions. For example a firm can raise output by increasing the amount of labour through overtime.

    a. 4-4-5 Calendar
                 b. Short-run

    c. Long-run
                     d. 529 plan

2.   Working capital requirements of a business should be monitored at all times to ensure that there are sufficient funds available to meet short-term expenses.

The _____ is basically a detailed plan that shows all expected sources and uses of cash

    a. Loans and interest, in Judaism
          b. Mitigating Control

    c. Rate of return
                    d. Cash budget

3.   In accounting, a _____ is an asset on the balance sheet which is expected to be sold or otherwise used up in the near future, usually within one year, or one business cycle - whichever is longer. Typical _____s include cash, cash equivalents, accounts receivable, inventory, the portion of prepaid accounts which will be used within a year, and short-term investments.

On the balance sheet, assets will typically be classified into _____s and long-term assets.

    a. Current asset
                 b. Historical cost

    c. Write-off
                    d. Long-term liabilities

4.   In accounting, _____ are considered liabilities of the business that are to be settled in cash within the fiscal year or the operating cycle, whichever period is longer.

For example accounts payable for goods, services or supplies that were purchased for use in the operation of the business and payable within a normal period of time would be _____.

Bonds, mortgages and loans that are payable over a term exceeding one year would be fixed liabilities.

    a. Gross sales
                 b. Current liabilities

    c. Closing entries
                 d. Net income

5.   In business and accounting, _____s are everything of value that is owned by a person or company. The balance sheet of a firm records the monetary value of the _____s owned by the firm. The two major _____ classes are tangible _____s and intangible _____s.

    a. Accounts payable
               b. Income

    c. Asset
                     d. EBITDA

6.   In financial accounting, a _____ or statement of financial position is a summary of a person's or organization's balances. Assets, liabilities and ownership equity are listed as of a specific date, such as the end of its financial year. A _____ is often described as a snapshot of a company's financial condition.

a. Statement on Auditing Standards No. 70: Service Organizations

b. Financial statements

c. Balance sheet

d. Statement of retained earnings

7. _____ is a financial metric which represents operating liquidity available to a business. Along with fixed assets such as plant and equipment, _____ is considered a part of operating capital. It is calculated as current assets minus current liabilities.

a. 529 plan

b. Working capital

c. Working capital management

d. 4-4-5 Calendar

8. _____, in bookkeeping, refers to assets, liabilities, income, and expenses recorded on individual pages of the so called book of final entry or ledger. Changes in _____ value are made by chronologically posting debit (DR) and credit (CR) entries to its page. Examples of _____s are cash, _____s receivable, mortgages, loans, land and buildings, common stock, sales, services provided, wages, and payroll overhead.

a. Accretion

b. Alpha

c. Option

d. Account

9. _____ is a file or account that contains money that a person or company owes to suppliers, but hasn't paid yet (a form of debt.) When you receive an invoice you add it to the file, and then you remove it when you pay. Thus, the A/P is a form of credit that suppliers offer to their purchasers by allowing them to pay for a product or service after it has already been received.

a. Earnings before interest, taxes, depreciation and amortization

b. Accrual

c. Outstanding balance

d. Accounts payable

10. _____ is one of a series of accounting transactions dealing with the billing of customers who owe money to a person, company or organization for goods and services that have been provided to the customer. In most business entities this is typically done by generating an invoice and mailing or electronically delivering it to the customer, who in turn must pay it within an established timeframe called credit or payment terms.

An example of a common payment term is Net 30, meaning payment is due in the amount of the invoice 30 days from the date of invoice.

a. Income

b. Accounting methods

c. Impaired asset

d. Accounts receivable

11. _____ is a list for goods and materials held available in stock by a business. It is also used for a list of the contents of a household and for a list for testamentary purposes of the possessions of someone who has died. In accounting _____ is considered an asset.

a. ABN Amro

b. A Random Walk Down Wall Street

c. Inventory

d. AAB

12. _____ is the balance of the amounts of cash being received and paid by a business during a defined period of time, sometimes tied to a specific project. Measurement of _____ can be used

- to evaluate the state or performance of a business or project.
- to determine problems with liquidity. Being profitable does not necessarily mean being liquid. A company can fail because of a shortage of cash, even while profitable.
- to generate project rate of returns. The time of _____s into and out of projects are used as inputs to financial models such as internal rate of return, and net present value.
- to examine income or growth of a business when it is believed that accrual accounting concepts do not represent economic realities. Alternately, _____ can be used to 'validate' the net income generated by accrual accounting.

_____ as a generic term may be used differently depending on context, and certain _____ definitions may be adapted by analysts and users for their own uses. Common terms include operating _____ and free _____.

_____s can be classified into:

1. Operational _____s: Cash received or expended as a result of the company's core business activities.
2. Investment _____s: Cash received or expended through capital expenditure, investments or acquisitions.
3. Financing _____s: Cash received or expended as a result of financial activities, such as interests and dividends.

All three together - the net _____ - are necessary to reconcile the beginning cash balance to the ending cash balance. Loan draw downs or equity injections, that is just shifting of capital but no expenditure as such, are not considered in the net _____.

a. Corporate finance
c. Real option

b. Shareholder value
d. Cash flow

13. The _____ is an equation that equals the cost of goods sold divided by the average inventory. Average inventory equals beginning inventory plus ending inventory divided by 2.

The formula for _____:

$$\text{Inventory Turnover} = \frac{\text{Cost of Goods Sold}}{\text{Average Inventory}}$$

The formula for average inventory:

$$\text{Average Inventory} = \frac{\text{Beginning inventory} + \text{Ending inventory}}{2}$$

A low turnover rate may point to overstocking, obsolescence, or deficiencies in the product line or marketing effort.

a. Earnings yield

b. Information ratio

c. Operating leverage

d. Inventory turnover

14. _____ is one of the Accounting Liquidity ratios, a financial ratio. This ratio measures the number of times, on average, the inventory is sold during the period. Its purpose is to measure the liquidity of the inventory.

a. ABN Amro

b. AAB

c. Inventory turnover ratio

d. A Random Walk Down Wall Street

15. _____ is one of the accounting liquidity ratios, a financial ratio. This ratio measures the number of times, on average, receivables (e.g. Accounts Receivable) are collected during the period. A popular variant of the _____ is to convert it into an Average Collection Period in terms of days.

a. Sharpe ratio

b. Return on equity

c. PEG ratio

d. Receivables turnover ratio

16. _____ or financing is to provide capital (funds), which means money for a project, a person, a business or any other private or public institutions.

Those funds can be allocated for either short term or long term purposes. The health fund is a new way of _____ private healthcare centers.

a. Proxy fight

b. Funding

c. Product life cycle

d. Synthetic CDO

17. In marketing, _____ refers to the total cost of holding inventory. This includes warehousing costs such as rent, utilities and salaries, financial costs such as opportunity cost, and inventory costs related to perishibility, shrinkage and insurance.

a. 4-4-5 Calendar

b. 529 plan

c. Carrying cost

d. 7-Eleven

18. In economics, business, and accounting, a _____ is the value of money that has been used up to produce something, and hence is not available for use anymore. In business, the _____ may be one of acquisition, in which case the amount of money expended to acquire it is counted as _____. In this case, money is the input that is gone in order to acquire the thing.

a. Fixed costs

b. Sliding scale fees

c. Marginal cost

d. Cost

19. _____ refinancing (in the case of real property) occurs when a loan is taken out on property already owned, and the loan amount is above and beyond the cost of transaction, payoff of existing liens, and related expenses.

Strictly speaking all refinancing of debt is '_____', when funds retrieved are utilized for anything other than repaying an existing lien.

In the case of common usage of the term, _____ refinancing refers to when equity is liquidated from a property above and beyond sum of the payoff of existing loans held in lien on the property, loan fees, costs associated with the loan, taxes, insurance, tax reserves, insurance reserves, and in the past any other non-lien debt held in the name of the owner being paid by loan proceeds.

a. Conforming loan   b. Home equity line of credit
c. Fixed rate mortgage   d. Cash-out

20.   A mutual shareholder or _____ is an individual or company (including a corporation) that legally owns one or more shares of stock in a joint stock company. A company's shareholders collectively own that company. Thus, the typical goal of such companies is to enhance shareholder value.
a. Stockholder   b. Stock market bubble
c. Limit order   d. Trading curb

21.   In political science and economics, the _____ or agency dilemma treats the difficulties that arise under conditions of incomplete and asymmetric information when a principal hires an agent. Various mechanisms may be used to try to align the interests of the agent with those of the principal, such as piece rates/commissions, profit sharing, efficiency wages, performance measurement (including financial statements), the agent posting a bond, or fear of firing. The _____ is found in most employer/employee relationships, for example, when stockholders hire top executives of corporations.
a. 529 plan   b. 7-Eleven
c. 4-4-5 Calendar   d. Principal-agent problem

22.   _____ is a form of corporation equity ownership represented in the securities. It is dangerous in comparison to preferred shares and some other investment options, in that in the event of bankruptcy, _____ investors receive their funds after preferred stockholders, bondholders, creditors, etc. On the other hand, common shares on average perform better than preferred shares or bonds over time.
a. Stock split   b. Stock market bubble
c. Stop-limit order   d. Common stock

23.   In financial accounting, the term _____ is most commonly used to describe any part of shareholders' equity, except for basic share capital. Sometimes, the term is used instead of the term provision; such a use, however, is inconsistent with the terminology suggested by International Accounting Standards Board. For more information about provisions, see provision (accounting.)
a. Reserve   b. Treasury stock
c. FIFO and LIFO accounting   d. Closing entries

24.   _____ is a life of security. It may also refer to the final payment date of a loan or other financial instrument, at which point all remaining interest and principal is due to be paid.

1, 3, 6 months _____ band can be calculated by using 30-day per month periods.

a. Maturity   b. Primary market
c. Replacement cost   d. False billing

25.   In finance, the _____ between two currencies specifies how much one currency is worth in terms of the other. For example an _____ of 102 Japanese yen to the United States dollar means that JPY 102 is worth the same as USD 1. The foreign exchange market is one of the largest markets in the world.

a. A Random Walk Down Wall Street
b. ABN Amro
c. AAB
d. Exchange rate

26.   _____ is a form of risk that arises from the change in price of one currency against another. Whenever investors or companies have assets or business operations across national borders, they face _____ if their positions are not hedged.

- Transaction risk is the risk that exchange rates will change unfavourably over time. It can be hedged against using forward currency contracts;
- Translation risk is an accounting risk, proportional to the amount of assets held in foreign currencies. Changes in the exchange rate over time will render a report inaccurate, and so assets are usually balanced by borrowings in that currency.

The exchange risk associated with a foreign denominated instrument is a key element in foreign investment. This risk flows from differential monetary policy and growth in real productivity, which results in differential inflation rates.

a. Credit risk
b. Market risk
c. Tracking error
d. Currency risk

27.   _____ is a fee paid on borrowed assets. It is the price paid for the use of borrowed money , or, money earned by deposited funds . Assets that are sometimes lent with _____ include money, shares, consumer goods through hire purchase, major assets such as aircraft, and even entire factories in finance lease arrangements.

a. A Random Walk Down Wall Street
b. Insolvency
c. AAB
d. Interest

28.   An _____ is the price a borrower pays for the use of money they do not own, and the return a lender receives for deferring the use of funds, by lending it to the borrower. _____s are normally expressed as a percentage rate over the period of one year.

_____s targets are also a vital tool of monetary policy and are used to control variables like investment, inflation, and unemployment.

a. A Random Walk Down Wall Street
b. Interest rate
c. ABN Amro
d. AAB

29.   _____ is a measure of the ability of a debtor to pay their debts as and when they fall due. It is usually expressed as a ratio or a percentage of current liabilities.

For a corporation with a published balance sheet there are various ratios used to calculate a measure of liquidity.

a. Accounting liquidity

b. Operating leverage

c. Invested capital

d. Operating profit margin

30.   A _____ is any credit facility extended to a business by a bank or financial institution. A _____ may take several forms such as cash credit, overdraft, demand loan, export packing credit, term loan, discounting or purchase of commercial bills etc. It is like an account that can readily be tapped into if the need arises or not touched at all and saved for emergencies.

a. Default Notice

b. Cash credit

c. Debt-snowball method

d. Line of credit

31.   _____ is a type of credit that does not have a fixed number of payments, in contrast to installment credit. Examples of _____s used by consumers include credit cards. Corporate _____ facilities are typically used to provide liquidity for a company's day-to-day operations.

a. Reverse stock split

b. Commercial finance

c. Package loan

d. Revolving credit

32.   _____ is the provision of resources (such as granting a loan) by one party to another party where that second party does not reimburse the first party immediately, thereby generating a debt, and instead arranges either to repay or return those resources (or material(s) of equal value) at a later date. The first party is called a creditor, also known as a lender, while the second party is called a debtor, also known as a borrower.

Movements of financial capital are normally dependent on either _____ or equity transfers.

a. Credit

b. Clearing house

c. Comparable

d. Warrant

33.   An _____ is a loan that is not backed by collateral. Also known as a signature loan or personal loan.

_____s are based solely upon the borrower's credit rating.

a. Event of default

b. Annualcreditreport.com

c. Intelliscore

d. Unsecured loan

34.   _____ is a form of short-term borrowing often used to improve a company's working capital and cash flow position.

_____ allows a business to draw money against its sales invoices before the customer has actually paid. To do this, the business borrows a percentage of the value of its sales ledger from a finance company, effectively using the unpaid sales invoices as collateral for the borrowing.

a. AAB

b. A Random Walk Down Wall Street

c. Invoice discounting

d. ABN Amro

35.   _____ is a financial transaction whereby a business sells its accounts receivable (i.e., invoices) at a discount. _____ differs from a bank loan in three main ways. First, the emphasis is on the value of the receivables (essentially a financial asset), not the firm's credit worthiness.

a. Financial Literacy Month

c. Debt-for-equity swap

b. Credit card balance transfer

d. Factoring

36. A standard, commercial _____ is a document issued mostly by a financial institution, used primarily in trade finance, which usually provides an irrevocable payment undertaking.

The _____ can also be the source of payment for a transaction, meaning that redeeming the _____ will pay an exporter. Letters of credit are used primarily in international trade transactions of significant value, for deals between a supplier in one country and a customer in another.

a. Bond indenture

c. Letter of credit

b. Duty of loyalty

d. McFadden Act

37. In the global money market, _____ is an unsecured promissory note with a fixed maturity of one to 270 days. _____ is a money-market security issued (sold) by large banks and corporations to get money to meet short term debt obligations (for example, payroll), and is only backed by an issuing bank or corporation's promise to pay the face amount on the maturity date specified on the note. Since it is not backed by collateral, only firms with excellent credit ratings from a recognized rating agency will be able to sell their _____ at a reasonable price.

a. Trade-off theory

c. Book building

b. Commercial paper

d. Financial distress

38. _____ exists when one firm provides goods or services to a customer with an agreement to bill them later, or receive a shipment or service from a supplier under an agreement to pay them later. It can be viewed as an essential element of capitalization in an operating business because it can reduce the required capital investment to operate the business if it is managed properly. _____ is the largest use of capital for a majority of business to business (B2B) sellers in the United States and is a critical source of capital for a majority of all businesses.

a. 4-4-5 Calendar

c. 529 plan

b. Going concern

d. Trade credit

39. In law, a _____ is a form of security interest granted over an item of property to secure the payment of a debt or performance of some other obligation. The owner of the property, who grants the _____, is referred to as the lienor and the person who has the benefit of the _____ is referred to as the _____ee.

The etymological root is: Anglo-French _____, loyen bond, restraint, from Latin ligamen, from ligare to bind.

a. Joint venture

c. Family and Medical Leave Act

b. Sarbanes-Oxley Act

d. Lien

40. Decisions relating to working capital and short term financing are referred to as _____. These involve managing the relationship between a firm's short-term assets and its short-term liabilities. The goal of _____ is to ensure that the firm is able to continue its operations and that it has sufficient cash flow to satisfy both maturing short-term debt and upcoming operational expenses.

a. Working capital

c. Working capital management

b. 4-4-5 Calendar

d. 529 plan

1.   _____ is a measure of the ability of a debtor to pay their debts as and when they fall due. It is usually expressed as a ratio or a percentage of current liabilities.

For a corporation with a published balance sheet there are various ratios used to calculate a measure of liquidity.

a. Invested capital   b. Accounting liquidity
c. Operating profit margin   d. Operating leverage

2.   In economics, business, and accounting, a _____ is the value of money that has been used up to produce something, and hence is not available for use anymore. In business, the _____ may be one of acquisition, in which case the amount of money expended to acquire it is counted as _____. In this case, money is the input that is gone in order to acquire the thing.

a. Marginal cost   b. Fixed costs
c. Sliding scale fees   d. Cost

3.   In banking and finance, _____ denotes all activities from the time a commitment is made for a transaction until it is settled. _____ is necessary because the speed of trades is much faster than the cycle time for completing the underlying transaction.

In its widest sense _____ involves the management of post-trading, pre-settlement credit exposures, to ensure that trades are settled in accordance with market rules, even if a buyer or seller should become insolvent prior to settlement.

a. Share   b. Clearing house
c. Procter ' Gamble   d. Clearing

4.   The free _____ of a public company is an estimate of the proportion of shares that are not held by large owners and that are not stock with sales restrictions (restricted stock that cannot be sold until they become unrestricted stock.)

The free _____ or a public _____ is usually defined as being all shares held by investors other than:

- shares held by owners owning more than 5% of all shares (those could be institutional investors, 'strategic shareholders,' founders, executives, and other insiders' holdings)
- restricted stocks (granted to executives that can be, but don't have to be, registered insiders)
- insider holdings (it is assumed that insiders hold stock for the very long term)

The free _____ is an important criterion in quoting a share on the stock market.

To _____ a company means to list its shares on a public stock exchange through an initial public offering (or 'flotation'.)

- Open market
- Outstanding shares
- Market capitalization
- Public _____ *loat*
- Reverse takeover

a. Float

c. Synthetic CDO

b. Trade finance

d. Golden parachute

5.   A _____ is the principal book for recording transactions. Originally, the term referred to a large volume of Scripture/service book kept in one place in church and accessible.

According to Charles Wriothesley's Chronicle (1538):

> the curates should provide a booke of the bible in Englishe, of the largest volume, to be a lidger in the same church for the parishioners to read on.

It is an application of this original meaning that is found in the commercial usage of the term for the principal book of account in a business house, the general _____ or nominal _____ and also in the terms purchase _____ and sales _____.

a. Journal entry

c. General ledger

b. Ledger

d. General journal

6.   _____, in bookkeeping, refers to assets, liabilities, income, and expenses recorded on individual pages of the so called book of final entry or ledger. Changes in _____ value are made by chronologically posting debit (DR) and credit (CR) entries to its page. Examples of _____s are cash, _____s receivable, mortgages, loans, land and buildings, common stock, sales, services provided, wages, and payroll overhead.

a. Option

c. Alpha

b. Accretion

d. Account

7.   _____ is the transfer of funds from diverse accounts into a central account to improve the efficiency of cash management. The consolidation of cash into a single account allows a company to maintain smaller cash balances overall, and to identify excess cash available for short term investments. The cash available in different bank accounts are pooled into a master account.The advantages of _____ are 1) Cash control 2) Cash visibility .

a. Capitalization rate

c. Profitability index

b. Conditional prepayment rate

d. Cash concentration

8. A _____ is a financial services company that provides clearing and settlement services for financial transactions, usually on a futures exchange, and often acts as central counterparty (the payor actually pays the _____, which then pays the payee). A _____ may also offer novation, the substitution of a new contract or debt for an old, or other credit enhancement services to its members.

The term is also used for banks like Suffolk Bank that acted as a restraint on the over-issuance of private bank notes.

a. Warrant	b. Valuation
c. Clearing house	d. Bucket shop

9. In finance, the _____ is the global financial market for short-term borrowing and lending. It provides short-term liquidity funding for the global financial system. The _____ is where short-term obligations such as Treasury bills, commercial paper and bankers' acceptances are bought and sold.

a. Debt-for-equity swap	b. Cramdown
c. Consumer debt	d. Money market

10. A _____ is a fungible, negotiable instrument representing financial value. They are broadly categorized into debt securities (such as banknotes, bonds and debentures), and equity securities; e.g., common stocks. The company or other entity issuing the _____ is called the issuer.

a. Securities lending	b. Tracking stock
c. Book entry	d. Security

11. _____ (also trust indenture or deed of trust) is a legal document issued to lenders and describes key terms such as the interest rate, maturity date, convertibility, pledge, promises, representations, covenants, and other terms of the bond offering. When the Offering Memorandum is prepared in advance of marketing a Bond, the indenture will typically be summarised in the 'Description of Notes' section.

a. Bond indenture	b. Fair Labor Standards Act
c. McFadden Act	d. Court of Audit of Belgium

12. _____ is a fee paid on borrowed assets. It is the price paid for the use of borrowed money , or, money earned by deposited funds . Assets that are sometimes lent with _____ include money, shares, consumer goods through hire purchase, major assets such as aircraft, and even entire factories in finance lease arrangements.

a. Interest	b. A Random Walk Down Wall Street
c. Insolvency	d. AAB

13. An _____ is the price a borrower pays for the use of money they do not own, and the return a lender receives for deferring the use of funds, by lending it to the borrower. _____s are normally expressed as a percentage rate over the period of one year.

_____s targets are also a vital tool of monetary policy and are used to control variables like investment, inflation, and unemployment.

a. A Random Walk Down Wall Street	b. ABN Amro
c. Interest rate	d. AAB

14. _____ is the risk (variability in value) borne by an interest-bearing asset, such as a loan or a bond, due to variability of interest rates. In general, as rates rise, the price of a fixed rate bond will fall, and vice versa. _____ is commonly measured by the bond's duration.

   a. A Random Walk Down Wall Street   b. International Fisher effect

   c. Official bank rate   d. Interest rate risk

15. _____ is a life of security. It may also refer to the final payment date of a loan or other financial instrument, at which point all remaining interest and principal is due to be paid.

1, 3, 6 months _____ band can be calculated by using 30-day per month periods.

   a. Replacement cost   b. Primary market

   c. Maturity   d. False billing

16. In economics, the concept of the _____ refers to the decision-making time frame of a firm in which at least one factor of production is fixed. Costs which are fixed in the _____ have no impact on a firms decisions. For example a firm can raise output by increasing the amount of labour through overtime.

   a. Long-run   b. 529 plan

   c. 4-4-5 Calendar   d. Short-run

17. In finance, a _____ is a debt security, in which the authorized issuer owes the holders a debt and, depending on the terms of the _____, is obliged to pay interest (the coupon) and/or to repay the principal at a later date, termed maturity.

Thus a _____ is a loan: the issuer is the borrower, the _____ holder is the lender, and the coupon is the interest. _____s provide the borrower with external funds to finance long-term investments, or, in the case of government _____s, to finance current expenditure.

   a. Catastrophe bonds   b. Convertible bond

   c. Puttable bond   d. Bond

18. A _____s a time deposit, a financial product commonly offered to consumers by banks, thrift institutions, and credit unions.

They are similar to savings accounts in that they are insured and thus virtually risk-free; they are 'money in the bank'. They are different from savings accounts in that they have a specific, fixed term (often three months, six months, or one to five years), and, usually, a fixed interest rate.

   a. Reserve requirement   b. Time deposit

   c. Certificate of deposit   d. Variable rate mortgage

19. _____ mature in one year or less. Like zero-coupon bonds, they do not pay interest prior to maturity; instead they are sold at a discount of the par value to create a positive yield to maturity. Many regard _____ as the least risky investment available to U.S. investors.

a. Treasury securities   b. Treasury bills
c. 4-4-5 Calendar   d. Treasury Inflation Protected Securities

20. _____ means regulating, adapting or settling in a variety of contexts:

In commercial law, _____ means the settlement of a loss incurred on insured goods. The calculation of the amounts of compensation to be paid by or to the several interests is a complicated matter. It involves much detail and arithmetic, and requires a full and accurate knowledge of the principles of the subject.

a. Asset recovery   b. Intelligent investor
c. Equity method   d. Adjustment

21. In United States banking, _____ is a marketing term for certain services offered primarily to larger business customers. It may be used to describe all bank accounts (such as checking accounts) provided to businesses of a certain size, but it is more often used to describe specific services such as cash concentration, zero balance accounting, and automated clearing house facilities. Sometimes, private banking customers are given _____ services.
a. Profitability index   b. Global tactical asset allocation
c. Capitalization rate   d. Cash management

22. The institution most often referenced by the word '_____' is a public or publicly traded _____, the shares of which are traded on a public stock exchange (e.g., the New York Stock Exchange or Nasdaq in the United States) where shares of stock of _____s are bought and sold by and to the general public. Most of the largest businesses in the world are publicly traded _____s. However, the majority of _____s are said to be closely held, privately held or close _____s, meaning that no ready market exists for the trading of shares.
a. Corporation   b. Protect
c. Federal Home Loan Mortgage Corporation   d. Depository Trust Company

23. _____ or economic opportunity loss is the value of the next best alternative foregone as the result of making a decision. _____ analysis is an important part of a company's decision-making processes but is not treated as an actual cost in any financial statement. The next best thing that a person can engage in is referred to as the _____ of doing the best thing and ignoring the next best thing to be done.
a. A Random Walk Down Wall Street   b. AAB
c. Opportunity cost   d. ABN Amro

24. In economics, and cost accounting, _____ describes the total economic cost of production and is made up of variable costs, which vary according to the quantity of a good produced and include inputs such as labor and raw materials, plus fixed costs, which are independent of the quantity of a good produced and include inputs (capital) that cannot be varied in the short term, such as buildings and machinery. _____ in economics includes the total opportunity cost of each factor of production in addition to fixed and variable costs.

The rate at which _____ changes as the amount produced changes is called marginal cost.

a. 529 plan   b. 7-Eleven
c. 4-4-5 Calendar   d. Total cost

1. _____ is the provision of resources (such as granting a loan) by one party to another party where that second party does not reimburse the first party immediately, thereby generating a debt, and instead arranges either to repay or return those resources (or material(s) of equal value) at a later date. The first party is called a creditor, also known as a lender, while the second party is called a debtor, also known as a borrower.

Movements of financial capital are normally dependent on either _____ or equity transfers.

a. Comparable	b. Clearing house
c. Warrant	d. Credit

2. _____ is the method by which one calculates the creditworthiness of a business or organization. The audited financial statements of a large company might be analyzed when it issues or has issued bonds. Or, a bank may analyze the financial statements of a small business before making or renewing a commercial loan.

a. Credit crunch	b. Credit report monitoring
c. Credit analysis	d. Capital note

3. _____ exists when one firm provides goods or services to a customer with an agreement to bill them later, or receive a shipment or service from a supplier under an agreement to pay them later. It can be viewed as an essential element of capitalization in an operating business because it can reduce the required capital investment to operate the business if it is managed properly. _____ is the largest use of capital for a majority of business to business (B2B) sellers in the United States and is a critical source of capital for a majority of all businesses.

a. Going concern	b. Trade credit
c. 529 plan	d. 4-4-5 Calendar

4. _____ is the balance of the amounts of cash being received and paid by a business during a defined period of time, sometimes tied to a specific project. Measurement of _____ can be used

- to evaluate the state or performance of a business or project.
- to determine problems with liquidity. Being profitable does not necessarily mean being liquid. A company can fail because of a shortage of cash, even while profitable.
- to generate project rate of returns. The time of _____s into and out of projects are used as inputs to financial models such as internal rate of return, and net present value.
- to examine income or growth of a business when it is believed that accrual accounting concepts do not represent economic realities. Alternately, _____ can be used to 'validate' the net income generated by accrual accounting.

_____ as a generic term may be used differently depending on context, and certain _____ definitions may be adapted by analysts and users for their own uses. Common terms include operating _____ and free _____.

_____s can be classified into:

1. Operational _____s: Cash received or expended as a result of the company's core business activities.
2. Investment _____s: Cash received or expended through capital expenditure, investments or acquisitions.
3. Financing _____s: Cash received or expended as a result of financial activities, such as interests and dividends.

All three together - the net _____ - are necessary to reconcile the beginning cash balance to the ending cash balance. Loan draw downs or equity injections, that is just shifting of capital but no expenditure as such, are not considered in the net _____.

a. Cash flow	b. Corporate finance
c. Shareholder value	d. Real option

5. _____ are formal records of a business' financial activities.

_____ provide an overview of a business' financial condition in both short and long term. There are four basic _____:

1. **Balance sheet**: also referred to as statement of financial position or condition, reports on a company's assets, liabilities, and net equity as of a given point in time.
2. **Income statement**: also referred to as Profit and Loss statement (or a 'P'L'), reports on a company's income, expenses, and profits over a period of time.
3. **Statement of retained earnings**: explains the changes in a company's retained earnings over the reporting period.
4. **Statement of cash flows**: reports on a company's cash flow activities, particularly its operating, investing and financing activities.

a. Financial statements	b. Notes to the Financial Statements
c. Statement of retained earnings	d. Statement on Auditing Standards No. 70: Service Organizations

6. _____ measures the nominal future sum of money that a given sum of money is 'worth' at a specified time in the future assuming a certain interest rate rate of return; it is the present value multiplied by the accumulation function.

The **value does** not include corrections for inflation or other factors that affect the true value of money in the future. This is used in **time value** of money calculations.

a. Discounted cash flow	b. Future value
c. Present value of costs	d. Future-oriented

7. _____, in bookkeeping, refers to assets, liabilities, income, and expenses recorded on individual pages of the so called book of final entry or ledger. Changes in _____ value are made by chronologically posting debit (DR) and credit (CR) entries to its page. Examples of _____s are cash, _____s receivable, mortgages, loans, land and buildings, common stock, sales, services provided, wages, and payroll overhead.

a. Accretion	b. Option
c. Alpha	d. Account

8. _____ is one of a series of accounting transactions dealing with the billing of customers who owe money to a person, company or organization for goods and services that have been provided to the customer. In most business entities this is typically done by generating an invoice and mailing or electronically delivering it to the customer, who in turn must pay it within an established timeframe called credit or payment terms.

An example of a common payment term is Net 30, meaning payment is due in the amount of the invoice 30 days from the date of invoice.

a. Impaired asset
c. Accounting methods

b. Income
d. Accounts receivable

9. An _____ or bill is a commercial document issued by a seller to the buyer, indicating the products, quantities, and agreed prices for products or services the seller has provided the buyer. An _____ indicates the buyer must pay the seller, according to the payment terms.

In the rental industry, an _____ must include a specific reference to the duration of the time being billed, so rather than quantity, price and discount the invoicing amount is based on quantity, price, discount and duration.

a. ABN Amro
c. A Random Walk Down Wall Street

b. AAB
d. Invoice

10. _____ is the long dimension of any object. The _____ of a thing is the distance between its ends, its linear extent as measured from end to end. This may be distinguished from height, which is vertical extent, and width or breadth, which are the distance from side to side, measuring across the object at right angles to the _____.

a. Length
c. 529 plan

b. 4-4-5 Calendar
d. 7-Eleven

11. In lending agreements, _____ is a borrower's pledge of specific property to a lender, to secure repayment of a loan. The _____ serves as protection for a lender against a borrower's risk of default - that is, a borrower failing to pay the principal and interest under the terms of a loan obligation. If a borrower does default on a loan (due to insolvency or other event), that borrower forfeits (gives up) the property pledged as _____ *ollateral* - and the lender then becomes the owner of the _____.

a. Collateral
c. Nominal value

b. Future-oriented
d. Refinancing risk

12. _____ is the risk of loss due to a debtor's non-payment of a loan or other line of credit (either the principal or interest (coupon) or both)

Most lenders employ their own models (credit scorecards) to rank potential and existing customers according to risk, and then apply appropriate strategies. With products such as unsecured personal loans or mortgages, lenders charge a higher price for higher risk customers and vice versa. With revolving products such as credit cards and overdrafts, risk is controlled through careful setting of credit limits.

a. Transaction risk
c. Liquidity risk

b. Market risk
d. Credit risk

13.   A '_____' is a 'Charge' that is paid to obtain the right to delay a payment. Essentially, the payer purchases the right to make a given payment in the future instead of in the Present. The '_____', or 'Charge' that must be paid to delay the payment, is simply the difference between what the payment amount would be if it were paid in the present and what the payment amount would be paid if it were paid in the future.

a. Value at risk

b. Risk aversion

c. Risk modeling

d. Discount

14.   _____ is a list for goods and materials held available in stock by a business. It is also used for a list of the contents of a household and for a list for testamentary purposes of the possessions of someone who has died. In accounting _____ is considered an asset.

a. A Random Walk Down Wall Street

b. AAB

c. ABN Amro

d. Inventory

15.   In economics, business, and accounting, a _____ is the value of money that has been used up to produce something, and hence is not available for use anymore. In business, the _____ may be one of acquisition, in which case the amount of money expended to acquire it is counted as _____. In this case, money is the input that is gone in order to acquire the thing.

a. Cost

b. Sliding scale fees

c. Marginal cost

d. Fixed costs

16.   A _____, referred to as a note payable in accounting, is a contract where one party (the maker or issuer) makes an unconditional promise in writing to pay a sum of money to the other (the payee), either at a fixed or determinable future time or on demand of the payee, under specific terms. They differ from IOUs in that they contain a specific promise to pay, rather than simply acknowledging that a debt exists.

The terms of a note typically include the principal amount, the interest rate if any, and the maturity date.

a. Financial plan

b. Credit repair software

c. Title loan

d. Promissory note

17.   In business, _____ is income that a company receives from its normal business activities, usually from the sale of goods and services to customers. Some companies also receive _____ from interest, dividends or royalties paid to them by other companies. _____ may refer to business income in general, or it may refer to the amount, in a monetary unit, received during a period of time, as in 'Last year, Company X had _____ of $32 million.'

In many countries, including the UK, _____ is referred to as turnover.

a. Furniture, Fixtures and Equipment

b. Bottom line

c. Matching principle

d. Revenue

18.   A _____ can require immediate payment by the second party to the third upon presentation of the _____. This is called a sight _____. A Cheques is a sight _____. An importer might write a _____ promising payment to an exporter for delivery of goods with payment to occur 60 days after the goods are delivered. Such a _____ is called a time _____.

a. Gross profit margin

b. Draft

c. Second lien loan

d. Cashflow matching

19. In finance, a _____ is a debt security, in which the authorized issuer owes the holders a debt and, depending on the terms of the _____, is obliged to pay interest (the coupon) and/or to repay the principal at a later date, termed maturity.

Thus a _____ is a loan: the issuer is the borrower, the _____ holder is the lender, and the coupon is the interest. _____s provide the borrower with external funds to finance long-term investments, or, in the case of government _____s, to finance current expenditure.

a. Bond

b. Puttable bond

c. Catastrophe bonds

d. Convertible bond

20. _____ is that which is owed; usually referencing assets owed, but the term can cover other obligations. In the case of assets, _____ is a means of using future purchasing power in the present before a summation has been earned. Some companies and corporations use _____ as a part of their overall corporate finance strategy.

a. Credit cycle

b. Cross-collateralization

c. Partial Payment

d. Debt

21. _____ or net present worth (NPW) is defined as the total present value (PV) of a time series of cash flows. It is a standard method for using the time value of money to appraise long-term projects. Used for capital budgeting, and widely throughout economics, it measures the excess or shortfall of cash flows, in present value terms, once financing charges are met.

a. Tax shield

b. Negative gearing

c. Present value of costs

d. Net present value

22. In economics and business, specifically cost accounting, the _____ is the point at which cost or expenses and revenue are equal: there is no net loss or gain, and one has 'broken even'. A profit or a loss has not been made, although opportunity costs have been paid, and capital has received the risk-adjusted, expected return.

For example, if the business sells less than 200 tables each month, it will make a loss, if it sells more, it will be a profit.

a. Defined contribution plan

b. Market microstructure

c. Fixed asset turnover

d. Break-even point

23. _____ is the value on a given date of a future payment or series of future payments, discounted to reflect the time value of money and other factors such as investment risk. _____ calculations are widely used in business and economics to provide a means to compare cash flows at different times on a meaningful 'like to like' basis.

The most commonly applied model of the time value of money is compound interest.

a. Present value of benefits

b. Net present value

c. Negative gearing

d. Present value

24. _____, refers to consumption opportunity gained by an entity within a specified time frame, which is generally expressed in monetary terms. However, for households and individuals, '_____ is the sum of all the wages, salaries, profits, interests payments, rents and other forms of earnings received... in a given period of time.' For firms, _____ generally refers to net-profit: what remains of revenue after expenses have been subtracted.

a. Annual report   b. OIBDA
c. Income   d. Accrual

25. An _____ is a financial statement for companies that indicates how Revenue is transformed into net income The purpose of the _____ is to show managers and investors whether the company made or lost money during the period being reported.

The important thing to remember about an _____ is that it represents a period of time.

a. ABN Amro   b. A Random Walk Down Wall Street
c. AAB   d. Income statement

26. In marketing, _____ refers to the total cost of holding inventory. This includes warehousing costs such as rent, utilities and salaries, financial costs such as opportunity cost, and inventory costs related to perishibility, shrinkage and insurance.

a. 4-4-5 Calendar   b. 529 plan
c. 7-Eleven   d. Carrying cost

27. _____s are goods that have completed the manufacturing process but have not yet been sold or distributed to the end user.

Manufacturing has three classes of inventory:

1. Raw material
2. Work in process
3. _____s

A good purchased as a 'raw material' goes into the manufacture of a product. A good only partially completed during the manufacturing process is called 'work in process'. When the good is completed as to manufacturing but not yet sold or distributed to the end-user is called a '_____'.

a. 4-4-5 Calendar   b. Finished good
c. 529 plan   d. 7-Eleven

28. _____ is the level of inventory that minimizes the total inventory holding costs and ordering costs. The framework used to determine this order quantity is also known as Wilson _____ Model. The model was developed by F. W. Harris in 1913.

a. AAB   b. A Random Walk Down Wall Street
c. ABN Amro   d. Economic order quantity

29. _____ is an accounting concept used most often in mining, timber, petroluem, or other similar industries. The _____ deduction allows an owner or operator to account for the reduction of a product's reserves. _____ is similar to depreciation in that, it is a cost recovery system for accounting and tax reporting.

a. Net profit   b. Current liabilities
c. Deferred income   d. Depletion

30.   In economics, and cost accounting, _____ describes the total economic cost of production and is made up of variable costs, which vary according to the quantity of a good produced and include inputs such as labor and raw materials, plus fixed costs, which are independent of the quantity of a good produced and include inputs (capital) that cannot be varied in the short term, such as buildings and machinery. _____ in economics includes the total opportunity cost of each factor of production in addition to fixed and variable costs.

The rate at which _____ changes as the amount produced changes is called marginal cost.

a. 4-4-5 Calendar   b. 529 plan
c. 7-Eleven   d. Total cost

31.   The _____ is the level of inventory when a fresh order should be made with suppliers to bring the inventory up by the Economic order quantity ('EOQ'.)

The _____ for replenishment of stock occurs when the level of inventory drops down to zero. In view of instantaneous replenishment of stock the level of inventory jumps to the original level from zero level.

a. 7-Eleven   b. 529 plan
c. 4-4-5 Calendar   d. Reorder point

32.   _____ is a term used by inventory specialists to describe a level of extra stock that is maintained below the cycle stock to buffer against stockouts. _____ exists to counter uncertainties in supply and demand. _____ is defined as extra units of inventory carried as protection against possible stockouts .(shortfall in raw material or packaging.)

a. Safety stock   b. Counting house
c. Golden parachute   d. Funding

33.   In business and finance, a _____ (also referred to as equity _____) of stock means a _____ of ownership in a corporation (company.) In the plural, stocks is often used as a synonym for _____s especially in the United States, but it is less commonly used that way outside of North America.

In the United Kingdom, South Africa, and Australia, stock can also refer to completely different financial instruments such as government bonds or, less commonly, to all kinds of marketable securities.

a. Procter ' Gamble   b. Bucket shop
c. Share   d. Margin

34.   _____ is an inventory strategy implemented to improve the return on investment of a business by reducing in-process inventory and its associated carrying costs. In order to achieve _____ the process must have signals of what is going on elsewhere within the process. This means that the process is often driven by a series of signals, which can be Kanban, that tell production processes when to make the next part.

a. Pac-Man defense   b. Greed and fear
c. Debtor-in-possession financing   d. Just-in-time

35.   A _____ is a set of companies with interlocking business relationships and shareholdings. It is a type of business group.

The prototypical _____ are those which appeared in Japan during the 'economic miracle' following World War II.

a. Zero-coupon bond   b. Relative strength Index
c. Stock split   d. Keiretsu

36.   _____ (also trust indenture or deed of trust) is a legal document issued to lenders and describes key terms such as the interest rate, maturity date, convertibility, pledge, promises, representations, covenants, and other terms of the bond offering. When the Offering Memorandum is prepared in advance of marketing a Bond, the indenture will typically be summarised in the 'Description of Notes' section.
a. Bond indenture   b. Court of Audit of Belgium
c. Fair Labor Standards Act   d. McFadden Act

37.   In finance, _____ occurs when a debtor has not met its legal obligations according to the debt contract, e.g. it has not made a scheduled payment, or has violated a loan covenant (condition) of the debt contract. _____ may occur if the debtor is either unwilling or unable to pay their debt. This can occur with all debt obligations including bonds, mortgages, loans, and promissory notes.
a. Debt validation   b. Credit crunch
c. Vendor finance   d. Default

1. _____ is an area of finance dealing with the financial decisions corporations make and the tools and analysis used to make these decisions. The primary goal of _____ is to maximize corporate value while managing the firm's financial risks. Although it is in principle different from managerial finance which studies the financial decisions of all firms, rather than corporations alone, the main concepts in the study of _____ are applicable to the financial problems of all kinds of firms.

  a. Special purpose entity   b. Gross profit

  c. Cash flow   d. Corporate finance

2. _____ are a currency pair that does not include USD, such as GBP/JPY. Pairs that involve the EUR are called euro crosses, such as EUR/GBP. All other currency pairs (those that don't involve USD or EUR) are generally referred to as

_____.

  a. Cross rates   b. 4-4-5 Calendar

  c. Foreign exchange risk   d. 529 plan

3. A _____ is an international bond that is denominated in a currency not native to the country where it is issued. It can be categorised according to the currency in which it is issued. London is one of the centers of the _____ market, but _____s may be traded throughout the world - for example in Singapore or Tokyo.

  a. Economic entity   b. Interest rate option

  c. Education production function   d. Eurobond

4. _____ is the term used to describe deposits residing in banks that are located outside the borders of the country that issues the currency the deposit is denominated in. For example a deposit denominated in US dollars residing in a Japanese bank is a _____ deposit, or more specifically a Eurodollar deposit.

Key points are the location of the bank and the denomination of the currency, not the nationality of the bank or the owner of the deposit/loan.

  a. Eurocurrency   b. ABN Amro

  c. A Random Walk Down Wall Street   d. AAB

5. _____s are deposits denominated in United States dollars at banks outside the United States, and thus are not under the jurisdiction of the Federal Reserve. Consequently, such deposits are subject to much less regulation than similar deposits within the United States, allowing for higher margins. There is nothing 'European' about _____ deposits; a US dollar-denominated deposit in Tokyo or Caracas would likewise be deemed _____ deposits.

  a. ABN Amro   b. AAB

  c. A Random Walk Down Wall Street   d. Eurodollar

6. _____ are bonds issued by the governments of the United Kingdom, South Africa, or Ireland. The term is of British origin, and refers to the debt securities issued by the Bank of England, which had a gilt (or gilded) edge. Hence, they are called gilt-edged securities, or _____ for short.

These are the simplest form of UK government bond and make up the largest share of UK government debt. A conventional gilt is a bond issued by the UK government which pays the holder a fixed cash payment (or coupon) every six months until maturity, at which point the holder receives their final coupon payment and the return of the principal.

a. Bond fund

b. Zero coupon bond

c. Zero-coupon bond

d. Gilts

7. In finance, a _____ is a debt security, in which the authorized issuer owes the holders a debt and, depending on the terms of the _____, is obliged to pay interest (the coupon) and/or to repay the principal at a later date, termed maturity.

Thus a _____ is a loan: the issuer is the borrower, the _____ holder is the lender, and the coupon is the interest. _____s provide the borrower with external funds to finance long-term investments, or, in the case of government _____s, to finance current expenditure.

a. Puttable bond

b. Catastrophe bonds

c. Bond

d. Convertible bond

8. _____ refers to a business or organization attempting to acquire goods or services to accomplish the goals of the enterprise. Though there are several organizations that attempt to set standards in the _____ process, processes can vary greatly between organizations. Typically the word '_____' is not used interchangeably with the word 'procurement', since procurement typically includes Expediting, Supplier Quality, and Traffic and Logistics (T'L) in addition to _____.

a. Purchasing

b. 529 plan

c. 7-Eleven

d. 4-4-5 Calendar

9. _____ is the value of goods/services compared to the amount paid with a currency. Currency can be either a commodity money, like gold or silver, or fiat currency like US dollars which are the world reserve currency. As Adam Smith noted, having money gives one the ability to 'command' others' labor, so _____ to some extent is power over other people, to the extent that they are willing to trade their labor or goods for money or currency.

a. 4-4-5 Calendar

b. 529 plan

c. 7-Eleven

d. Purchasing power

10. The _____ theory uses the long-term equilibrium exchange rate of two currencies to equalize their purchasing power. Developed by Gustav Cassel in 1920, it is based on the law of one price: the theory states that, in ideally efficient markets, identical goods should have only one price.

This purchasing power SEM rate equalizes the purchasing power of different currencies in their home countries for a given basket of goods.

a. 4-4-5 Calendar

b. Gross national product

c. TED spread

d. Purchasing power parity

11. A _____ is a foreign exchange agreement between two parties to exchange principal and fixed rate interest payments on a loan in one currency for principal and fixed rate interest payments on an equal (regarding net present value) loan in another currency. They are motivated by comparative advantage.

a. Foreign exchange market

b. Currency pair

c. Forex swap

d. Currency swap

12.   The _____ is where currency trading takes place. It is where banks and other official institutions facilitate the buying and selling of foreign currencies. FX transactions typically involve one party purchasing a quantity of one currency in exchange for paying a quantity of another.

a. Foreign exchange option

b. Floating exchange rate

c. Foreign exchange market

d. Spot market

13.   _____ is a fee paid on borrowed assets. It is the price paid for the use of borrowed money , or, money earned by deposited funds . Assets that are sometimes lent with _____ include money, shares, consumer goods through hire purchase, major assets such as aircraft, and even entire factories in finance lease arrangements.

a. AAB

b. A Random Walk Down Wall Street

c. Insolvency

d. Interest

14.   An _____ is the price a borrower pays for the use of money they do not own, and the return a lender receives for deferring the use of funds, by lending it to the borrower. _____s are normally expressed as a percentage rate over the period of one year.

_____s targets are also a vital tool of monetary policy and are used to control variables like investment, inflation, and unemployment.

a. A Random Walk Down Wall Street

b. ABN Amro

c. Interest rate

d. AAB

15.   An _____ is a derivative in which one party exchanges a stream of interest payments for another party's stream of cash flows. _____s can be used by hedgers to manage their fixed or floating assets and liabilities. They can also be used by speculators to replicate unfunded bond exposures to profit from changes in interest rates.

a. International Swaps and Derivatives Association

b. Equity swap

c. Implied volatility

d. Interest rate swap

16.   In finance, a _____ is a derivative in which two counterparties agree to exchange one stream of cash flows against another stream. These streams are called the legs of the _____.

The cash flows are calculated over a notional principal amount, which is usually not exchanged between counterparties.

a. Local volatility

b. Volatility arbitrage

c. Volatility swap

d. Swap

17.   In finance, the _____ between two currencies specifies how much one currency is worth in terms of the other. For example an _____ of 102 Japanese yen to the United States dollar means that JPY 102 is worth the same as USD 1. The foreign exchange market is one of the largest markets in the world.

a. A Random Walk Down Wall Street

b. AAB

c. ABN Amro

d. Exchange rate

18.   _____ refers to taking advantage of a state of imbalance between three foreign exchange markets: a combination of matching deals are struck that exploit the imbalance, the profit being the difference between the market prices.

_____ offers a risk-free profit (in theory), so opportunities for _____ usually disappear quickly, as many people are looking for them, or simply never occur as everybody knows the pricing relation.

Consider the three foreign exchange rates among the Canadian dollar, the U.S. dollar, and the Australian dollar.

a. Floating exchange rate	b. Currency pair
c. Currency future	d. Triangular arbitrage

19.   In economics and finance, _____ is the practice of taking advantage of a price differential between two or more markets: striking a combination of matching deals that capitalize upon the imbalance, the profit being the difference between the market prices. When used by academics, an _____ is a transaction that involves no negative cash flow at any probabilistic or temporal state and a positive cash flow in at least one state; in simple terms, a risk-free profit.

a. Initial margin	b. Issuer
c. Arbitrage	d. Efficient-market hypothesis

20.   The _____ or spot rate of a commodity, a security or a currency is the price that is quoted for immediate (spot) settlement (payment and delivery.) Spot settlement is normally one or two business days from trade date. This is in contrast with the forward price established in a forward contract or futures contract, where contract terms (price) are set now, but delivery and payment will occur at a future date.

a. Cost of carry	b. Central Securities Depository
c. Market price	d. Spot price

21.   _____ is a term used in accounting relating to the increase in value of an asset. In this sense it is the reverse of depreciation, which measures the fall in value of assets over their normal life-time.

_____ is a rise of a currency in a floating exchange rate.

a. Operating cash flow	b. A Random Walk Down Wall Street
c. Other Comprehensive Basis of Accounting	d. Appreciation

22.   _____ is a term used in accounting, economics and finance to spread the cost of an asset over the span of several years.

In simple words we can say that _____ is the reduction in the value of an asset due to usage, passage of time, wear and tear, technological outdating or obsolescence, depletion or other such factors.

In accounting, _____ is a term used to describe any method of attributing the historical or purchase cost of an asset across its useful life, roughly corresponding to normal wear and tear.

a. Deferred financing costs	b. Bottom line
c. Matching principle	d. Depreciation

23. _____ is the investment strategy where an investor buys a financial instrument denominated in a foreign currency, and hedges his foreign exchange risk by selling a forward contract in the amount of the proceeds of the investment back into his base currency. The proceeds of the investment are only known exactly if the financial instrument is risk-free and only pays interest once, on the date of the forward sale of foreign currency. Otherwise, some foreign exchange risk remains.

a. Currency future

b. Covered interest arbitrage

c. Triangular arbitrage

d. Floating exchange rate

24. _____ is an economic concept, expressed as a basic algebraic identity that relates interest rates and exchange rates. The identity is theoretical, and usually follows from assumptions imposed in economics models. There is evidence to support as well as to refute the concept.

a. A Random Walk Down Wall Street

b. AAB

c. Unit price

d. Interest rate parity

25. _____ is a form of risk that arises from the change in price of one currency against another. Whenever investors or companies have assets or business operations across national borders, they face _____ if their positions are not hedged.

- Transaction risk is the risk that exchange rates will change unfavourably over time. It can be hedged against using forward currency contracts;
- Translation risk is an accounting risk, proportional to the amount of assets held in foreign currencies. Changes in the exchange rate over time will render a report inaccurate, and so assets are usually balanced by borrowings in that currency.

The exchange risk associated with a foreign denominated instrument is a key element in foreign investment. This risk flows from differential monetary policy and growth in real productivity, which results in differential inflation rates.

a. Tracking error

b. Currency risk

c. Market risk

d. Credit risk

26. The _____ or forward rate is the agreed upon price of an asset in a forward contract. Using the rational pricing assumption, we can express the _____ in terms of the spot price and any dividends etc., so that there is no possibility for arbitrage.

The _____ is given by:

where

F is the _____ to be paid at time T
e^x is the exponential function
r is the risk-free interest rate
q is the cost-of-carry
S_0 is the spot price of the asset (i.e. what it would sell for at time 0)
D_i is a dividend which is guaranteed to be paid at time t_i where $0 < t_i < T$.

The two questions here are what price the short position (the seller of the asset) should offer to maximize his gain, and what price the long position (the buyer of the asset) should accept to maximize his gain?

At the very least we know that both do not want to lose any money in the deal.

a. Financial Gerontology	b. Biweekly Mortgage
c. Security interest	d. Forward price

27.   The _____ of a commodity, a security or a currency is the price that is quoted for immediate (spot) settlement (payment and delivery.) Spot settlement is normally one or two business days from trade date. This is in contrast with the forward price established in a forward contract or futures contract, where contract terms (price) are set now, but delivery and payment will occur at a future date.

a. Limits to arbitrage	b. Long position
c. Spot rate	d. Market anomaly

28.   In economics, the _____ is the proposition by Irving Fisher that the real interest rate is independent of monetary measures, especially the nominal interest rate. The Fisher equation is

$$r_r = r_n >- >\pi^e.$$

This means, the real interest rate (r_r) equals the nominal interest rate (r_n) minus expected rate of inflation ($>\pi^e$.) Here all the rates are continuously compounded.

a. 529 plan	b. 4-4-5 Calendar
c. 7-Eleven	d. Fisher hypothesis

29.   The _____ is a hypothesis in international finance that says that the difference in the nominal interest rates between two countries determines the movement of the nominal exchange rate between their currencies, with the value of the currency of the country with the lower nominal interest rate increasing. This is also known as the assumption of Uncovered Interest Parity.

The Fisher hypothesis says that the real interest rate in an economy is independent of monetary variables.

a. Interest rate risk

b. International Fisher effect

c. Official bank rate

d. A Random Walk Down Wall Street

30. _____ is the planning process used to determine whether a firm's long term investments such as new machinery, replacement machinery, new plants, new products, and research development projects are worth pursuing. It is budget for major capital, or investment, expenditures.

Many formal methods are used in _____, including the techniques such as

- Net present value
- Profitability index
- Internal rate of return
- Modified Internal Rate of Return
- Equivalent annuity

These methods use the incremental cash flows from each potential investment, or project. Techniques based on accounting earnings and accounting rules are sometimes used - though economists consider this to be improper - such as the accounting rate of return, and 'return on investment.' Simplified and hybrid methods are used as well, such as payback period and discounted payback period.

a. Shareholder value

b. Preferred stock

c. Capital budgeting

d. Financial distress

31. In economics, the concept of the _____ refers to the decision-making time frame of a firm in which at least one factor of production is fixed. Costs which are fixed in the _____ have no impact on a firms decisions. For example a firm can raise output by increasing the amount of labour through overtime.

a. Long-run

b. 4-4-5 Calendar

c. 529 plan

d. Short-run

32. _____ is the balance of the amounts of cash being received and paid by a business during a defined period of time, sometimes tied to a specific project. Measurement of _____ can be used

- to evaluate the state or performance of a business or project.
- to determine problems with liquidity. Being profitable does not necessarily mean being liquid. A company can fail because of a shortage of cash, even while profitable.
- to generate project rate of returns. The time of _____s into and out of projects are used as inputs to financial models such as internal rate of return, and net present value.
- to examine income or growth of a business when it is believed that accrual accounting concepts do not represent economic realities. Alternately, _____ can be used to 'validate' the net income generated by accrual accounting.

_____ as a generic term may be used differently depending on context, and certain _____ definitions may be adapted by analysts and users for their own uses. Common terms include operating _____ and free _____.

_____s can be classified into:

1. Operational _____s: Cash received or expended as a result of the company's core business activities.
2. Investment _____s: Cash received or expended through capital expenditure, investments or acquisitions.
3. Financing _____s: Cash received or expended as a result of financial activities, such as interests and dividends.

All three together - the net _____ - are necessary to reconcile the beginning cash balance to the ending cash balance. Loan draw downs or equity injections, that is just shifting of capital but no expenditure as such, are not considered in the net

_____.

a. Corporate finance   b. Shareholder value
c. Real option   d. Cash flow

33.   _____ are formal records of a business' financial activities.

_____ provide an overview of a business' financial condition in both short and long term. There are four basic _____:

1. **Balance sheet**: also referred to as statement of financial position or condition, reports on a company's assets, liabilities, and net equity as of a given point in time.
2. **Income statement**: also referred to as Profit and Loss statement (or a 'P'L'), reports on a company's income, expenses, and profits over a period of time.
3. **Statement of retained earnings**: explains the changes in a company's retained earnings over the reporting period.
4. **Statement of cash flows**: reports on a company's cash flow activities, particularly its operating, investing and financing activities.

a. Notes to the Financial Statements   b. Statement on Auditing Standards No. 70: Service
                                                    Organizations
c. Statement of retained earnings   d. Financial statements

34.   In economic models, the _____ time frame assumes no fixed factors of production. Firms can enter or leave the marketplace, and the cost (and availability) of land, labor, raw materials, and capital goods can be assumed to vary. In contrast, in the short-run time frame, certain factors are assumed to be fixed, because there is not sufficient time for them to change.
a. 529 plan   b. Short-run
c. 4-4-5 Calendar   d. Long-run

35.   The role of the _____ is to issue accounting standards in the United Kingdom. It is recognised for that purpose under the Companies Act 1985. It took over the task of setting accounting standards from the Accounting Standards Committee (ASC) in 1990.

a. A Random Walk Down Wall Street

b. AAB

c. ABN Amro

d. Accounting Standards Board

36.   The _____ is a private, not-for-profit organization whose primary purpose is to develop generally accepted accounting principles (GAAP) within the United States in the public's interest. The Securities and Exchange Commission (SEC) designated the _____ as the organization responsible for setting accounting standards for public companies in the U.S. It was created in 1973, replacing the Accounting Principles Board and the Committee on Accounting Procedure of the American Institute of Certified Public Accountants. The _____'s mission is 'to establish and improve standards of financial accounting and reporting for the guidance and education of the public, including issuers, auditors, and users of financial information.'

The _____ is not a governmental body.

a. Credit karma

b. FASB

c. MRU Holdings

d. PlaNet Finance

37.   _____ is the field of accountancy concerned with the preparation of financial statements for decision makers, such as stockholders, suppliers, banks, employees, government agencies, owners, and other stakeholders. The fundamental need for _____ is to reduce principal-agent problem by measuring and monitoring agents' performance and reporting the results to interested users.

_____ is used to prepare accounting information for people outside the organization or not involved in the day to day running of the company.

a. 7-Eleven

b. 4-4-5 Calendar

c. 529 plan

d. Financial Accounting

38.   The _____ is a private, not-for-profit organization whose primary purpose is to develop generally accepted accounting principles (GAAP) within the United States in the public's interest. The Securities and Exchange Commission (SEC) designated the _____ as the organization responsible for setting accounting standards for public companies in the U.S. It was created in 1973, replacing the Accounting Principles Board and the Committee on Accounting Procedure of the American Institute of Certified Public Accountants. The _____'s mission is 'to establish and improve standards of financial accounting and reporting for the guidance and education of the public, including issuers, auditors, and users of financial information.'

The _____ is not a governmental body.

a. KPMG

b. Financial Accounting Standards Board

c. Federal Deposit Insurance Corporation

d. World Congress of Accountants

39.   _____ is a type of risk faced by investors, corporations, and governments. It is a risk that can be understood and managed with proper aforethought and investment.

Broadly, _____ refers to the complications businesses and governments may face as a result of what are commonly referred to as political decisions--or 'any political change that alters the expected outcome and value of a given economic action by changing the probability of achieving business objectives.' .

a. Mid price   b. Single-index model

c. Political risk   d. Capital asset

40.   In finance, a _____ is a type of bond that can be converted into shares of stock in the issuing company, usually at some pre-announced ratio. It is a hybrid security with debt- and equity-like features. Although it typically has a low coupon rate, the holder is compensated with the ability to convert the bond to common stock, usually at a substantial discount to the stock's market value.

a. Gilts   b. Corporate bond

c. Bond fund   d. Convertible bond

1. _____ is simply a practice of systematically selecting cost effective approaches for minimizing the effect of threat realization to the organization. All risks can never be fully avoided or mitigated simply because of financial and practical limitations. Therefore all organizations have to accept some level of residual risks.

   a. Thing

   c. Undefined

   b. Risk management1

   d. Undefined

2. _____ comprises directing and controlling a group of one or more people or entities for the purpose of coordinating and harmonizing that group towards accomplishing a goal. _____ often encompasses the deployment and manipulation of human resources, financial resources, technological resources, and natural resources. _____ can also refer to the person or people who perform the act(s) of _____.

   a. Management2

   c. Undefined

   b. Thing

   d. Undefined

3. A _____ is a generic term for specific types of investments from which payoffs over time are derived from the performance of assets, interest rates, exchange rates, or indices or an index of weather conditions).

   a. Thing

   c. Undefined

   b. Derivative3

   d. Undefined

4. _____ is a strategy designed to minimize exposure to an unwanted business risk, while still allowing the business to profit from an investment activity.

   a. Hedging4

   c. Undefined

   b. Thing

   d. Undefined

5. A _____ is a fungible, negotiable instrument representing financial value. They are broadly categorized into debt and equity securities such as bonds and common stocks, respectively.

   a. Security5

   c. Undefined

   b. Thing

   d. Undefined

6. _____ most frequently refers to the standard deviation of the change in value of a financial instrument with a specific time horizon. It is often used to quantify the risk of the instrument over that time period.

   a. Thing

   c. Undefined

   b. Volatility6

   d. Undefined

7. The _____ conference, was a gathering of 730 delegates from all 45 Allied nations at the Mount Washington Hotel, situated in _____, New Hampshire to regulate the international monetary and financial order after the conclusion of World War II.

   a. Event

   c. Undefined

   b. Bretton Woods7

   d. Undefined

8. The _____ of international monetary management established the rules for commercial and financial relations among the world's major industrial states. The _____ was the first example of a fully negotiated monetary order intended to govern monetary relations among independent nation-states.

   a. Thing

   c. Undefined

   b. Bretton Woods system8

   d. Undefined

9. The _____ System was created via the _____ Act of December 23rd, 1913. All national banks were required to join the system and other banks could join. The Reserve Banks opened for business on November 16th, 1914. _____ Notes were created as part of the legislation, to provide an elastic supply of currency.

   a. Federal Reserve9   b. Thing

   c. Undefined   d. Undefined

10. In finance, a _____ is a collection of investments held by an institution or a private individual. Holding but not always a _____ is part of an investment and risk-limiting strategy called diversification. By owning several assets, certain types of risk (in particular specific risk) can be reduced.

   a. Thing   b. Portfolio10

   c. Undefined   d. Undefined

11. _____ is a financial condition experienced by a person or business entity when their assets no longer exceed their liabilities, commonly referred to as 'balance-sheet' _____, or when the person or entity can no longer meet its debt obligations when they come due, commonly referred to as 'cash-flow' _____.

   a. Insolvency11   b. Thing

   c. Undefined   d. Undefined

12. _____ is a fee paid on borrowed money. The fee is a compensation to the lender for foregoing other useful investments that could have been made with the loaned money.

   a. Interest12   b. Thing

   c. Undefined   d. Undefined

13. The rate of return on bonds, loans, or deposits. When one speaks of 'the' _____, it is usually in a model where there is only one.

   a. Interest rate13   b. Thing

   c. Undefined   d. Undefined

14. A _____ is a special kind of ratio, indicating a relationship between two measurements with different units, such as miles to gallons or cents to pounds. For example, suppose one spends 9 dollars on 2 pounds of candy. The _____ $9 / 2 pounds compares the money spent to the number of pounds of candy.or money

   a. Thing   b. Rate14

   c. Undefined   d. Undefined

15. A _____ is a financial institution which specializes in accepting savings deposits and making mortgage loans. They are often mutually held, meaning that the depositors and borrowers are members with voting rights and have the ability to direct the financial and managerial goals of the organization.

   a. Thing   b. Savings and loan15

   c. Undefined   d. Undefined

16. A _____ is something that can be relatively easily traded, be physically delivered and be stored for a reasonable period of time. A characteristic of these is that their prices are determined on the basis of an active market, rather than by the supplier (or other seller) on a "cost-plus" basis.

   a. Commodity16   b. Thing

   c. Undefined   d. Undefined

17.   The risk related to the inability of the firm to meet its debt obligations as they come due is called _____.
a. Thing
b. Financial risk17
c. Undefined
d. Undefined

18.   A group of firms that produce identical or similar products is an _____. It is also used specifically to refer to an area of economic production focused on manufacturing which involves large amounts of capital investment before any profit can be realized, also called "heavy _____".
a. Thing
b. Industry18
c. Undefined
d. Undefined

19.   A _____ is a type of debt. Like all debt instruments, it entails the redistribution of financial assets over time, between the lender and the borrower.
a. Thing
b. Loan19
c. Undefined
d. Undefined

20.   In finance, _____ is the probability that an investment's actual return will be different than expected. This includes the possibility of losing some or all of the original investment. It is usually measured by calculating the standard deviation of the historical returns or average returns of a specific investment.
a. Risk20
b. Thing
c. Undefined
d. Undefined

21.   A financial _____ involves a change in the status of the finances of two or more businesses or individuals.
a. Transaction21
b. Thing
c. Undefined
d. Undefined

22.   In economics, business, and accounting, a _____ is the value of money that has been used up to produce something, and hence is not available for use anymore.
a. Cost22
b. Thing
c. Undefined
d. Undefined

23.   A _____ is an agreement between two parties to buy or sell an asset at a pre-agreed future point in time. Therefore, the trade date and delivery date are separated.
a. Forward contract23
b. Thing
c. Undefined
d. Undefined

24.   _____ of securities is the process whereby securities or interests in securities are delivered, usually against payment, to fulfill contractual obligations, such as those arizing under securities trades. In the context of trusts, a _____ is a deed whereby real estate, land, or other property is given by a settlor into trust so that the beneficiary only has the limited right to the property, but usually has no right to transfer the land to another or leave it in their own will.
a. Settlement24
b. Thing
c. Undefined
d. Undefined

25.   A _____ is a legally binding exchange of promises or agreement between parties that the law will enforce.
a. Thing
b. Contract25
c. Undefined
d. Undefined

26. In finance, a _____ is a standardized contract, traded on a futures exchange, to buy or sell a certain underlying instrument at a certain date in the future, at a pre-set price. The

  a. Futures contract26   b. Thing

  c. Undefined   d. Undefined

27. _____ refers to a recording as positive in the balance of payments, any transaction that gives rise to a payment into the country, such as an export, the sale of an asset, or borrowing from abroad.

  a. Thing   b. Credit27

  c. Undefined   d. Undefined

28. The risk of loss due to a counterparty defaulting on a contract, or more generally the risk of loss due to some "credit event" is called _____.

  a. Thing   b. Credit risk28

  c. Undefined   d. Undefined

29. A _____ is a social arrangement that allows buyers and sellers to discover information and carry out a voluntary exchange of goods or services.

  a. Thing   b. Market29

  c. Undefined   d. Undefined

30. The _____ is the world's oldest futures and options exchange. More than 50 different options and futures contracts are traded by over 3,600 CBOT members through open outcry and eTrading.

  a. Place   b. Chicago Board of Trade30

  c. Undefined   d. Undefined

31. The _____ is the largest futures exchange in the United States. It has four major product areas: short term interest rates, stock market indexes, foreign exchange, and commodities. It has the largest options and futures contracts open interest (number of contracts outstanding) of any futures exchange in the world, which indicates a very high liquidity. This is vital to the success of any stock or futures exchange.

  a. Chicago Mercantile Exchange31   b. Thing

  c. Undefined   d. Undefined

32. The _____ was the name of a futures exchange based in London, prior to its takeover by Euronext in January 2002.

  a. Place   b. London International Financial Futures and Options Exchange32

  c. Undefined   d. Undefined

33. The _____ is the world's largest physical commodity futures exchange, located in New York City.

  a. New York Mercantile Exchange33   b. Place

  c. Undefined   d. Undefined

34. The number of contracts outstanding is an _____. That is, the total contracts for a specific strike price and expiration date, that have been traded, but have not yet expired or been terminated via early exercise.

a. Thing
c. Undefined

b. Open interest34
d. Undefined

35. A contract that gives the purchaser the _____ to buy or sell the underlying financial instrument at a specified price, called the exercise price or strike price, within a specific period of time.
a. Thing
c. Undefined

b. Option35
d. Undefined

36. An _____ is defined as "a promise which meets the requirements for the formation of a contract and limits the promisor's power to revoke an offer."
a. Option contract36
c. Undefined

b. Thing
d. Undefined

37. In finance a _____ is a derivative, where two counterparties exchange one stream of cash flows against another stream. These streams are called the legs of the _____. The cash flows are calculated over a notional principal amount. Swaps are often used to hedge certain risks, for instance interest rate risk. Another use is speculation.
a. Thing
c. Undefined

b. Swap37
d. Undefined

38. _____ is the voluntary exchange of goods, services, or both. _____ is also called commerce. A mechanism that allows _____ is called a market. The original form of _____ was barter, the direct exchange of goods and services. Modern traders instead generally negotiate through a medium of exchange, such as money. As a result, buying can be separated from selling, or earning. The invention of money (and later credit, paper money and non-physical money) greatly simplified and promoted _____. _____ between two traders is called bilateral _____, while _____ between more than two traders is called multilateral _____.
a. Thing
c. Undefined

b. Trade38
d. Undefined

39. A _____ is an exchange which provides a marketplace where one can buy and sell futures; that is a contract to buy specific quantities of a commodity or financial instrument at a specified price with delivery set at a specified time in the future.
a. Thing
c. Undefined

b. Futures exchange39
d. Undefined

40. A _____ is a unit of exchange, facilitating the transfer of goods and services. It is one form of money, where money is anything that serves as a medium of exchange, a store of value, and a standard of value.
a. Thing
c. Undefined

b. Currency40
d. Undefined

41. _____ refers to the exchange of a set of payments in one currency for a set of payments in another currency.
a. Thing
c. Undefined

b. Currency swap41
d. Undefined

42. A popular form of swap is the _____, in which one party exchanges a stream of interest for another party's stream. These were originally created to allow multi-national companies to evade exchange controls. They are normally 'fixed against floating', but can also be 'floating against floating' rate.

a. Thing   b. Interest rate swap42
c. Undefined   d. Undefined

43.   A stock option that can be exercized at any time up to the expiration date of the contract is referred to as _____.
a. Thing   b. American option43
c. Undefined   d. Undefined

44.   _____ refers to an option contract that provides the right to buy a security at a specified price within a certain time period.
a. Call option44   b. Thing
c. Undefined   d. Undefined

45.   An option that can be exercized only at the expiration date of the contract is referred to as _____.
a. European option45   b. Thing
c. Undefined   d. Undefined

46.   The _____ is a key variable in a derivatives contract between two parties. Where the contract requires delivery of the underlying instrument, the trade will be at the strike price, regardless of the spot price of the underlying instrument at that time.
a. Thing   b. Exercise price46
c. Undefined   d. Undefined

47.   An option contract that provides the right to sell a security at a specified price within a specified period of time is a _____.
a. Put option47   b. Thing
c. Undefined   d. Undefined

48.   The withholding of labor services by an organized group of workers is referred to as a _____.
a. Strike48   b. Thing
c. Undefined   d. Undefined

49.   The _____ is a key variable in a derivatives contract between two parties. Where the contract requires delivery of the underlying instrument, the trade will be at the _____, regardless of the spot price of the underlying at that time.
a. Strike price49   b. Thing
c. Undefined   d. Undefined

50.   _____ is the concept or idea of fairness or justice in economics, particularly in terms of taxation and welfare economics. It has been studied in experimental economics as inequity aversion.
a. Equity50   b. Thing
c. Undefined   d. Undefined

51.   _____ refers to the price at which one country's currency trades for another, typically on the exchange market.
a. Exchange rate51   b. Thing
c. Undefined   d. Undefined

52. _____ is a form of risk that arises from the change in price of one currency against another. Whenever investors or companies have assets or business operations across national borders, they face currency risk if their positions are not hedged.

a. Exchange rate risk52   b. Thing

c. Undefined   d. Undefined

53. _____ is the risk that the relative value of a security, especially a bond, will worsen due to an interest rate increase. This risk is commonly measured by the bond's duration.

a. Interest rate risk53   b. Thing

c. Undefined   d. Undefined

54. A _____ is an investment strategy that uses options to limit the possible range of positive or negative returns on an investment in an underlying asset to a specific range. To do this, an investor simultaneously buys a put option and sells writes a call option on that asset. The strike price on the call needs to be above the strike price for the put, and the expiration dates should be the same.

a. Collar54   b. Thing

c. Undefined   d. Undefined

55. A _____ is a financial instrument granting the owner an option to enter into an interest rate swap. A _____ gives the buyer the right but not the obligation to enter into the underlying swap.

a. Swaption55   b. Thing

c. Undefined   d. Undefined

56. _____ refers to a note payable issued for property, such as a house, usually repaid in equal installments consisting of part principle and part interest, over a specified period.

a. Mortgage56   b. Thing

c. Undefined   d. Undefined

1. _____, Inc. is an American e-commerce company based in Seattle, Washington. It was one of the first major companies to sell goods over the Internet and was one of the iconic stocks of the late 1990s dot-com bubble. After the bubble burst Amazon faced skepticism about its business model, but it made its first annual profit in 2003.
   a. Person
   b. Amazon.com1
   c. Undefined
   d. Undefined

2. A _____ is a commercial or state institution that provides financial services, including issuing money in form of coins, banknotes or debit cards, receiving deposits of money, lending money and processing transactions.
   a. Bank2
   b. Person
   c. Undefined
   d. Undefined

3. _____ and Mellon Financial Corporation merged on July 2, 2007. The merged corporation is named The _____ Mellon Corporation. The _____ was founded by Alexander Hamilton in 1784, making it the oldest bank in the United States.
   a. Thing
   b. Bank of New York3
   c. Undefined
   d. Undefined

4. The _____ is one of the world's largest options exchanges with an annual trade of over 450 million options contracts, covering more than 1200 companies, 50 stock indexes, and 50 exchange-traded funds.
   a. Place
   b. Chicago Board Options Exchange4
   c. Undefined
   d. Undefined

5. _____ comprises directing and controlling a group of one or more people or entities for the purpose of coordinating and harmonizing that group towards accomplishing a goal. _____ often encompasses the deployment and manipulation of human resources, financial resources, technological resources, and natural resources. _____ can also refer to the person or people who perform the act(s) of _____.
   a. Management5
   b. Thing
   c. Undefined
   d. Undefined

6. A contract that gives the purchaser the _____ to buy or sell the underlying financial instrument at a specified price, called the exercise price or strike price, within a specific period of time.
   a. Option6
   b. Thing
   c. Undefined
   d. Undefined

7. In financial terminology, _____ is the capital raised by a corporation, through the issuance and sale of shares. A shareholder is any person or organization which owns one or more shares of a corporation's _____.
   a. Thing
   b. Stock7
   c. Undefined
   d. Undefined

8. In finance, _____ is the process of estimating the market value of a financial asset or liability. They can be done on assets (for example, investments in marketable securities such as stocks, options, business enterprises, or intangible assets such as patents and trademarks) or on liabilities (e.g., Bonds issued by a company).
   a. Valuation8
   b. Thing
   c. Undefined
   d. Undefined

9.   The _____ is a key variable in a derivatives contract between two parties. Where the contract requires delivery of the underlying instrument, the trade will be at the strike price, regardless of the spot price of the underlying instrument at that time.
   a. Thing   b. Exercise price9
   c. Undefined   d. Undefined

10.   _____ Corporation is an American multinational computer technology corporation with 76,000 employees in 102 countries and global annual revenue of US $44.28 billion. It develops, manufactures, licenses and supports a wide range of software products for computing devices.
   a. Person   b. Microsoft10
   c. Undefined   d. Undefined

11.   In financial mathematics, _____ defines a relationship between the price of a call option and a put option - both with the identical strike price and expiry.
   a. Put-call parity11   b. Thing
   c. Undefined   d. Undefined

12.   The withholding of labor services by an organized group of workers is referred to as a _____.
   a. Strike12   b. Thing
   c. Undefined   d. Undefined

13.   The _____ is a key variable in a derivatives contract between two parties. Where the contract requires delivery of the underlying instrument, the trade will be at the _____, regardless of the spot price of the underlying at that time.
   a. Thing   b. Strike price13
   c. Undefined   d. Undefined

14.   In economics, purchasing power _____ is an estimate of the exchange rate required to equalise the purchasing power of different currencies, given the prices of goods and services in the countries concerned.
   a. Parity14   b. Thing
   c. Undefined   d. Undefined

15.   _____ refers to an option contract that provides the right to buy a security at a specified price within a certain time period.
   a. Thing   b. Call option15
   c. Undefined   d. Undefined

16.   In economics, a _____ is a theoretical construct that represents economic processes by a set of variables and a set of logical and quantitative relationships between them. As in other fields, models are simplified frameworks designed to illuminate complex processes, often but not always using mathematical techniques.
   a. Thing   b. Model16
   c. Undefined   d. Undefined

17.   _____ is the manual or automatic process of applying prices to purchase and sales orders, based on factors such as: a fixed amount, quantity break, promotion or sales campaign, specific vendor quote, price prevailing on entry, shipment or invoice date, combination of multiple orders or lines, and many others.

a. Pricing17

b. Thing

c. Undefined

d. Undefined

18.   An option contract that provides the right to sell a security at a specified price within a specified period of time is a

_____.

a. Thing

b. Put option18

c. Undefined

d. Undefined

19.   A stock option that can be exercized at any time up to the expiration date of the contract is referred to as _____.

a. Thing

b. American option19

c. Undefined

d. Undefined

20.   _____ is the term denoting either an entrance or changes which are inserted into a system and which
activate/modify a process. It is an abstract concept, used in the modeling, system(s) design and system(s) exploitation.

a. Input20

b. Thing

c. Undefined

d. Undefined

21.   _____ is a legal contract written in duplicate on the same sheet, with the copies separated by cutting along a jagged
line so that the teeth of the two parts could later be refitted to confirm authenticity.

a. Indenture21

b. Thing

c. Undefined

d. Undefined

22.   _____ refers to as applied to a warrant, this represents the market value of common stock minus the exercise price.
The difference is then multiplied by the number of shares each warrant entitles the holder to purchase.

a. Intrinsic value22

b. Thing

c. Undefined

d. Undefined

23.   In finance, _____ is a representation of the risk associated with a given security or the risk of a portfolio of securities.

a. Thing

b. Standard deviation23

c. Undefined

d. Undefined

24.   A _____ is a special kind of ratio, indicating a relationship between two measurements with different units, such as
miles to gallons or cents to pounds. For example, suppose one spends 9 dollars on 2 pounds of candy. The _____ $9 / 2
pounds compares the money spent to the number of pounds of candy.or money

a. Rate24

b. Thing

c. Undefined

d. Undefined

25.   _____ refers to an account, usually for a year, of the planned expenditures and the expected receipts of an entity.
For a government, the receipts are tax revenues.

a. Budget25

b. Thing

c. Undefined

d. Undefined

26.   A _____ is an investment transaction by which the entire or a controlling part of the stock of a company is sold. A
firm buysout the stake of the company to strengthen its influence on the company's decision making body. A _____ can
take the forms of a leveraged _____ or a management _____.

a. Buyout26   b. Thing
c. Undefined   d. Undefined

27. _____ is the concept or idea of fairness or justice in economics, particularly in terms of taxation and welfare economics. It has been studied in experimental economics as inequity aversion.
a. Equity27   b. Thing
c. Undefined   d. Undefined

28. In finance, a _____ is a debt security, in which the authorized issuer owes the holders a debt and is obliged to repay the principal and interest at a later date, termed maturity.
a. Bond28   b. Thing
c. Undefined   d. Undefined

29. A _____ is a final product of a specific mental/cognitive process by an individual or group. Therefore it is a subjective concept. It is a mental object and can be an opinion, a rule or a task for execution/application.
a. Thing   b. Decision29
c. Undefined   d. Undefined

30. _____ refers to the aspect of corporate strategy, corporate finance and management dealing with the buying, selling and combining of different companies that can aid, finance, or help a growing company in a given industry grow rapidly without having to create another business entity.
a. Merger30   b. Thing
c. Undefined   d. Undefined

31. _____ is an insurance-related term that often describes a splitting or spreading of risk among multiple parties.
a. Thing   b. Coinsurance31
c. Undefined   d. Undefined

32. _____ generally refers to financial wealth, especially that used to start or maintain a business. In classical economics, _____ is one of four factors of production, the others being land and labor and entrepreneurship.
a. Thing   b. Capital32
c. Undefined   d. Undefined

33. _____ is the planning process used to determine a firm's long term investments such as new machinery, replacement machinery, new plants, new products, and research and development projects.
a. Thing   b. Capital budgeting33
c. Undefined   d. Undefined

34. An _____ is a stock option for the company's own stock that is often offered to upper-level employees as part of the executive compenzation package, especially by American corporations. An _____ is identical to a call option on the company's stock, with some extra restrictions.
a. Employee stock option34   b. Thing
c. Undefined   d. Undefined

35. A _____ is a specific type of option that uses the stock itself as an underlying instrument to determine the option's pay-off and therefore its value.

a. Stock option35   b. Thing

c. Undefined   d. Undefined

1.   The phrase _____ refers to the aspect of corporate finance strategy and management dealing with the merging and acquiring of different companies as well as other assets. Usually mergers occur in a friendly setting where executives from the respective companies participate in a due diligence process to ensure a successful combination of all parts.
    a. Mergers and acquisitions1   b. Thing
    c. Undefined   d. Undefined

2.   _____ refers to the aspect of corporate strategy, corporate finance and management dealing with the buying, selling and combining of different companies that can aid, finance, or help a growing company in a given industry grow rapidly without having to create another business entity.
    a. Merger2   b. Thing
    c. Undefined   d. Undefined

3.   A _____ is an obstacle which makes it difficult to achieve a desired goal, objective or purpose. It refers to a situation, condition, or issue that is yet unresolved. In a broad sense, a _____ exists when an individual becomes aware of a significant difference between what actually is and what is desired.
    a. Thing   b. Problem3
    c. Undefined   d. Undefined

4.   _____ is an offer of setting a price one is willing to pay for something. A price offer is called a bid. The term may be used in context of auctions, stock exchange or card games.
    a. Thing   b. Bidding4
    c. Undefined   d. Undefined

5.   In business, _____ often refers to the mergers or acquisitions of many smaller companies into much larger ones. The financial accounting term of _____ refers to the aggregated financial statements of a group company as consolidated account.
    a. Thing   b. Consolidation5
    c. Undefined   d. Undefined

6.   An item of property, such as land, capital, money, a share in ownership, or a claim on others for future payment, such as a bond or a bank deposit is an _____.
    a. Asset6   b. Thing
    c. Undefined   d. Undefined

7.   A public offer by a bidder to purchase a subject company's shares directly from its shareholders at a specified price for a fixed period of time is called _____.
    a. Tender offer7   b. Thing
    c. Undefined   d. Undefined

8.   In financial terminology, _____ is the capital raised by a corporation, through the issuance and sale of shares. A shareholder is any person or organization which owns one or more shares of a corporation's _____.
    a. Stock8   b. Thing
    c. Undefined   d. Undefined

9.   A _____ is a commercial or state institution that provides financial services, including issuing money in form of coins, banknotes or debit cards, receiving deposits of money, lending money and processing transactions.

a. Person

b. Bank9

c. Undefined

d. Undefined

10. A _____ is a large company that consists of divisions of often seemingly unrelated businesses.

a. Conglomerate10

b. Thing

c. Undefined

d. Undefined

11. A legal entity chartered by a state or the Federal government that is distinct and separate from the individuals who own it is a _____. This separation gives the _____ unique powers which other legal entities lack.

a. Thing

b. Corporation11

c. Undefined

d. Undefined

12. _____ comprises directing and controlling a group of one or more people or entities for the purpose of coordinating and harmonizing that group towards accomplishing a goal. _____ often encompasses the deployment and manipulation of human resources, financial resources, technological resources, and natural resources. _____ can also refer to the person or people who perform the act(s) of _____.

a. Thing

b. Management12

c. Undefined

d. Undefined

13. _____ refers to a note payable issued for property, such as a house, usually repaid in equal installments consisting of part principle and part interest, over a specified period.

a. Mortgage13

b. Thing

c. Undefined

d. Undefined

14. _____ Corporation, based in Charlotte, North Carolina is one of the largest banking chains in the United States. _____ is a diversified financial services company that provides a broad range of banking, asset management, wealth management, and corporate and investment banking products and services. It is one of the largest providers of financial services in the United States, operating financial centers in 21 states and Washington D.C., with locations from Connecticut to Florida and west to California.

a. Person

b. Wachovia14

c. Undefined

d. Undefined

15. A _____ is an investment transaction by which the entire or a controlling part of the stock of a company is sold. A firm buysout the stake of the company to strengthen its influence on the company's decision making body. A _____ can take the forms of a leveraged _____ or a management _____.

a. Buyout15

b. Thing

c. Undefined

d. Undefined

16. A _____ in business refers to one company purchasing another. In the UK the term properly refers to the acquisition of a public company whose shares are listed on a stock exchange, in contrast to the acquisition of a private company.

a. Takeover16

b. Thing

c. Undefined

d. Undefined

17. A financial _____ involves a change in the status of the finances of two or more businesses or individuals.

a. Thing
b. Transaction17
c. Undefined
d. Undefined

18.   A system that collects and processes financial information about an organization and reports that information to decision makers is referred to as _____ .
a. Thing
b. Accounting18
c. Undefined
d. Undefined

19.   _____ generally refers to financial wealth, especially that used to start or maintain a business. In classical economics, _____ is one of four factors of production, the others being land and labor and entrepreneurship.
a. Capital19
b. Thing
c. Undefined
d. Undefined

20.   _____ refers to the gain in value that the owner of an asset experiences when the price of the asset rises, including when the currency in which the asset is denominated appreciates.
a. Capital gain20
b. Thing
c. Undefined
d. Undefined

21.   _____ is the branch of accountancy concerned with the preparation of financial statements for external decision makers, such as stockholders, suppliers, banks and government agencies. The fundamental need for _____ is to reduce principal-agent problem by measuring and monitoring agents' performance.
a. Financial Accounting21
b. Thing
c. Undefined
d. Undefined

22.   _____ refers to an undertaking by two parties for a specific purpose and duration, taking any of several legal forms.
a. Joint venture22
b. Thing
c. Undefined
d. Undefined

23.   In finance, _____ is a profit or an increase in value of an investment such as a stock or bond. _____ is calculated by fair market value or the proceeds from the sale of the investment minus the sum of the purchase price and all costs associated with it.
a. Gain23
b. Thing
c. Undefined
d. Undefined

24.   A _____ is a formal relationship formed between two or more parties to pursue a set of agreed upon goals or to meet a critical business need while remaining independent organizations.
a. Thing
b. Strategic alliance24
c. Undefined
d. Undefined

25.   A _____ is a financial charge or other levy imposed on an individual or a legal entity by a state or a functional equivalent of a state for example, tribes, secessionist movements or revolutionary movements.
a. Tax25
b. Thing
c. Undefined
d. Undefined

26.   The role of the _____ is to issue accounting standards in the United Kingdom. It is recognized for that purpose under the Companies Act 1985. It took over the task of setting accounting standards from the Accounting Standards Committee (ASC) in 1990.

a. Organization   b. Accounting Standards Board26

c. Undefined   d. Undefined

27.   The _____ is a private, not-for-profit organization whose primary purpose is to develop generally accepted accounting principles within the United States in the public's interest.

a. Financial Accounting Standards Board27   b. Person

c. Undefined   d. Undefined

28.   _____ is an accounting term used to reflect the portion of the market value of a business entity not directly attributable to its assets and liabilities; it normally arises only in case of an acquisition. It reflects the ability of the entity to make a higher profit than would be derived from selling the tangible assets.

a. Goodwill28   b. Thing

c. Undefined   d. Undefined

29.   _____ refers to the method under which income and expenses are determined for tax purposes. Important accounting methods include the cash basis and the accrual basis.

a. Accounting method29   b. Thing

c. Undefined   d. Undefined

30.   The term _____ is the grouping together of assets, samples, equipment etc. for the purposes of maximizing advantage to the users. The term is used in many disciplines.

a. Pooling30   b. Thing

c. Undefined   d. Undefined

31.   _____ refers to a method of financial recording for mergers, in which the financial statements of the firms are combined, subject to minor adjustments, and goodwill is not created.

a. Thing   b. Pooling of interests31

c. Undefined   d. Undefined

32.   _____ is a fee paid on borrowed money. The fee is a compensation to the lender for foregoing other useful investments that could have been made with the loaned money.

a. Thing   b. Interest32

c. Undefined   d. Undefined

33.   Promoting and selling products or services to customers, or prospective customers, is referred to as _____.

a. Thing   b. Marketing33

c. Undefined   d. Undefined

34.   _____ is a business term for the amount of money that a company receives from its activities in a given period, mostly from sales of products and/or services to customers

a. Thing   b. Revenue34

c. Undefined   d. Undefined

35. In economics, returns to scale and _____ are related terms that describe what happens as the scale of production increases. They are different terms and not to be used interchangeably.
    a. Economies of scale35
    c. Undefined
    b. Thing
    d. Undefined

36. A _____ is a social arrangement that allows buyers and sellers to discover information and carry out a voluntary exchange of goods or services.
    a. Thing
    c. Undefined
    b. Market36
    d. Undefined

37. The ability of a single economic actor to have a substantial influence on market prices is _____.
    a. Concept
    c. Undefined
    b. Market power37
    d. Undefined

38. In economics, business, and accounting, a _____ is the value of money that has been used up to produce something, and hence is not available for use anymore.
    a. Cost38
    c. Undefined
    b. Thing
    d. Undefined

39. At least five definitions of _____ have been used in economics depending on its usage: purchasing _____, monopoly _____, bargaining _____, managerial _____, class _____ in Marxian political economy. In general, those with more _____ also have more freedom than others and may be able to exploit others in society and/or cause some sort of market failure.
    a. Power39
    c. Undefined
    b. Thing
    d. Undefined

40. A _____ is an individual or company (including a corporation) that legally owns one or more shares of stock in a joined stock company. The shareholders are the owners of a corporation. Companies listed at the stock market strive to enhance shareholder value.
    a. Thing
    c. Undefined
    b. Stockholder40
    d. Undefined

41. _____ refers to the process of dividing total fixed costs by more units of output. Average fixed cost declines as quantity rises.
    a. Spreading overhead41
    c. Undefined
    b. Thing
    d. Undefined

42. _____ refers to production of different stages of processing of a product within the same firm.
    a. Thing
    c. Undefined
    b. Vertical integration42
    d. Undefined

43. Economic _____ refers to reducing barriers among countries to transactions and to movements of goods, capital, and labor, including harmonization of laws, regulations, and standards. Integrated markets theoretically function as a unified market.

a. Thing
c. Undefined

b. Integration43
d. Undefined

44. In business, _____, _____ cost or _____ expense refers to an ongoing expense of operating a business.
a. Thing
c. Undefined

b. Overhead44
d. Undefined

45. _____ is the quantity of some thing that remains after activity relating to the production of that thing has been completed, or where the requirement to produce or possess the thing has been met. Anything which is redundant or no longer useful may be described as "_____ to requirements".
a. Surplus45
c. Undefined

b. Thing
d. Undefined

46. _____ is that which is owed; usually referencing assets owed, but the term can cover other obligations. In the case of assets, _____ is a means of using future purchasing power in the present before a summation has been earned.
a. Thing
c. Undefined

b. Debt46
d. Undefined

47. Any cost associated with bringing buyers and sellers together is referred to as _____.
a. Transactions cost47
c. Undefined

b. Thing
d. Undefined

48. _____ is the concept or idea of fairness or justice in economics, particularly in terms of taxation and welfare economics. It has been studied in experimental economics as inequity aversion.
a. Equity48
c. Undefined

b. Thing
d. Undefined

49. _____ refers to annual profit of the corporation divided by the number of shares outstanding.
a. Earnings per share49
c. Undefined

b. Thing
d. Undefined

50. In finance a _____ is a unit of account for various financial instruments including stocks, mutual funds, limited partnerships, and REIT's.
a. Thing
c. Undefined

b. Share50
d. Undefined

51. A _____ is a piece of land over which other people could exercise one of a number of traditional rights, such as allowing their cattle to graze upon it. By extension, the term has come to be applied to other resources which a community has rights or access.
a. Thing
c. Undefined

b. Common51
d. Undefined

52. _____ refers to the basic, normal, voting stock issued by a corporation; called residual equity because it ranks after preferred stock for dividend and liquidation distributions.

a. Thing   b. Common stock52
c. Undefined   d. Undefined

53.   A _____ is a document bestowing certain rights on a town, city, university, land or institution; sometimes used as a loan of money. The Canadian Charter of Rights and Freedoms is a bill of rights.
a. Person   b. Corporate charter53
c. Undefined   d. Undefined

54.   An arrangement whereby the Fed, or another party, purchases securities with the understanding that the seller will repurchase them in a short period of time, usually less than a week is a _____.
a. Repurchase agreement54   b. Thing
c. Undefined   d. Undefined

55.   _____ refers to a commitment to refrain from introducing new measures such as trade barriers that are not consistent with an agreement. Such commitments are usually offered at the start of multilateral trade negotiations as an indication of good faith.
a. Standstill55   b. Thing
c. Undefined   d. Undefined

56.   A _____ is usually an instrument of a hostile takeover defense, in which an unfriendly bidder agrees to limit its holdings of a target firm. In many cases, the target firm is willing to purchase the potential raider's shares at a premium price, thereby enacting a standstill or eliminating any takeover chance.
a. Standstill agreement56   b. Thing
c. Undefined   d. Undefined

57.   In business, a _____ may be a corporation, a private company, or a person that intends to help another firm. There are many types of white knights. Alternatively, a gray knight is an acquiring company that enters a bid for a hostile takeover in addition to the target firm and first bidder, perceived as more favorable than the black knight (unfriendly bidder), but less favorable than the _____ (friendly bidder).
a. Person   b. White knight57
c. Undefined   d. Undefined

58.   _____ is terminology, much like slang, that relates to a specific activity, profession, or group to express ideas that are frequently discussed between members.
a. Jargon58   b. Thing
c. Undefined   d. Undefined

59.   The _____ is a defensive option to stave off a hostile takeover. It is when a company that is under a hostile takeover acquires its would-be buyer.
a. Thing   b. Pac-man defense59
c. Undefined   d. Undefined

60.   _____ is a measurement of corporate or economic size equal to the share price times the number of shares outstanding of a public company. As owning stock represents owning the company, including all its assets, _____ could represent the public opinion of a company's net worth and is a determining factor in stock valuation.

a. Capitalization60　　　　　　　　　　b. Thing

c. Undefined　　　　　　　　　　　　　d. Undefined

61.　In finance and economics, _____ is the reduction of some kind of asset, for either financial or social goals. A divestment is the opposite of an investment.

a. Divestiture61　　　　　　　　　　　b. Thing

c. Undefined　　　　　　　　　　　　　d. Undefined

62.　A _____ is a new organization or entity formed by a split from a larger one, such as a television series based on a pre-existing one, or as a new company formed from a university research group or business incubator.

a. Spin-off62　　　　　　　　　　　　b. Thing

c. Undefined　　　　　　　　　　　　d. Undefined

63.　_____ is the corporate management term for the act of partially dismantling or otherwise reorganizing a company for the purpose of making it more efficient and therefore more profitable. It generally involves selling off portions of the company and making severe staff reductions.

a. Thing　　　　　　　　　　　　　　b. Restructuring63

c. Undefined　　　　　　　　　　　　d. Undefined

64.　The _____ are the result of the U.S. Department of Justice antitrust suit against American Telephone & Telegraph. AT&T settled the suit and agreed to divest its local exchange service operating companies in return for a chance to go into the Internet services industry. AT&T's local operations were split into seven independent _____.

a. Baby Bells64　　　　　　　　　　　b. Thing

c. Undefined　　　　　　　　　　　　d. Undefined

65.　_____ is a process that allows beings to exchange information by several methods requiring that some kinds of symbols from a kind of language are exchanged.

a. Communication65　　　　　　　　　b. Thing

c. Undefined　　　　　　　　　　　　d. Undefined

66.　_____ was founded in July 1802 as a gun powder mill by Eleuthère Irénée _____ on Brandywine Creek, near Wilmington, Delaware, USA. _____ is currently the world's second largest chemical company in terms of market capitalization and fourth in revenue.

a. Person　　　　　　　　　　　　　　b. DuPont66

c. Undefined　　　　　　　　　　　　d. Undefined

67.　_____ Roebuck and Company is an American mid-range chain of international department stores, founded by Richard _____ and Alvah Roebuck in the late 19th century. From its mail order beginnings, the company grew to become the largest retailer in the United States by the mid-20th century, and its catalogs became famous. Competition and changes in the demographics of its customer base challenged the company after World War II as its rural and inner city strongholds shrank and the suburban markets grew

a. Person　　　　　　　　　　　　　　b. Sears67

c. Undefined　　　　　　　　　　　　d. Undefined

1. The _____ Company, or GE is a multinational American technology and services conglomerate incorporated in the State of New York. In terms of market capitalization, G.E. is the world's second largest company. In the 1960s, aspects of U.S. tax laws and accounting practices led to a rise in the assembly of conglomerates.
   a. Thing
   b. General Electric1
   c. Undefined
   d. Undefined

2. _____ is the right to use or occupy personal property or real property given by a lessor to another person for a fixed or indefinite period of time, whereby the lessee obtains exclusive possession of the property in return for paying the lessor a fixed or determinable consideration.
   a. Leasing2
   b. Thing
   c. Undefined
   d. Undefined

3. A legal entity chartered by a state or the Federal government that is distinct and separate from the individuals who own it is a _____. This separation gives the _____ unique powers which other legal entities lack.
   a. Thing
   b. Corporation3
   c. Undefined
   d. Undefined

4. _____ studies and addresses the ways in which individuals, businesses, and organizations raise, allocate, and use monetary resources over time, taking into account the risks entailed in their projects.
   a. Thing
   b. Finance4
   c. Undefined
   d. Undefined

5. _____ Corporation, also known as GM is the world's 2nd largest auto company by sales revenue as of the first sales quarter of 2007 (behind Toyota Motor Company). Founded in 1908, in Flint, Michigan, GM employs approximately 284,000 people around the world. With global headquarters at the Renaissance Center in Detroit, Michigan, USA, GM manufactures its cars and trucks in 33 countries.
   a. General Motors5
   b. Person
   c. Undefined
   d. Undefined

6. A _____ is defined as a contractual agreement between a lessor and lessee that gives the lessee the right to use specific property, either owned by or in the possession of the lessor, for a specified period of time in return for stipulated, and generally periodic, cash payment.
   a. Lease6
   b. Thing
   c. Undefined
   d. Undefined

7. One who rents property from another. In the case of real estate, the _____ is also known as the tenant.
   a. Lessee7
   b. Thing
   c. Undefined
   d. Undefined

8. The _____ is the person or comapany who leases the building, car, or other property to the lessee
   a. Thing
   b. Lessor8
   c. Undefined
   d. Undefined

9. A _____ is a unit of exchange, facilitating the transfer of goods and services. It is one form of money, where money is anything that serves as a medium of exchange, a store of value, and a standard of value.

a. Currency9

b. Thing

c. Undefined

d. Undefined

10. In finance, a _____ is a debt security, in which the authorized issuer owes the holders a debt and is obliged to repay the principal and interest at a later date, termed maturity.

a. Thing

b. Bond10

c. Undefined

d. Undefined

11. A long-term, non-cancelable lease is a _____. The _____ has all the characteristics of long-term debt.

a. Thing

b. Financial lease11

c. Undefined

d. Undefined

12. In financial accounting, _____, refers to the amount of cash a company generates from the revenues it brings in, excluding costs associated with long-term investment on capital items or investment in securities.

a. Operating cash flow12

b. Thing

c. Undefined

d. Undefined

13. An _____ is a lease whose term is short compared to the useful life of the asset or piece of equipment an airliner, a ship etc. being leased. An _____ is commonly used to acquire equipment on a relatively short-term basis. Thus, for example, an aircraft which has an economic life of 25 years may be leased to an airline for 5 years on an _____.

a. Thing

b. Operating lease13

c. Undefined

d. Undefined

14. _____ generally refers to financial wealth, especially that used to start or maintain a business. In classical economics, _____ is one of four factors of production, the others being land and labor and entrepreneurship.

a. Capital14

b. Thing

c. Undefined

d. Undefined

15. _____ is a term that refers to the amount of cash being received and spent by a business during a defined period of time, sometimes tied to a specific project. The _____ statement is one of the four main financial statements of a company. The _____ statement can be examined to determine the short-term sustainability of a company.

a. Cash flow15

b. Thing

c. Undefined

d. Undefined

16. A _____ is a piece of land over which other people could exercise one of a number of traditional rights, such as allowing their cattle to graze upon it. By extension, the term has come to be applied to other resources which a community has rights or access.

a. Common16

b. Thing

c. Undefined

d. Undefined

17. _____ refers to the basic, normal, voting stock issued by a corporation; called residual equity because it ranks after preferred stock for dividend and liquidation distributions.

a. Thing

b. Common stock17

c. Undefined

d. Undefined

18. The _____ requires the tenant to pay, in addition to the fixed rent, some or all all of the property expenses which normally would be paid by the property owner. These include expenses such as real estate taxes, insurance, maintenance, repairs, utilities and other items.

   a. Net lease18   b. Thing

   c. Undefined   d. Undefined

19. _____ is the act of meeting prospective buyers and providing them with a product or service in turn of money or other required compensation.

   a. Thing   b. Selling19

   c. Undefined   d. Undefined

20. In financial terminology, _____ is the capital raised by a corporation, through the issuance and sale of shares. A shareholder is any person or organization which owns one or more shares of a corporation's _____.

   a. Thing   b. Stock20

   c. Undefined   d. Undefined

21. A system that collects and processes financial information about an organization and reports that information to decision makers is referred to as _____.

   a. Accounting21   b. Thing

   c. Undefined   d. Undefined

22. The role of the _____ is to issue accounting standards in the United Kingdom. It is recognized for that purpose under the Companies Act 1985. It took over the task of setting accounting standards from the Accounting Standards Committee (ASC) in 1990.

   a. Organization   b. Accounting Standards Board22

   c. Undefined   d. Undefined

23. _____ is a global financial services provider operating in Europe, United States, Middle East, Latin America, Australia, Asia and Africa. It is a holding company that is listed in London and New York. It consists almost solely of Barclays Bank plc. _____ is the 4th largest financial services provider in the world by Tier 1 capital and the 28th largest in the world by Market capitalization.

   a. Barclays PLC23   b. Thing

   c. Undefined   d. Undefined

24. _____ is the branch of accountancy concerned with the preparation of financial statements for external decision makers, such as stockholders, suppliers, banks and government agencies. The fundamental need for _____ is to reduce principal-agent problem by measuring and monitoring agents' performance.

   a. Thing   b. Financial Accounting24

   c. Undefined   d. Undefined

25. The _____ is a private, not-for-profit organization whose primary purpose is to develop generally accepted accounting principles within the United States in the public's interest.

   a. Financial Accounting Standards Board25   b. Person

   c. Undefined   d. Undefined

26. _____ usually means an asset or debt or financing activity not on the company's balance sheet. It could involve a lease or a separate subsidiary or a contingent liability such as a letter of credit. It also involves loan commitments, futures, forwards and other derivatives, when-issued securities and loans sold.

a. Thing
b. Off balance sheet26
c. Undefined
d. Undefined

27. In financial mathematics, _____ defines a relationship between the price of a call option and a put option - both with the identical strike price and expiry.

a. Thing
b. Put-call parity27
c. Undefined
d. Undefined

28. In economics, purchasing power _____ is an estimate of the exchange rate required to equalise the purchasing power of different currencies, given the prices of goods and services in the countries concerned.

a. Thing
b. Parity28
c. Undefined
d. Undefined

29. _____ is an American electronic stock exchange. It was founded in 1971 by the National Association of Securities Dealers who divested it in a series of sales in 2000 and 2001.

a. NASDAQ29
b. Thing
c. Undefined
d. Undefined

30. A _____ is a financial charge or other levy imposed on an individual or a legal entity by a state or a functional equivalent of a state for example, tribes, secessionist movements or revolutionary movements.

a. Thing
b. Tax30
c. Undefined
d. Undefined

31. A _____ is a type of debt. Like all debt instruments, it entails the redistribution of financial assets over time, between the lender and the borrower.

a. Loan31
b. Thing
c. Undefined
d. Undefined

32. _____ is a standard method in finance of capital budgeting – the planning of long-term investments. Using this method a potential investment project should be undertaken if the present value of all cash inflows minus the present value of all cash outflows (which equals the _____) is greater than zero.

a. Thing
b. Net present value32
c. Undefined
d. Undefined

33. The value today of a stream of payments and/or receipts over time in the future and/or the past, converted to the present using an interest rate. If X t is the amount in period t and r the interest rate, then _____ at time t=0 is V = ?T /t.

a. Present value33
b. Thing
c. Undefined
d. Undefined

34. _____ is the systematic determination of merit, worth, and significance of something or someone. _____ often is used to characterize and appraise subjects of interest in a wide range of human enterprises,

a. Evaluation34   b. Thing

c. Undefined   d. Undefined

35.   As used in economics, _____ means something unexpected, rather than the more extreme normal meaning of something seemingly impossible. Some paradoxes are just theoretical results that go against what one thinks of as normal.
 a. Paradox35   b. Thing
 c. Undefined   d. Undefined

36.   A _____ or commodity in economics is any object or service that increases utility, directly or indirectly, not be confused with _____ in a moral or ethical sense. A _____ that cannot be used by consumers directly, such as an office building or capital equipment, can also be referred to as a _____ as an indirect source of utility through resale value or as a source of income.
 a. Good36   b. Thing
 c. Undefined   d. Undefined

37.   _____ payments can refer to an ongoing stream of payments in respect of the completion of past achievements.
 a. Residual37   b. Thing
 c. Undefined   d. Undefined

38.   _____ is one of the constituents of a leasing calculus or operation. It describes the future value of a good in terms of percentage of depreciation of its initial value.
 a. Thing   b. Residual value38
 c. Undefined   d. Undefined

39.   In accounting, the _____ of an asset is its remaining value after depreciation. The estimated value of an asset at the end of its useful life.
 a. Salvage value39   b. Thing
 c. Undefined   d. Undefined

40.   The _____ was the name of a futures exchange based in London, prior to its takeover by Euronext in January 2002.
 a. Place   b. London International Financial Futures and Options Exchange40
 c. Undefined   d. Undefined

41.   In economics, business, and accounting, a _____ is the value of money that has been used up to produce something, and hence is not available for use anymore.
 a. Thing   b. Cost41
 c. Undefined   d. Undefined

42.   _____, generally defined, is the money that is received as a result of the normal business activities of an individual or a business.
 a. Income42   b. Thing
 c. Undefined   d. Undefined

43. A _____ is a fungible, negotiable instrument representing financial value. They are broadly categorized into debt and equity securities such as bonds and common stocks, respectively.

   a. Thing

   b. Security43

   c. Undefined

   d. Undefined

44. A financial _____ involves a change in the status of the finances of two or more businesses or individuals.

   a. Transaction44

   b. Thing

   c. Undefined

   d. Undefined

45. A _____ is a cost incurred in making an economic exchange. For example, most people, when buying or selling a stock, must pay a commission to their broker; that commission is a _____ of doing the stock deal.

   a. Thing

   b. Transaction cost45

   c. Undefined

   d. Undefined

46. A _____ is a final product of a specific mental/cognitive process by an individual or group. Therefore it is a subjective concept. It is a mental object and can be an opinion, a rule or a task for execution/application.

   a. Thing

   b. Decision46

   c. Undefined

   d. Undefined

47. _____ is a financial condition experienced by a person or business entity when their assets no longer exceed their liabilities, commonly referred to as 'balance-sheet' _____, or when the person or entity can no longer meet its debt obligations when they come due, commonly referred to as 'cash-flow' _____.

   a. Thing

   b. Insolvency47

   c. Undefined

   d. Undefined

Chapter 1

1. b	2. d	3. d	4. c	5. d	6. d	7. a	8. c	9. b	10. d
11. d	12. a	13. d	14. d	15. b	16. d	17. d	18. d	19. d	20. a
21. c	22. d	23. d	24. d	25. a	26. c	27. c	28. d	29. b	30. d
31. b	32. c	33. b	34. b	35. d	36. d	37. d	38. d	39. a	40. d
41. c	42. c	43. d	44. d	45. d	46. d	47. b	48. a	49. b	

Chapter 2

1. b	2. b	3. b	4. d	5. a	6. d	7. d	8. a	9. b	10. b
11. b	12. d	13. d	14. d	15. c	16. c	17. d	18. d	19. a	20. b
21. d	22. d	23. d	24. a	25. a	26. a	27. d	28. c	29. d	30. d
31. d	32. d	33. d	34. a	35. c	36. d	37. d	38. b	39. c	

Chapter 3

1. b	2. c	3. c	4. b	5. c	6. b	7. d	8. b	9. a	10. d
11. d	12. d	13. d	14. a	15. a	16. c	17. d	18. a	19. d	20. a
21. a	22. b	23. b	24. d	25. d	26. b	27. d	28. b	29. a	30. d
31. d	32. d	33. d	34. a	35. b	36. d	37. c	38. d	39. c	40. d
41. d	42. d	43. d	44. b	45. c	46. a	47. d	48. d	49. d	50. d
51. b	52. d	53. a	54. b	55. d	56. b	57. d			

Chapter 4

1. d	2. d	3. a	4. b	5. d	6. d	7. d	8. a	9. a	10. d
11. d	12. a	13. b	14. d	15. b	16. d	17. b	18. d	19. d	20. d
21. c	22. b	23. a	24. d	25. d	26. d	27. d			

Chapter 5

1. b	2. b	3. d	4. d	5. d	6. d	7. c	8. d	9. c	10. b
11. b	12. d	13. b	14. d	15. c	16. b	17. a	18. a		

Chapter 6

1. d	2. d	3. c	4. b	5. d	6. d	7. d	8. d	9. c	10. d
11. a	12. d	13. a	14. b	15. d	16. d	17. d	18. d	19. b	20. d
21. d	22. d	23. d	24. a						

Chapter 7

1. a	2. d	3. c	4. a	5. d	6. b	7. a	8. a	9. c	10. b
11. d	12. b	13. b	14. c	15. a	16. a	17. a	18. d	19. b	20. d
21. d	22. c	23. d	24. a	25. d	26. a	27. b	28. c	29. d	30. c
31. a	32. b	33. c	34. c	35. c	36. a	37. a	38. a	39. a	40. b
41. d	42. c	43. d	44. c	45. b	46. b	47. a	48. b	49. d	50. d
51. a	52. b	53. c	54. c	55. d	56. d	57. c	58. d	59. b	60. d
61. d	62. d	63. b	64. d	65. c	66. a	67. d	68. d	69. c	

Chapter 8

1. a	2. d	3. b	4. b	5. c	6. a	7. d	8. c	9. d	10. a
11. d	12. c	13. d	14. d	15. d	16. a	17. d	18. b	19. d	20. a
21. d	22. d	23. d	24. c	25. d	26. d	27. d	28. b	29. d	30. d
31. a	32. b	33. d	34. d	35. c	36. a	37. b	38. d	39. d	40. d
41. d	42. d	43. d	44. d	45. a	46. b	47. d	48. b	49. a	

Chapter 9

1. d	2. a	3. a	4. a	5. d	6. b	7. d	8. b	9. a	10. d
11. a	12. d	13. a	14. d	15. b	16. a	17. b	18. c	19. d	20. c

Chapter 10

1. b	2. c	3. b	4. d	5. d	6. d	7. d	8. d	9. a	10. a
11. b	12. d	13. d	14. d	15. d	16. a	17. c	18. a	19. d	20. d
21. a	22. d	23. d							

Chapter 11

1. d	2. d	3. c	4. b	5. d	6. a	7. d	8. d	9. c	10. c
11. d	12. b	13. a	14. d	15. d	16. d	17. d	18. d	19. b	20. a

Chapter 12

1. d	2. d	3. d	4. d	5. d	6. a	7. c	8. b	9. d	10. c
11. c	12. b	13. c	14. c	15. b	16. d				

Chapter 13

1. d	2. a	3. b	4. a	5. d	6. d	7. a	8. d	9. d	10. d
11. d	12. d	13. b	14. d	15. d	16. d	17. d	18. d	19. d	20. d

Chapter 14

1. a	2. d	3. b	4. c	5. d	6. a	7. a	8. d	9. d	10. a
11. d	12. d	13. a	14. c	15. b	16. c	17. b	18. a	19. d	20. d
21. a	22. d	23. d	24. c	25. d	26. c				

Chapter 15

1. a	2. d	3. d	4. d	5. d	6. d	7. d	8. d	9. d	10. a
11. a	12. b	13. d	14. d	15. d	16. a	17. d	18. b	19. a	20. d
21. a	22. d	23. c	24. d	25. c					

Chapter 16

1. a	2. b	3. d	4. d	5. d	6. d	7. d	8. d	9. c	10. d
11. d	12. b	13. b	14. d	15. a	16. d	17. a	18. b	19. b	20. b
21. a	22. b	23. b	24. b	25. c	26. b	27. c	28. c	29. b	30. c
31. d	32. d	33. d	34. d	35. c	36. c				

Chapter 17

1. d	2. a	3. d	4. d	5. a	6. b	7. b	8. a	9. b	10. d
11. d	12. d	13. d	14. a	15. d	16. a	17. d	18. d	19. d	20. d
21. d	22. c	23. b	24. b	25. a	26. a	27. d	28. a	29. d	

Chapter 18

1. b	2. b	3. b	4. d	5. a	6. d	7. d	8. b	9. c	10. d
11. d	12. d	13. b	14. b	15. d	16. d	17. d	18. a	19. a	20. a
21. d	22. a	23. d	24. c	25. d	26. c				

Chapter 19

1. b	2. d	3. a	4. b	5. c	6. c	7. b	8. d	9. d	10. d
11. c	12. d	13. d	14. c	15. d	16. b	17. c	18. d	19. d	20. a
21. d	22. d	23. a	24. a	25. d	26. d	27. d	28. b	29. a	30. d
31. d	32. a	33. d	34. c	35. d	36. c	37. b	38. d	39. d	40. c

Chapter 20

1. b	2. d	3. d	4. a	5. b	6. d	7. d	8. c	9. d	10. d
11. a	12. a	13. c	14. d	15. c	16. d	17. d	18. c	19. b	20. d
21. d	22. a	23. c	24. d						

Chapter 21

1. d	2. c	3. b	4. a	5. a	6. b	7. d	8. d	9. d	10. a
11. a	12. d	13. d	14. d	15. a	16. d	17. d	18. b	19. a	20. d
21. d	22. d	23. d	24. c	25. d	26. d	27. b	28. d	29. d	30. d
31. d	32. a	33. c	34. d	35. d	36. a	37. d			

Chapter 22

1. d	2. a	3. d	4. a	5. d	6. d	7. c	8. a	9. d	10. d
11. d	12. c	13. d	14. c	15. d	16. d	17. d	18. d	19. c	20. d
21. d	22. d	23. b	24. d	25. b	26. d	27. c	28. d	29. b	30. c
31. d	32. d	33. d	34. d	35. d	36. b	37. d	38. b	39. c	40. d

Chapter 23

1. b	2. a	3. b	4. a	5. a	6. b	7. b	8. b	9. a	10. b
11. a	12. a	13. a	14. b	15. b	16. a	17. b	18. b	19. b	20. a
21. a	22. a	23. a	24. a	25. b	26. a	27. b	28. b	29. b	30. b
31. a	32. b	33. a	34. b	35. b	36. a	37. b	38. b	39. b	40. b
41. b	42. b	43. b	44. a	45. a	46. b	47. a	48. a	49. a	50. a
51. a	52. a	53. a	54. a	55. a	56. a				

Chapter 24

1. b	2. a	3. b	4. b	5. a	6. a	7. b	8. a	9. b	10. b
11. a	12. a	13. b	14. a	15. b	16. b	17. a	18. b	19. b	20. a
21. a	22. a	23. b	24. a	25. a	26. a	27. a	28. a	29. b	30. a
31. b	32. b	33. b	34. a	35. a					

Chapter 25

1. a	2. a	3. b	4. b	5. b	6. a	7. a	8. a	9. b	10. a
11. b	12. b	13. a	14. b	15. a	16. a	17. b	18. b	19. a	20. a
21. a	22. a	23. a	24. b	25. a	26. b	27. a	28. a	29. a	30. a
31. b	32. b	33. b	34. b	35. a	36. b	37. b	38. a	39. a	40. b
41. a	42. b	43. b	44. b	45. a	46. b	47. a	48. a	49. a	50. b
51. b	52. b	53. b	54. a	55. a	56. a	57. b	58. a	59. b	60. a
61. a	62. a	63. b	64. a	65. a	66. b	67. b			

Chapter 26

1. b	2. a	3. b	4. b	5. a	6. a	7. a	8. b	9. a	10. b
11. b	12. a	13. b	14. a	15. a	16. a	17. b	18. a	19. b	20. b
21. a	22. b	23. a	24. b	25. a	26. b	27. b	28. b	29. a	30. b
31. a	32. b	33. a	34. a	35. a	36. a	37. a	38. b	39. a	40. b
41. b	42. a	43. b	44. a	45. b	46. b	47. b			

Breinigsville, PA USA
22 October 2009
226342BV00001B/11/P